© 2024 Joel G. Hancock

All rights reserved.

No part of this publication may be reproduced, distributed, or transmitted in any form or by any means, including photocopying, recording, or other electronic or mechanical methods, without the prior written permission of the author, except in the case of brief quotations embodied in critical reviews and certain other noncommercial uses permitted by the copyright law. For permission requests, write to the author, addressed "Attention: Permissions" at the address below.

Joel G. Hancock
204 Lewis St.
Harkers Island, NC 28531
joelghancock@gmail.com

Printed in the United States of America
ISBN: 9798344360102

Unless otherwise noted, photos are part of my personal collection.

The Education of an Island Boy
Growing up on Harkers Island, NC in the 50s & 60s

Stories for those who

Lived it,

Loved it,

Or long for it~

Joel G. Hancock

Contents

Contents -- 5
Dedication -- 9
Foreword --- 11
Acknowledgments --- 15
Preface -- 17
Prologue --- 27
   Where Is It You Say You Are Going? ------------------------------- 27
From the Banks to the Island --- 33
   From Tidewater & New England to Harkers Island ------------------ 33
   Shackleford Banks --- 37
   The Storms of 1896 and 1899 ------------------------------------- 39
   Leaving the Banks --- 42
   Making Harkers Island Home -------------------------------------- 46
   The Landing and The Shore --------------------------------------- 50
   Neighborhoods of Kinfolks --------------------------------------- 55
   Brothers, Sisters, Cousins, and a World at War ------------------ 57
   Life at the Landing --- 59
A New Home and Way of Life --- 65
   Tradition! -- 65
   Shell Point --- 66
   Academy Field --- 69
   Red Hill -- 70
   Annis & Mississippi --- 77
   More Than Just a Store -- 82
   Prince and the Fudgesicles -------------------------------------- 90
   Barbershop Lessons -- 92
   "Lying Willie" -- 95
   The Island "Showhouse" -- 97
Ol' Pa's Neighborhood and Bertha's Legacy ---------------------------- 103
   The Path to the Landing --------------------------------------- 103
   Our Neighborhood -- 106
   Becoming Ol' Pa --- 107

The Education of an Island Boy

    Ol' Pa's Crowd ------ *111*
    Life After Aggie ------ *123*
    Bertha's Legacy ------ *127*
    A Part Of — but Apart From ------ *136*

Charlie and Margarette ------ 139

    Making a Family of Their Own ------ *144*
    Working Away from Home ------ *150*
    The Last of Ten Children ------ *158*
    The Loss of a Son and Brother ------ *163*
    Halcyon Days ------ *167*
    What My Parents Wanted, and Expected of Me ------ *170*

Livin', Learnin', and Playin' ------ 173

    HIS (Harkers Island School) ------ *174*
    Ridin' the School Bus ------ *179*
    The Bittersweet ------ *182*
    Not Completely Detached ... ------ *184*
    School's Out! ------ *187*
    Washin' Off with a Water Hose ------ *189*
    Made-up Games ------ *191*
    My Rooster that was a "Chicken" ------ *192*
    Hollering For (Not At) Your Children! ------ *195*
    My Daddy's Very Personal "GPS" Monitor ------ *197*
    Harkers Island Cowboys ------ *200*
    Horsepenning ------ *205*

Playin' Ball and Workin' the Water ------ 209

    We Didn't Even Get a Chance to Bat! ------ *210*
    That Ball was High! ------ *213*
    A League of Our Own ------ *216*
    Yet Another Generation ------ *221*
    Learning to "Work the Water" ------ *224*
    How Much Would you Take Right Now For the Whole Mess? -- *228*
    Joining a Fishing Crew ------ *231*

Kith & Kin — Women & Men ------ 239

    Aunt Gracie's Scrambled Eggs ------ *241*
    "Dack" and the Egg Man ------ *244*
    The Prettiest Sound in the Whole World ------ *246*
    Pickin' Mule Hairs ------ *248*

Donald Guthrie- We Ain't Gonna Get Nowhere if You Keep Stopping ---- *249*
Blind Lilly ---- *252*
They Were Keeping Me Awake at Night ---- *254*
A Goat in Bed with Me! ---- *257*
The Closest I Ever Come to Having a Job. ---- *259*
The "Booze Yacht," A Journey, and the Sweetest Fumes I Ever Smelled ---- *261*

The Wisdom and Wit of Ordinary Days ---- 269

Telford Willis & Brady Lewis – You Can't Have it Both Ways! - *274*
Telford Willis - You'll Freeze to Death This Winter ---- *278*
The Handsomest Man in the World ---- *279*
Are You Now or Have You Ever Been ...? ---- *280*
Dallas Rose- In Two Hours, We'll Be Headed Out Again ---- *282*
Cletus Rose- Why Don't You Fly Somewhere? ---- *283*
My Mama's Aunt Mary- Just Look at You Crowd ---- *286*
Ed Russell- What About that Oak Tree Over There ---- *288*
Fishing with Calvin Rose- All I Wanted Was a Chance ---- *289*
An Unexpected Holiday Visitor ---- *290*
Disappointed at Her Proofs ---- *292*
Do You Wanna Cut the Grass, or ... ---- *293*
Wouldn't That Be an Unsafe Movement? ---- *295*
Dead Man's Curve ---- *296*
I Didn't Have a Dime in my Pocket, So ... ---- *298*
Some Lines That Ought to Never Be Forgotten ---- *300*

Special People and Their Stories — Life Lessons Lived Large ---- 303

Has there been a blow or something? Tom C. and The Storm of '33 ---- *304*
Danny Boy Lewis- I Know Twice as Much as My Father! ---- *307*
Loke and Lemmis- "Stewed Loons" and "Tied-up Chickens" ---- *309*
The "Tiny World" of Cecil Nelson ---- *312*
The Sad Story of Abram Lewis ---- *316*
Archie Fulford- You Look Enough Alike ---- *318*
Harkers Island "Professionals" — Charlie Nelson, Raymond Guthrie, and Maxwell Willis ---- *320*
Earl Davis- Hardened Oak and Iron Nails ---- *324*
Miss Ollie & Dr. Moore ---- *327*
Manus Fulcher was Headed Home ---- *332*

The Education of an Island Boy

    Luther Willis- Mullet Fishing, an Old Man, & The War to End all Wars --- *335*

Leaving and Coming Back -------------------------- 339
    Over the Bridge -- *339*
    Off to College -- *344*
    A Serious Student --- *347*
    "Love in the Library" with a Shout-Out to Jimmy Buffett ------- *351*
    The More Things Change --- *356*

Epilogue -- 365

Dedication

To Charlie & Margarette

And to Ralph, Ella Dee, June, Tommy, Bill, Sister, Mike, Denny, & Teff

It's their story too!

The Education of an Island Boy

Foreword

I've been homesick for Harkers Island for a long time; now I've been ...

Through the images and voices of Joel's carefully written stories, I have laughed and cried, remembering and reliving in my mind (and heart) those precious Island days ... pony pennings and mullet blows, the smell of rain coming across the sound, the sunburned backs of men working at the Landing, and the women standing in the scallop house on those cold mornings in December.

With these stories, I've been able to reconnect with the people and places I once took for granted. I've listened again to characters whose voices I have not heard in decades, almost forgotten —but now revisited with an appreciation only the passing of time can make possible.

For a few moments I have heard once again the names of places that used to be every day ... the Sand Hole, the Old Road, the Showhouse, Edith's Store ... and the names of people who would be lost if not for this powerful tribute to the lessons their lives taught an entire community for a generation, maybe more. I am reminded of so many of the small day-to-day realities of our growing up that I miss the most — the unlocked doors, the wide expanse of sand along the Banks-facing shore, the assurance of knowing who belonged to who ...

I have been comforted by reunions with people I loved as a child and experienced for a moment the return to the Island filled with fish houses and community stores, gathering places needed by generations of families living and dying together, taking care of one another, no matter how hard the struggle.

The Education of an Island Boy

Once again, I have seen the glistening amber sand of Red Hill. I have smelled the scallop house. I have tasted a stale honeybun from Clarence's store. I have felt the closeness of a community of family neighborhoods that faced the Landing where wives and mothers waited to see what was caught or gathered, only then to know what she would cook for supper; would it be a mess of fish, a bucket of shrimp, a peck of oysters?

For anyone who remembers "when Harkers Island was Harkers Island" Joel's beautifully woven collection of stories is not only his story but our story too. Only the names changed from one family neighborhood to the next as all Islander's lives were determined by the same forces. No matter which hammock of the island we called home, we shared in the same "education" for life that Joel affectionately retells. The common threads of family, security, and a deep sense of "Islandness" are the main themes of Harkers Island's story, a story told here with reverence and honesty revealing that his — and our — "island education" runs much deeper than anything learned from a book.

Joel's years of listening are so well told that we will be called to read it over and over, to ourselves and to our children and their families in the years to come. We will be reminded each time that we cannot ever forget what a gift growing up on Harkers Island has been to us, a "shared education" that is the foundation of all our lives.

To others who will read this book, I personally hope it will help you understand why we hold onto this place like we do. For those of us growing up on the Harkers Island of the 50s and 60s, it is more than an amazing story of interesting and independent characters. It is a reassurance that yes, that life was truly as good as we remember, but it was not easy or trivial. With these stories in retrospect, we realize that we have been molded by the hardships of the past one hundred years, giving us strong reason to be proud of all that Island people have accomplished, overcoming challenges, strengthened by victories and sorrows, great and small.

For Islanders, much of what we knew of our Island home is gone. Many of these stories would have been forgotten in another generation save for Joel's years of work creating this much-needed

Foreword

book, reminding us again what a privilege it has been "just to be here."

As Joel's last pages admonishes us, we cannot forget their names, those men and women who taught us, cared for us, and made us who we are. Nor can we forget the places, the days and times of our growing up, the lessons we learned, the values that were instilled in us from people and places now seen and unseen. It is an "education" that we cannot allow to be lost with our generation.

Thank you, Joel Hancock – Charlie William's boy – for following your heart back home to be the Island's scribe, the gatherer and keeper of our stories, and for reminding us who and whose we are .... And now allowing us all to "go home again." This is a gift only you could have given.

I kin ye ...

Karen Willis Amspacher
Director, Core Sound Waterfowl Museum & Heritage Center

The Education of an Island Boy

Acknowledgments

Friends and family who have helped in bringing this story to life are "way yonder" too many to name individually. So, I thank them as a group. Yet, I would be remiss if I did not mention a few who were generous and insightful in reading and revising various sections of the book to help me make it better. Those included, but were not limited to my niece, Deena Lynk, who teaches English at our community college; Dr. Carmine Prioli, a retired professor at North Carolina State University; Lyle Frederick Robinson, a retired professor at Graceland College now living in Brazil; and Richard Bell, MD, a personal friend who has become my fellow traveler in this latest portion of my life.

Then there is Dr. Anthony Papalas, a retired professor of History at East Carolina University. He was my advisor both as an undergraduate and graduate student at the school. He advised and even coaxed me in preparing my senior Honors Paper and then my Master's Thesis. Now, half a century later, he graciously volunteered to reprise that role in helping me to conceive and then to compose this manuscript. Few, if any, of the leaders or educators I have known in my life have fulfilled the role of a "mentor" so well as he.

My daughter Leah made an invaluable contribution that involved lots of both time and effort. Standing beside me at our home, or while connected to me by phone from her home 200 miles away, she read aloud to me the entire manuscript. She wanted to be comfortable that the text, and especially the stories, appeared on the page true to how they sounded when spoken by the teller. If she had her way, it would have started as an audio book and only later to be printed.

The Education of an Island Boy

I owe a special debt of gratitude to the Core Sound Waterfowl Museum and Heritage Center (hereafter shown as CSWM&HC) here on Harkers Island for allowing me free access to their photo collection of several thousand original photos accumulated over the years. In it I found visual reminders of faces and places that brightened my memory.

Finally, I extend my deepest gratitude to two incredible women who have been instrumental in bringing this project to fruition. First, my grade school and lifelong friend Karen Willis Amspacher. She has been a steadfast source of support, guidance, and insight throughout this journey, and long before. Without her, this work would look and feel vastly different. Lastly, my wife Susan has been unwavering in her support, always ready to help in any way needed. From the initial idea to the final formatting, her influence is felt at every step. To be completely fair, her name truly deserves a place on the title page. Karen and Susan together helped to turn what was a "loose and rough" draft into a much "smoother and tighter" product.

Preface

This is a story, or more correctly, a collection of stories about my "coming of age" on Harkers Island, NC, in the 1950s and 60s. Many, if not most such narratives are written by someone who left and later came back, or at least wanted to. You should know in advance that this one is written by someone who stayed — in body and in mind. Though I did leave for a few years to attend college, Harkers Island has remained my home both physically and emotionally.

During my working years, I left the Island every workday to earn a living, but always with the anticipation and understanding that I would be back home that same evening. In fact, in one of my early jobs before settling into my career as an insurance agent, I once was offered a promotion with a sizable raise in salary. But my acceptance would have meant relocating to another part of the state. In declining the offer, I remarked, not totally in jest, "Why would I ever leave a place where so many people work their entire lives trying to get to?"

I have come to appreciate that such an attachment to a home place is not just uncommon but rare. It is especially so in a country populated by people among whom pulling up stakes in search of advancement and a better life is often considered a founding principle. Why my sentiments are so different is understandable only in the context of how my experience has been so unique and even peculiar in the view of many. Over the past half-century, as I have watched and been a part of how the routines of daily living that shaped me now have changed forever, I have attempted to remember and chronicle what that lifestyle once was like. These stories are the culmination of that effort.

It should be understood that this is not a documentary history, at least not in the classical sense, as it is not built upon written, printed, or historical documents. But that should not be taken to mean that it is not factual. Rather, it is based upon my own experiences and recollections, and upon accounts, tales, and even yarns I heard growing up, and were just as real to me as they were to the people who told them.

The singer-songwriter James Taylor asserted in his brief audio autobiography, "Break Shot," that "Memory is tricky! We remember how it felt and not necessarily how it was." My recollections of events as they happened are necessarily colored by what I have experienced in the interim. I appreciate that my description of those events and my rendering of some stories may not be the same as that of some of my contemporaries. But I can assert with assurance that my account, especially as it relates to my own feelings, is precisely correct as to the way I remember them — and on that subject I am the world's foremost authority!

Likewise, though it may seem like an autobiography, it is not just about me. I include stories about myself and my immediate and extended family to provide context for a broader depiction of the community and lifestyle I aim to describe. In that sense, it could be seen as an autobiography of my Harkers Island home. Two introductory chapters are a narrative about why and how the people of Shackleford Banks abandoned their ancestral homes as the 19th century gave way to the 20th. Three following chapters tell the story of my immediate family both on the Banks and after establishing at Harkers Island, extending to the midpoint of the century when their story became mine as well. I attempt to describe daily life and how work, school, and play were intertwined to make every day an exciting experience.

Three later chapters are collections of stories and yarns told by and about some of the special people who gave the Island much of its unique character. They are written and presented so that, if need be, they can stand alone for reading or telling. Indeed, I suggest that these three chapters might best be appreciated when read aloud. Necessarily, some of the details they include are repetitions of information incorporated in the main narrative and descriptions. A final chapter and the Epilogue are my attempt to summarize and

Preface

explain some of the more profound changes the Island and its people have witnessed in the past fifty plus years.

Sensitive to matters of privacy, except for my immediate and close extended family, dates of birth and passing are shown only for persons already deceased, and then only for those whose role is integral to the event or story being told.

My generation of Harkers Islanders was the first for which life on Shackleford Banks, where our grandparents and many of our parents had been born, was a collection of stories rather than a mixture of memories. For us and those who have come after us, searching for whales in the ocean and schools of fish in the sounds was part of our heritage rather than an everyday exercise. Still, much more than for my children and grandchildren, I and other mid-20th century children on Harkers Island grew up surrounded by our past. Everything around us seemed to be a part of something else — something bigger than ourselves.

That something else was the unique heritage we shared. An awareness of that heritage emanated not from community celebrations, reunions, or even public bulletin boards of pictures and charts. In fact, there wasn't any need to try and describe it with written accounts. That was because we were surrounded by our common past and culture everywhere and all the time. It stared us in our faces, and we could not ignore it, even if we had wanted to. It was somewhat like the old baseball games for which the results never were recorded or reported. There was no need to — because everybody, or someone they knew, had been at the game when it was played.

Every day we were confronted with expressions like:

"Take this to Ole' Pa's house," "find him on Aunt Gracie's porch," or "go play games in Rennie's field."

"Something is happening down there at the end of Ferry Dock Road."

"He rode his bike all the way to Shell Point."

The Education of an Island Boy

We were swimming off "Danky's dock," and played baseball on "Johnson's cow pasture."

We walked and played games on the "Old Road" and pulled tin cans in the middle of the "New Road."

Every time we went to the Landing we looked across to "Bells Island," "Whale Creek Bay," "Wade's Shore," "Sam Windsor's Lump," "The Horse Pen," or "Whitehurst's Island."

As we crossed the bridge, we noticed the lump of cedar trees on the very edge of what we called "Brown's Island," or focused on the other direction at the vines and tall trees of "Harkers Point."

But it wasn't just places or things that had names with a story.

A tall man was "longer than Lonzo Lewis."

A heavy man was "bigger than Bull Hunter."

Someone else might be smarter than Charlie Nelson, or could oar a skiff faster than Luther Willis, or told more made-up stories than "Lying Willie," or could throw a baseball harder than Moe Willis, or play and sing like the Rose crowd, or loved to eat loon more than Loch, or could run faster than Billie Hancock.

Most of us were called by both our first and middle names because most everyone was named after someone else. At other times people were labeled by their nearest kinship. You wouldn't just say that something happened or belonged to Mary. You felt a need to be more specific.

Was it Mary Anne, Mary Francis, Mary Catherine, or even Norman's Mary, Weldon's Mary, Tommy Lewis's Mary, or Iddy's Mary? There was also Luther's Mary, who when she was married became William's Mary, and who had a son called Mary's Michael.

He lived almost next door to Elsie Mae's Johnny William, who was not to be confused with Johnny Lane, Johnny Wayne, Johnny Michael, Johnny Manley — the son of Johnny Boo, or Johnny Vann — the son of Alena's Johnny.

Preface

If Mama sent me to get something from Ollie, she had to be more specific — was it Big Ollie or Little Ollie?

In a hundred ways every day, I was reminded of who I was and what and where our crowd had been. Knowing those things made me feel that I was part of something special and something that mattered. It gave me a reason to do my best to avoid bringing discredit or pain to others who were a part of my crowd, and who shared those names and feelings with me.

"Be careful and don't get hurt" my mama would remind me whenever I left our house. But with my father it was a little different. "Remember who you are," he would utter as a plea and a caution about the possible consequences whenever I set out for anything away from our family and neighborhood. With loving respect for the pleas of my mother, it was my father's counsel that kept, and keeps, echoing in my mind. Trying to avoid bringing shame on him, on our crowd, was and is something that has constantly prompted me to consider long and hard the consequences of my life decisions — big and small.

In the final year of the 19th century the entire population of Shackleford Banks had been obliged to find new homes to escape the ravages of several major storms. The larger groupings of those refugees came to be known as "crowds." For several generations, those who landed in Morehead City to help build an ocean-going port at the end of a railroad line, later known as the "Promise Landers," were first called "The Crowd from the Banks" by their new neighbors.

Another group made their way westward along Bogue Banks and squatted on land belonging to the family of John A. Royall, who two decades later sold his holdings to a wealthy New York City heiress, Alice Hoffman. She and her successors, including the grandson of President Theodore Roosevelt, would later contend with the "squatters" from the Banks for more than half a century before real ownership was granted to the newcomers — or more specifically to their heirs.

That community eventually was called "Salter Path" and even today, more than a century later, their descendants are lumped

The Education of an Island Boy

together as that "crowd of Salter Pathers" by newcomers to that stretch of beach. By far the largest group were the ones that moved just across Back Sound to Harkers Island and that included my grandparents. Over the years I have been reminded many times, on both sides of the bridge that connects us to the mainland, that I am one of "that crowd of Harkers Islanders."

Still further, when the "crowds" from the Banks reached their new homes, they assembled as extended families. Ledgers of census takers for the next fifty years offer the appearance of having been "sorted" by a specific key-field of "surnames" in their registers and lists. Instead, the written records merely list the names in the order they found them, one extended family, or more especially one "crowd," following directly after another.

Because there was of necessity so much intermarriage, someone could be, and usually was, part of more than one crowd, linked to their mother and their father. The names for those crowds generally would morph with each passing generation to focus on grandparents more than the immediate family. Thus, by the time I came along, I was one of Charlie Hancock's crowd during the week, but on Sunday I was part of Bertha Willis's crowd. In more ways than might be imagined, I still am.

What follows is why and how that came to be, and how those two extended families, along with a host of neighbors and friends, fashioned my character and my life.

Acquiring the accounts, descriptions, and especially the stories and yarns that comprise this book has been a lifelong endeavor. Compiling them into some semi-coherent form has involved both brief and much longer stints of the last two decades. Having written for books, magazines, and online articles about local history since the late 1980s, I have amassed a sizable amount of previous material that I have been able to incorporate into this more comprehensive portrait.

A section of Chapter Five describing attending Harkers Island Elementary School dates back to 1982 when I was asked to provide a summary and to offer remarks at an event celebrating the 25th anniversary of its opening. To emphasize how the mechanics of

Preface

preparing documents have changed in the interim, the document was typed using an IBM Selectric typewriter. Describing life at Diamond City and Shackleford Banks dates back to 1989 when I published a full-length book, *Strengthened by the Storm*, telling the story of the earliest Mormon members and missionaries on the Island and the Banks. It began on a Commodore 64, one of the earliest home computers. It was completed and formatted on an IBM XT clone using an MS-DOS version of the WordPerfect word processor and Ventura Publisher.

Several of my stories about memorable characters and events of previous generations of Islanders were originally included in a quarterly journal of local life and lore called "The Mailboat" (1990-1992). They were done on a later model of an IBM AT clone, still using WordPerfect and Ventura Publisher but now powered by the Windows 3 operating system. By the end of that decade, I was thoroughly immersed in the array of graphic interfaces that have been deployed in succession up to and including Windows 11. I eventually settled on a combination of MS Word and Google Docs for entering, editing, and formatting this final product.

It was not until 2013 that, having been impressed by the popularity of internet blogs dedicated to various subjects of particular interest, I decided to get serious about my own project. Adopting the "blogosphere" platform, I began posting some of my stories to an internet blog titled "The Education of an Island Boy." Over the next few years, I submitted several dozen brief accounts and stories, each intending to be included in this book when it was finally published. Two dozen or more of those are here, but they have been edited and expanded to allow them to fit within the story and pattern of the overall narrative.

In the spring of 1982, I happened upon a newly published paperback copy of a "coming of age" story told by Russell Baker (1925-2019), a Pulitzer Prize-winning columnist with the New York Times. It was called "Growing Up." In it, he told of his youth in Virginia and of his mother's resilience and resolve during the Great Depression. It won the Pulitzer Prize for Biography or Autobiography in 1983. It was while reading and thoroughly enjoying that book that I had the idea of doing a similar account of the life I knew growing up on Harkers Island. None of the events or people he chronicled would be considered remarkable or unique in and of themselves. But taken together, they created an enjoyable, even comforting, affirmation of the sublime pleasure to be found in everyday events and things. I imagined what a recreation of the world I once knew would be like.

A decade later, in 1992, I attended a basketball game at the Smith Center on the campus of the University of North Carolina. The printed lineup and program for the game included short biographies of each player. For some reason, I noticed that one of the players mentioned that his favorite book was called "The Education of Little Tree" by Forrest Carter. A few days later, recalling that title, I searched for and found it online and was intrigued by the summaries and reviews that described it. I immediately ordered a copy and began thumbing through the pages as soon as it arrived. I could not help but start reading and soon became totally captivated by the story and how it was told. Originally presented as an autobiography, it was later discovered to be primarily a fictional account, and that the author's real name was Asa Carter.

Fact or fiction, the tales it tells of a boy adopted by his Cherokee grandparents and raised in the mountains of eastern Tennessee during the Great Depression are mesmerizing. It is filled with stories that make you both cry and laugh — sometimes simultaneously. It is permeated by the wisdom of his elders, and especially his grandfather. Just as with Baker's "Growing Up," I began consciously to think of similar stories and similar counsel I had received 500 miles to the east and a quarter century later. Family, kinship, and neighborhoods were the heart of our story too.

Still, the ultimate determination that I should compile and combine all my stories had its true genesis in October of 2007. My wife, Susan, and I were driving home from visiting our daughter Alyson's family in Utah. Susan demands that she be behind the wheel when we ride together. So, riding shotgun, I had lots of time to enjoy the beautiful scenery and to read from the digital library of books and essays I had acquired over the years. Somewhere between Laramie and Cheyenne, Wyoming, I happened upon this quote attributed to

Preface

Mark Twain explaining how he was moved to tell stories of his youth when he visited his hometown of Hannibal many years later:

"The old life has swept before me like a panorama; the old days have trooped by in their old glory, again; the old faces have looked out of the mists of the past; old footsteps have sounded in my listening ears; old hands have clasped mine, old voices have greeted me, and the songs I loved ages and ages ago have come wailing down the centuries!" Mark Twain, "Letter to Will Bowen."

Pondering that quote was a catalyst that inspired me to begin a serious attempt to compose an account conveying to others some understanding and appreciation of the childhood I knew growing up when and where I did. There, on US Interstate 85, nearly two thousand miles away from my home, I was struck with a desire to "see again the faces and hear again the voices" ingrained in my memory a half-century earlier. By the time we reached the Black Hills of South Dakota and set out for Mount Rushmore, I had pulled out my laptop and begun to describe in my own words the neighborhood I had known as a boy. Every completed paragraph seemed to open one or more doors to other memories that would further describe the story being told. Three days later, as we arrived home, I had prepared in my mind an outline of what I have spent two decades, off and on, trying to complete.

I hope that for some of you, this will be a happy reminder of the life you once knew. Finally, I hope all of you will both enjoy and appreciate what follows.

The Education of an Island Boy

The path from "the Landing" heading up to my home from the shore. My parents raised ten children in the little white house at the end of this well-worn path.

Prologue

"No man is himself. He is the sum of his past. There is no such thing really as 'was' because the past 'is.' It is a part of every man, every woman, and every moment. All of his or her ancestry, background, is all a part of himself and herself at any moment."

William Faulkner

"The Child is Father of the Man."

William Wordsworth

Where Is It You Say You Are Going?

Early one morning in August of 1970, I hurried down the dirt and shell path that ran beside our house to the nearby shoreline we called "the Landing." My sister's '62 Oldsmobile was already parked by the road in front of the house and packed with all my belongings. She was getting ready to deliver me to Greenville, NC, and to East Carolina University where I was to report the next day and prepare to play freshman football. I already had said my goodbyes to my mama as she stood on the back porch of our house, but my father was at the Landing and in his boat that was moored at the family dock.

He was working to cull the keepers from what he earlier had unloaded from his shrimp trawl into the cockpit of "The Montgomery," his open twenty-two-foot Harkers Island fishing boat. The best time for shrimping in the inland waters was from sundown to sunup, and the daylight "tow" or drag was usually the best one of the whole night. From the looks of what was there on the stern of the boat, this morning's catch had been no exception.

The Education of an Island Boy

When I got there, the culling board was still over half-full and the wire basket beside it was brimming with green-tailed shrimp, the kind that show up generally only when summer is giving way to fall.

The water that morning was "slick cam" and a flock of seagulls surrounded and circled over and around my father and his catch, mostly swimming close by, waiting to pounce every time he raked another cull of scrap off of the culling board and into the shallow water that lapped at the nearby water's edge. In the distance, on the south horizon, the bright sandy shorelines and green marshes of Shackleford Banks, just a two-mile straight shot across Back Sound, glistened in the morning sun that was now hovering in the sky well above East'ard (Core) Banks.

As I hopped up from the beach sand at the foot of the wooden dock and made my way towards him, Daddy stood up, but slowly, as was usually the case when he had been perched in one place and position for more than a few minutes. He now was standing on the deck of his boat with his waist and legs hidden below the edge of the wooden pier. Even before I got to where he was now climbing from the gunwale and up onto the edge of the wharf, I began to explain to him, "I'm ready to leave now, Daddy; Sister is waiting, and I've come to say 'bye.'"

Once he was upright on the dock, he reached up to grab my shoulders, and to "smell my neck." That gesture, "smelling your neck," was the ultimate show of affection for him and many of his generation. Kisses and long embraces were reserved for more private and intimate moments, but a quick nod to breathe in the scent of someone's upper torso was how he, as well as my aunts and uncles, and almost all the old folks of the neighborhood, usually expressed their fondness. As he reached towards me, he uttered the very same injunction that he had offered every single time I had said goodbye to him, for as long as I could remember, even if I was headed out only for a date or to meet up with friends. "Remember who you are," he repeated to me yet again. Once more reminding me to make sure that I do nothing to besmirch his, or more importantly, his family's good name. Then, just as he let go of my shoulders, he asked me with all the emotion he could allow

Prologue

himself to show anyone other than my mother, "Where is it you say you are going?"

Looking back, and keeping in mind that it was 1970, and that many other boys of my age-group, including my brother, Telford, had already left or soon were leaving for Vietnam or other places far more dangerous and exciting than was freshman football at a college just two hours away, it may seem strange that he didn't already know my plans, if not my schedule. But most fathers of his era were not as involved with their children, especially their teenage sons, as I and many other dads came to be just a generation later. In fact, his obligation to my brothers and me could be summed up in one oft-repeated line that I still remember. "A shirt on your back, shoes on your feet, a roof overhead, and something to eat," was the sum and total of what a father of his day and time was obliged to offer. My father gave me more, much more than that, but it was understood that this was something extra that he was adding, and not anything that might have been demanded or expected. Affection and nurturing were assumed to be the responsibility of mothers, and even sisters, and in our family they more than upheld their end of the bargain.

As he let go of my arms, ready to head back to the end of the dock and his unfinished task of sorting what remained on the culling board, I responded, "I'm going to Greenville, to East Carolina, to play football, to college, to get an education."

Turning back toward me and while nodding his approval and patting me once again on the same shoulder he had moments before lodged under his chin, he responded, "That's good son." And then, just as he moved to squat back down and into his boat, he reminded me yet again of something he had tried to instill into each of his children, or at least his sons. "Good," he said, "everybody needs some kind of education." By "education" he did not necessarily mean schooling or "book learning." Rather, his feeling was that each of us should acquire a recognized skill that would allow us to make a living and provide for a family, just as he had done by working in the water and building boats. But he also intended that we acquire the life skills that would allow us to survive in and preserve the world — small as it was — that he had helped to build for us.

And so off I went with his words still ringing in my head. As I turned and hurried back up the path and towards a waiting two-toned Oldsmobile sedan, I did not fully appreciate, as I later would, my father's parting advice. I had known for a long time, for as long as I could remember, that I wanted an education. So, starting that morning I was heading out on my own to get one. But in the decades since, especially as I have reflected more on that farewell and on my father's words, I have come to know that in a very real sense, and in a way I couldn't fully have appreciated at the time, I already had received an education. What that was, and how I came to get it, is what this book is about.

In the eighteen years that preceded my one and only long-term departure from my Island home, I had been part of a unique way of life and thinking. More precisely, I belonged to a family and neighborhood, and a greater Harkers Island community that my grandparents and their contemporaries had molded after their exodus from Diamond City and Shackleford Banks following the great hurricane of 1899. A whole generation of Island children had been my classmates. The shoreline, paths, and woods had been my classroom. Older men and women had been my teachers. And the shallow waters of Back Sound and the marshes and beaches of Shackleford Banks had been my playground.

Through the loving tutelage of my parents and siblings, and scores of uncles, aunts, and cousins, I was schooled in what it meant to be part of what was called the "Charlie Hancock crowd," named after my paternal grandfather, and also of the "Bertha Lewis crowd," in reference to my maternal grandmother. Taken together the lessons I learned shaped, and still shape, who I became and what I am.

The pages that follow are my attempt to tell something of what I had seen and heard and, ultimately, what I learned. It is a narrative made up of a web of smaller stories that, taken together, hopefully, will weave a tapestry of the world I knew and loved and that still shapes my thoughts and character.

That is why I call my stories *"The Education of an Island Boy."*

Prologue

The author, Joel Hancock, at 6 years old in the first grade. School pictures meant dressing in your finest and even having your teacher comb your hair just before the camera was clicked.

The Education of an Island Boy

Cape Lookout Region
Of Coastal North Carolina

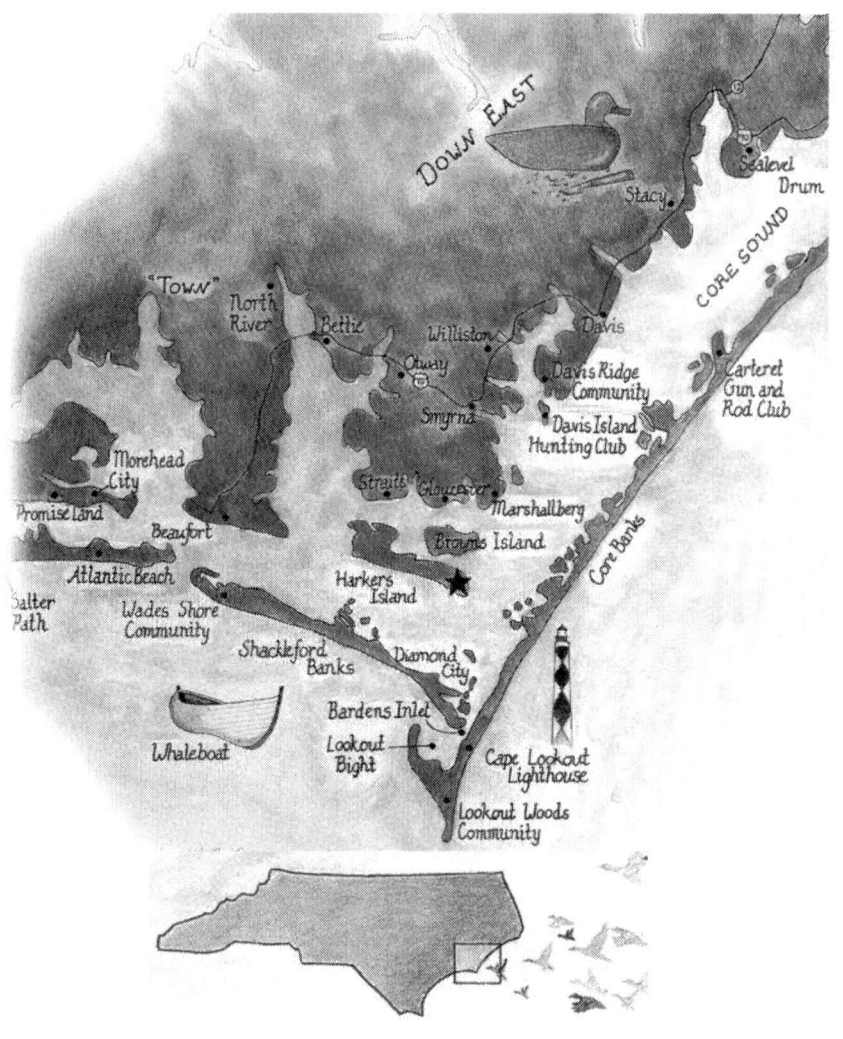

Map by Kimberly Schott
CSWM&HC Collection

1

From the Banks to the Island

... The knowledge of a place that comes from working in it in all weathers, making a living from it, suffering from its catastrophes, loving its mornings or evenings or hot noons, valuing it for the profound investment of labor and feeling that you, your parents and grandparents, your all-but-unknown ancestors have put into it.

Wallace Stegner, "The Sense of Place"

From Tidewater & New England to Harkers Island

The largest part of my almost entirely English ancestry must have had at least some wanderlust in their spirits, or else they might never have agreed to make the long and arduous journey across the Atlantic to find a new life in what they all viewed as a new world. But for most of my direct forbearers, that same wanderlust was all but spent by the time they landed on the southeast coast of Virginia in the early 1600s. Somewhere between the crowded docks of Southampton and Portsmouth on their way to the ramshackle moorings that dotted the James and York Rivers entrance into the Virginia Tidewater, they had a change of heart. I can easily imagine their anxiety as they voyaged day after day and week after week across the wide and sometimes stormy North Atlantic. I can even envision one or more of them saying to themselves or their fellow passengers, "If ever I get to set my feet on dry land once more, I will never again venture far enough offshore that I cannot set my eyes to see the solid ground!"

That conclusion didn't mean they had found a permanent home among the transplanted English aristocracy and noblemen who had turned the Jamestown colony into their personal fiefdom and whose descendants, the Randolphs, Jeffersons, Washingtons, and the like, moved farther and farther westward to expand their holdings and find better soil. As for the masses of settlers those fledgling aristocrats left behind, it has been estimated that as many as 80% of the English men and women who came to Virginia in the 1600s were servants. Like so many others whose labor later would be replaced by imported African slaves, my ancestors were unwilling to continue in servitude, indentured or otherwise, to their planter overlords. But unlike the future planter class, they and their descendants soon began to make their way not westward but southward and away from the Virginia settlements with their rigid class structures.

Where they eventually landed and put down roots along the shoreline of coastal North Carolina was much farther removed in social order than the mere physical distance would have suggested. Sitting between the Royalist and Cavalier Commonwealth of Virginia to the north and the near-feudal Proprietorship of South Carolina to the south, North Carolina has been labeled a "Valley of Humility between two Mountains of Conceit" since soon after it was settled. During their movement south, they eventually abandoned the livelihoods that had sustained them amid the farmlands of southeastern Virginia. Left behind was prospecting for gold and other minerals, an enterprise that had been the foremost interest of their original sponsors. Even farming and foraging eventually took a backseat to fishing, shellfishing, and hunting waterfowl as their primary means of sustenance.

The first of my known forebearers native to Carteret County, one of the oldest in the State, was my fifth great-grandfather, Hector Hancock, born here in 1712. His father, William Hancock II, had been born in Norfolk, VA, in 1675 and eventually relocated down the coast just beyond the state border. Many of my other ancestors were in no hurry to finish their journey. It would take them more than a century and several more generations to migrate less than two hundred miles to where their journey finally ended.

Their route was mainly down the barrier islands that lined the North Carolina Coast from Corolla to Cape Lookout. At this nexus point, the Outer Banks turns from a north-south direction to one that, at least for a stretch of thirty miles, follows a route directly east-west. Amid the sand hills and salt marshes of North Carolina's lower islands and banks, they found a freedom and independence, if not a prosperity, which had eluded them as underlings to the Tidewater elite. And once they settled near the base of the Cape Lookout lighthouse, the first one having been completed in 1812, most of them never moved again — unless you consider it movement to build a small home on an adjoining plot within easy walking distance of the shacks or huts in which they had been born and raised.

Within a few generations, they had lost or forsaken most of their ties to their Tidewater and English roots. There was one noticeable exception to their cultural evolution. That was how they clung to what would become an archaic oral dialect that retained vowel pronunciations and other grammatical anomalies long after they had passed out of the more standard American English vernacular. For instance, the word "time" is pronounced as if it were spelled "toime." There are dozens of other examples. That peculiarity endures even today.

Their move south and away from the land of the Virginia planters had another, albeit unplanned and unforeseen, consequence. It allowed them to escape most of the ravages caused by the Civil War that followed less than two generations after their final settlement at the convergence of Core and Back Sounds. The portion of the Outer Banks between Hatteras Inlet to the north down to Fort Macon on Bogue Banks to the south and west was relatively untouched by the deadly conflict that lasted from early 1861 until April of 1865. After the fall of Fort Macon to Federal troops in 1862, life for the people of eastern Carteret County, including Shackleford Banks and Harkers Island, returned to normal. And because there had been and were so few slaves among the population — most communities had none at all, the "Reconstruction" years that followed the war were likewise much less eventful than what was experienced farther inland.

The Education of an Island Boy

The descendants of at least one of my forefathers followed a different course after he arrived nearly a thousand miles farther north in Massachusetts Bay as part of the first great wave of settlers in Puritan New England. Anthony Harker was born in 1606 in the town of Sibsey in Lincolnshire, near the northeastern corner of England. By the time he was thirty, he was married and living in Boston, where he and his wife, Mary, would raise a family of two sons and four daughters.

Their third child, John Ebenezer, remained in the Boston area and, in 1680, married Patience Folger, whose sister, Abiah, would become the mother of the renowned Benjamin Franklin (my first cousin - nine times removed.) John and Patience were not so blessed, at least in terms of historical recognition, but their son Ebenezer, born in Boston in 1689, would do something to make the family's name enduring, if not famous.

As the second of his father's sons and barred by the rules of primogeniture from inheriting any of his father's estate, he chose to look farther south to find his fortune. Like several of his neighbors in the Boston area at around the same time, he decided to come to the vicinity of Beaufort, North Carolina, where a fledgling shore-based whaling industry had begun to take hold. Some of the others were named Chadwick, Whitehurst, Pigott, and Leffers and those surnames are still everywhere to be found in eastern Carteret County. Once settled, Ebenezer quickly showed that he had brought with him the vaunted Yankee ethic of work and industry that eventually afforded him the resources to buy not just a plot or even an estate, but a whole island that would be home to him and his children for generations to come.

In 1730, when he was forty-one years old, he purchased an island from George Pollock of Beaufort that lay barely five miles east of the town and was protected by barrier islands to the east and south. His purchase cost him £400 and a twenty-foot boat. He soon settled there, building a home on the far northwest corner amid a cluster of tall oak trees, and took for his wife a local girl from the nearby community of Straits named Elizabeth Brooks, with whom he eventually had six children.

From the Banks to the Island

The island had earlier been known as Craney Island, but from that time on it has been known to residents and visitors alike as Harkers Island, and with no apostrophe, as the concluding "s" was intended to denote plurality even more than possession. But Ebenezer and his descendants would spawn far fewer "Y" chromosomes than did those of his friends, such that eventually, the lone reminder of him in the place where he settled would be that place's name.

It would be seven generations and five surnames later that I arrived on the scene and on an Island named for my intrepid great-grandfather, less than two miles from where he had built his large home. At the same moment, my parents could look from a south-facing upstairs window and get a clear view of the towering lighthouse that overlooked Cape Lookout and the remains of a village where the greater part of my other ancestors had ended up.

Shackleford Banks

Shackleford Banks lies at the corner and southernmost point of a 250-mile-long string of barrier islands that make up what are called North Carolina's Outer Banks. At the turn of the 20th century, several settlements lined the north side shoreline that fronted what was called Back Sound. They extended from near the foot of the Cape Lookout lighthouse at the east end to Beaufort Inlet at the west.

A settlement known as Diamond City, taking its name from the large diamond shapes that adorn the nearby lighthouse, was the largest of several communities on Shackleford Banks. Just to the east of the village, and across the small "Drain" that eventually became Barden's Inlet, was the small hamlet of Cape Lookout. It sometimes was called "Cape Hills," but as the former name suggests, this neighborhood was centered around the large lighthouse that had been constructed there a century earlier.

Later the United States Life Saving Service built a station in the same vicinity. Cape Lookout technically was a part of Core Banks, but the closest community northward along the shore was at Portsmouth Island, some thirty miles distant. Because of this geographical separation, the inhabitants of Cape Lookout were more closely associated commercially, socially, and by bloodline with the westward-lying communities and people of Shackleford Banks than with Portsmouth Village.

Just to the west of Diamond City was the community of Bell's Island. Renowned for the large and bountiful persimmon trees that grew wild there, it was somewhat smaller than its sister village. Later tradition would consider it as part of that larger settlement. Still further west was a tiny hamlet known as Sam Windsor's Lump. It took its name from the only African American, or "Colored," family living on the Banks. To the south of the Lump was the dipping station used to disinfect cattle and other livestock from all over the Banks.

The westernmost part of Shackleford Banks was known as Wade's Shore. It extended for more than two miles and was the most densely wooded part of the entire Island. To this day that area is covered with thick patches of cedar that nestle neatly among the large and rolling dunes. The east end of Wade's Shore was called "Whale Creek Bay," a reference to it having been the shipping point for most of the by-products taken from whales and moved overland from the ocean side. At Whale Creek Bay the fig trees grew dense and wild. A very small church, "Jones Chapel," had been built there by the Southern Methodists, but it was used by any denomination that needed its facilities.

The west end of Wade's Shore was the "Mullet Pond." Here, at the edge of the Beaufort Bar, mullet would school in abundance in late summer and early fall. Like Bell's Island and Cape Lookout, the communities at Wade's Shore were very closely associated with Diamond City. In fact, the residents of the entire Island might properly have been considered as having been citizens of Diamond City.

The basic pattern of life all over the Banks was very much the same. It was almost entirely on the shores of the surrounding sounds and ocean that all were left to carve out their existence. That pattern was somewhat unique. They were not bound to the soil as were the dirt farmers of the mainland. Dry land was sometimes viewed as merely a bridge between the waters. Yet neither were they wedded entirely to the sea like many other seamen who spent weeks and even months on oceangoing vessels. Seldom, if ever, did the fishermen of Shackleford Banks venture far enough from shore that they could not return to their homes by nightfall.

Rather, the "proggers" along Back Sound made most of their living amid the marshes and on the tidal plain that skirted their Island home. Neither the land nor the water completely ruled the setting. With northerly winds and a high tide, the sea predominated as acre after acre ultimately gave way to the deluge of the tides. But sou'westers and ebb tides saw the shoals rise again and appear once more as dry land. Rich with bottom fish, finfish, shellfish, shrimp, flounder, and crabs, the tide plain offered a cornucopia of all that was to be harvested from the shallow sound.

There, literally at the water's edge, was nearly everything necessary to sustain their humble manner of living. Of necessity, that shoreline became the focal point of their lives. Within the expanse of just a few hundred feet was found what was at once their homes and their gardens, their schools and their workshops, their theaters and their playgrounds.

That unique pattern of life proceeded placidly and undisturbed on Shackleford Banks for several generations prior to the fall of 1896. Everything still might have appeared peaceful and serene to the people there as they approached the end of the last decade of the 19th century. But a series of events had already begun that, within five years, would leave Diamond City and its sister communities nothing more than ghost towns and memories.

The Storms of 1896 and 1899

Many longtime residents of Harkers Island will recall the 1996 hurricanes, especially Fran in September of that year. Three years later, Floyd, in the same month of 1999, was one of the most destructive natural disasters ever to hit the Tarheel state. However, similar storms exactly a century earlier, in 1896 and again in 1899, might have been equally powerful — and even more disruptive, at least to the people who lived at Shackleford Banks on North Carolina's lower Outer Banks. Like every coastal community before and since, the residents were familiar with the wrath of sudden and violent ocean storms.

The Education of an Island Boy

The fury of fierce winds and treacherous offshore shoals had given their section of the Atlantic coastline the infamous title of "Graveyard of the Atlantic." But even the most storm hardened inhabitants of Shackleford Banks were unprepared for the monster storms that closed out the 19th Century. These storms would have been labeled as hurricanes by modern meteorologists. However, accurate and long-range weather forecasting was entirely unavailable at that early date, and the fact that these storms had come unannounced made them even more destructive.

How the hurricanes worked their devastation was simple. Winds and water combined to build a storm surge of ocean water that eventually inundated the entire Island. The immediate impact was flooded homes and lost horses, sheep, goats, and cattle. Yet these same effects were sometimes felt by every other community along the Atlantic Coast. Taken alone, they might have been insufficient to cause the disruption of life that eventually resulted.

The latent consequences of the storms proved particularly devastating on Shackleford Banks. Barren beach sand soon replaced what had been fertile soil. Fresh water wells turned brackish, trees and shrubbery died, and vegetables refused to grow. After the storm of 1896, many residents of the Banks openly considered moving inland or to higher ground. Some families determined even then that it would be wise to look for a safer place to make their homes. From that time forward, the Banks' population began steadily declining.

If there was any uncertainty among those who remained on the Banks as to whether or not such a move would be necessary, those doubts were removed in 1899 with what would later be called the San Cieraco hurricane. That August brought a storm to which all subsequent storms would be compared for more than a generation. Throughout Carteret County, havoc and destruction were left in its path. And nowhere was the damage so consequential as at Shackleford Banks. There, the wind and tides of the South Atlantic left more than battered homes as their legacy. Instead, they rang a death knell for the communities that had grown and flourished on what had been a comfortable and hospitable island.

More than half a century later, the few remaining storm survivors could describe it as vividly as if it had occurred the previous evening. "The wind blew from the northeast at first and brought in tides from the sound," one explained to Lillian Davis, my maternal Aunt, who wrote a detailed newspaper article describing the storm and its aftermath. "Then, following hours of that, all was perfectly calm for a short while. Suddenly the winds shifted to the southwest and again blew as hard or harder than before. With those southwest winds came the waters from the ocean and the two waters met. This time few, if any, homes were without water in them."

Even the giant sand dune that ran through the center of the community had been nearly washed away by the storm. To add insult to the already intolerable injury, the ransacking waters had uncovered graves in the local cemetery and left bones and caskets strewn everywhere.

What had previously been contingency proposals now became the order of the day. From Cape Lookout in the east to Wade's Shore in the west, the residents of Shackleford Banks scurried to find new places to live. Some pulled up stakes and moved their families to the mainland. Many Cape Lookout residents ended up at Marshallberg. Several families from Wade's Shore found their way to Broad Creek and the "Promise' Land" section of Morehead City. Still others moved west across the Beaufort Bar to Bogue Banks and settled as squatters among the sand hills of Salter Path.

Lillian Davis

But for most people of Shackleford Banks, the choice of where to go was simple. They realized they could no longer stay on the Banks without risking their property and the safety of their families. But they were unwilling to affect a total separation from the only home most of them had ever known. Their best option for

The Education of an Island Boy

a place to rebuild and start anew was directly across Back Sound at a place known as Harkers Island.

Leaving the Banks

Harkers "Island" is not just a name; it is a description. It is surrounded by water on every side and blessed with natural outlets at every corner to allow rising water to pass it by. It is protected from the damaging forces of wind and water of the ocean by Shackleford Banks to the south and Core Banks to the east. It seemed an obvious place where those forced to flee the Banks hoped to be spared from the destruction caused by the high tides and flooding that had prompted their exodus.

There were communities and settlements beyond the sounds to the east and south and channels to the west and north. In most cases, there also were relatives both on the Island and on the mainland. So, some of the people and families who left the Banks for the Island after the 1899 storm were actually "coming back" when they set up their houses on the Island's southern shore.

From the time of Ebenezer Harker and before, there had been constant resettlement of people and families back and forth across Back Sound and to the mainland communities to the north and the village of Lennoxville to the west. It was not until well into the 20th century that the national census even saw fit to distinguish between what was divided by the various channels and marshes that demarcated the lower Down East settlements. There was little variation in family names from Marshallberg, on the eastern tip of the mainland, southward to Cape Lookout at the farthest southeast point of the Banks. The same was true of the Mullet Pond, on the west end of Shackleford, northward to the Straits community just across a channel from the westernmost section of the Island.

Unlike what was later experienced by the generation of my parents, the pattern of life my grandparents left behind at the Banks had changed little from when my ancestors first arrived there in the 18th century. With hardly any exceptions, all work was for subsistence. The closest real stores were in Beaufort, but that was miles away and separated from most of the Banks by bending and often treacherous channels that wound around marshes, shoals, and sandbars. As a result, the population was as devoid of social classes as can ever be imagined. The only hierarchy among the laborers was in whaling crews, where one of the older or more experienced crew members was viewed as a captain. But that was for only a few weeks each springtime. For the remainder of the year, each of the fishermen worked mostly alone or for equal shares when joined by his neighbors.

Yet one significant economic change was on the horizon, and had already begun even before the first Bankers began leaving after the storms of the 1890s. The recent widespread discovery and use of petroleum and the worldwide depletion of whale stock, taken together, had signaled a death knell for whaling in the North Atlantic. That industry had been the primary source of hard currency for most people on Shackleford Banks for over a Century.

As late as February of 1898, a Mormon missionary (The Church of Jesus Christ of Latter-day Saints) was proselyting at Harkers Island when word arrived that a local crew had brought in a whale on the beach side of Shackleford. Anxious to see the cause of all the commotion, the visitor and his companion accompanied a party to the Banks. That evening, he wrote in his journal.

"We soon found ourselves in a boat and shortly were landed on what was called "The Banks," where we beheld the whale. It was lying partly in the water and partly out of the water; seven feet were in the water, and eight feet above water, making the whale fifteen feet through. The whale was sixty feet long and weighed about fifty tons. The crew anticipated securing from its body about 4,800 gallons of oil. The bones in the whale's mouth, which is the most expensive part of the whale, were eleven feet long, three feet wide, and thirty inches thick. With the oil and the bones, the crew

William Hansen

expected to realize about $1,800.00." (Journal of Elder William Hansen)

The young visitor from Utah added some interesting things he had been told by the Bankers who worked all day and night to complete their harvest. "There is something very peculiar about a whale," he recorded in his journal. "It has fifty-two joints in its backbone, the same number as the weeks in a year. And it has three hundred and sixty-five bones in its mouth, the same number as the days in a year." He concluded with one final observation that epitomized his excitement at what he had witnessed that day. "When on top of this fish it seemed as though we were on a small island."

Little did the visitor from the West realize he had witnessed one of the very last whales taken off the shore of Shackleford Banks. What he had seen and described would be nothing more than a distant but still vivid memory in the years to come.

Although the Banks was home to hundreds of horses, most were wild and feral, and there are hardly any accounts of Bankers using them for draft, pulling a wagon, or even riding. My father would relate stories of fishermen carrying heavy sacks of fish on their backs and dealing with curious horses blocking their paths. Still, he never mentioned anyone having resorted to using the horses to help in carrying their loads. On land, just as had been the case for time immemorial, people and cargo moved only at the speed a person could walk, or maybe run if in an emergency or for a short distance. On the surrounding sound and ocean, depending on the wind or the skill of an oarsman, movement was somewhat faster but not by much, and was dependent on the prevailing breeze, the direction of the tide, or the depth of the water.

There also were cattle, goats, and sheep. Some of their stories mention using cattle and goats for milk, but there is hardly evidence of either being used for meat. Pigs, on the other hand, were everywhere, and late fall is still sometimes referred to as "hog-killing weather," as that practice came with the Bankers when they arrived at the Island. There are also tales of wild pigs or "boars" roaming freely among the lush woodlands at a spot called Wade's Shore and points to the westward.

Lamps were lit by whale oil stored and saved from the "springtime" harvest. But whale oil "saved" was necessarily whale oil "not sold," so it was used sparingly and often supplemented by homemade candles. Thus, nights were long and dark in late fall and winter, or anytime the skies were overcast, but they were short and brightened by stars and moonlight the rest of the year.

Life was spartan by any standard. The diet was largely of fish and shellfish, supplemented by waterfowl in the colder months and garden vegetables in the spring and summer. The wind howled from one direction, or another almost daily and sometimes blew sand particles so fine they would penetrate the skin and cause bleeding in tender spots around the cheeks and nose. But that same wind also provided a welcomed relief from the mosquitos, flies, and other airborne bugs that could make calm summer nights an extended nightmare.

In David McCullough's recent account of the Wright Brothers and their visits to Kitty Hawk, farther up the Outer Banks, between 1900 and 1903, he quotes from their journals and letters home. In describing the environment and terrain surrounding them, Orville Wright wrote in his journal that "the only thing that thrived on the Outer Banks were bedbugs, mosquitoes, and wood ticks."

Houses were small, seldom more than two or three rooms, and built close to the ground to block the constant north winds of winter from flowing underneath and making the cold months even more uncomfortable. Evidence of the rustic character of their furnishings is the story of the visit by a property tax collector and his effort to settle delinquent accounts. It was said that none of the "Bankers" had any money to pay, so the tax collector began to seize their personal property in payment. At the home of Tom Styron (1843-1920), they took his mattress. Since all their mattresses were filled and stuffed mainly with the dried seaweed readily available all along the shore, Tom offered no resistance and hollered at the taxman as he left, "Don't make no difference to me. I'll make me another one as soon as the tide goes out!"

With a few exceptions, houses were grouped together in clusters. Most couples lived literally in the shadow of their families, so interacting with siblings and cousins, as well as aunts and uncles,

The Education of an Island Boy

was a part of daily living. Family lives, even for extended families, were so intertwined that there was little privacy stemming from both proximity and the interdependence of families and generations.

Also, in author McCullough's story of the Wright brothers and their visits to Kitty Hawk, he recounts a letter Wilbur Wright wrote to his brother Orville. In it, the elder brother elaborated on the physical environment he found upon his arrival in 1900, at almost the exact moment Shackleford Banks, barely a hundred miles south along the Outer Banks, was being evacuated. McCullough summarized Wilbur's description in four sentences. If you substitute "Diamond City" for "Kitty Hawk," he was also describing Shackleford Banks.

"... the scene from the tent door—the scene from almost any point—was spectacular, with great stretches of water and sand dunes and beach and a tremendous sky overhead, with cumulus clouds rising like castles, thrilling to behold against the blue. Long flat horizons reached far in the distance in every direction. And then there was the wind, always the wind. It was not just that it blew nearly all the time, it was the same force that had sculpted the sand hills and great dunes of Kitty Hawk that shaped and kept shaping the whole surrounding landscape." David McCullogh, "The Wright Brothers"

As the 19th century gave way to the 20th, it was that same wind, compacted and energized into a destructive hurricane, that left Diamond City and all of Shackleford Banks unlivable. For most of the inhabitants, there was an obvious choice as to where they should look to start their new lives.

Making Harkers Island Home

Only a few families lived on Harkers Island before the storm of 1896 caused some to flee from the Banks. When the first Mormon missionaries visited in 1898, Elder William Hansen noted that twenty-eight families called the Island home. They also observed that the Island's residents were "good, humble, but very poor

From the Banks to the Island

people. All they lived on was a few fish they would catch, then sell them, and not worry any more until all the money was gone."

By late 1899, the exodus from the Banks had begun in earnest. Raw acreage on Harkers Island sold for one dollar per acre, allowing even the humblest of families to start anew with adequate land. Local tradition has it that William Henry Guthrie (1865-1935) was the first to leave the Banks after the 1899 storm. Within a month, the flow of families across the Sound became a flood. Some houses were torn down board by board, loaded on skiffs, transported across the water, and then hastily rebuilt. Other homes were left intact, laid upon dories, and floated across. By 1910, there was not a home left at Diamond City. A few structures remained on Shackleford Banks until many years later, but they were used only as fishing and hunting camps or as summer retreats.

When the "crowd from the Banks" began arriving at the Island, they usually found a place close to family already at the Island. My grandfather Charlie, later called Ol' Pa, arrived in late 1900. He built his house directly beside where his mother-in-law and my great-grandmother, Emeline, had been established for twenty years. If anything, the exodus from the Banks allowed families that might have been scattered in previous generations to reassemble in even closer proximity than they had known before the recent upheavals. Within just a few years, patterns of settlement and resettlement were established that would last for more than half a century. By the time I came along, everyone I knew could still be identified with one or more family neighborhoods and with several surnames.

Many of the first generation that left the Banks for the Island did so grudgingly at best. They retained their memories, attachments, and longings for their erstwhile homes and neighborhoods. Perhaps no one I ever knew had missed it more and longer than did "Aunt Mary Willis" (1885-1987). She was not really my aunt, but like many other older women I knew, most people always preceded her name with that title, so I did too. It is believed that before her passing in 1987, Mary was the last living person born at the Banks. The following is a story about what she missed and why, and how she felt when finally, she made her way back.

The Education of an Island Boy

A salt marsh has an aroma all its own. Throw in the odors of the feral horses, cattle, and sheep that once populated the Banks, and what you sense is a smell unlike anything else you have ever known, and one you will never forget — especially not forgotten by Mary Willis!

She had been born and raised at Diamond City. She left with her family and all the others after the storm of 1899. Arriving at Harkers Island as a teenager with the possessions she had salvaged, Mary carved out a life on the south shore of the Island, less than a quarter mile from where I would later grow up. I knew her, but only as a much older woman who usually sat in a rocker on her porch, always wore a bonnet, and had her shoulders leaning sharply forward when she walked the road.

Mary Willis
from Almeta Gaskill Collection

After enduring that first exodus, Mary was blessed never to need to pull up stakes again. For the remainder of her century-long life, she stayed at or near the spot where the skiff carrying her family to the island had landed late in the fall of 1899. At first, she was drawn to the Landing, where Mary looked across to the southeast and where she had spent her childhood. It was less than three miles distant, and she could still see the hills and even the marshes that dotted the landscape on clear days in the spring and fall. Many of her family and friends, especially the men, often went back to fish, hunt, dig for clams, or reminisce.

But for Mary, such a time never came. She soon was raising a family of her own and may never have had the occasion, the means, or maybe even the yearning to return to a place she knew had changed so dramatically from what she remembered. Time passed, and old routines gave way to new ones, and none of them ever drew or sent her back to the Banks. Years turned into decades, and

From the Banks to the Island

eventually, so much time passed that she no longer gazed across the water to imagine old sights and sounds.

Then, for some unknown reason that doesn't really matter, when she was in her seventies, Mary went back. Her son, Willie Guyon (1918-1984), convinced her one day to climb into his open boat so that he could carry her again, just one more time, to what had once been Diamond City. It was a calm, almost "slick cam" summer day as they headed off for the half-hour boat ride across the channel and shoals into a small cove called Bell's Island. From there they wound their way eastward through a maze of marshes that eventually gave way to Banks Bay, and finally to the "horse pen" that marked the Landing of where her home had once stood less than fifty yards on shore.

As the mother and her son moved slowly through the marshes, one more time Mary saw sights, heard sounds, and sensed aromas that she had not known for more than sixty years. And as she did, the days came rushing back, and for a moment at least, she was a young girl once again — running on the shore, throwing shells in the wind, and watching horses and cattle make their way through vines and rushes.

It was there that Mary leaned forward in the slow-moving boat and took a deep breath of the salty air that hangs like a mist around the summer marshes. At least a part of the distinctive smell could be traced to those feral horses that roamed the marshes in search of grass and pond water. As the pungent aroma became more and more palpable, Aunt Mary stood up from where she had been seated on the forward "thought" (thwart) of the small skiff, assumed a broad smile, and with a loud and excited voice she turned to her son and asked, "Hon, don't that horse piss smell good?" Mary Willis was home again!

At least a portion of that sentiment has been carried forward several generations and continues even now. When my children arrive home after being away for extended periods, they are prone to lower the windows in their car as they approach the North River Bridge, sometimes called the "Gateway to the Original Down East," just to smell the marshes!

Wild ponies on Shackleford Banks

The Landing and The Shore

For the Islanders of my generation and earlier, place and location names of where they had been and now settled were specific, but did not always coincide with what might show on a map or an atlas. In addition, those designations were so familiar that they often were shortened for brevity and convenience. "The Cape" was understood to mean Cape Lookout. "The Banks," when used alone, always meant Shackleford Banks, and "The Sound" could be assumed to mean "Back Sound." Finally, the most obvious of all assumptions was that when someone mentioned "The Island," they could be referring to Harkers Island and nothing else, regardless of where they were from or where they might be going. To many of us, this last one was and remains non-negotiable.

Like at the Banks, the Island's southside shore was then a sandy and largely pristine beach. A significant difference was that here, the primarily calm water of Back Sound lapped the shoreline — unlike the sometimes-stormy ocean waves of Onslow Bay that splashed on the south side of Shackleford Banks. Again, just as at the Banks, grassy marshes dissected by narrow channels were consigned to the northside shore, called the Bay. That difference is far less noticeable now, with the modern structures visitors see when they approach the Island across a bridge from the north.

However, until the latter half of the 1970s, only the island's south side was settled with any density.

In a remarkable testament to the familial bonds shared both by the newcomers and the Island's earlier settlers, that shoreline would remain entirely communal for another seventy years or more. Regardless of who or what lay above the tideline, it was understood that the sandy beach and the water that adjoined it belonged to everyone equally. Other than a series of breakwaters laid to prevent erosion after the hurricanes and storms of the 1950s, there were no artificial barriers to block access to, or passage through, the shoreline in any direction. No matter how far his home might be inland from the water, every fisherman, along with his family and crew, had an accepted easement along paths and even through the yards of his neighbors that allowed unfettered access to his boats, skiffs, nets, and gear. Boats were anchored, moored, or tied to stakes in places that were the most convenient, and not necessarily adjacent to the property of their owners. And because there were no fences or barricades, the shore itself was a convenient and often-used pathway headed both east and west. For a long time, it was considered that the "shortest distance between any two points" was not a "straight line," but rather, "along the shore."

There were sentimental reasons, as well as more logical ones, that explained the pattern of staying as close as possible to the south-facing beach. The south shore of the Island has been called "The Landing" for as long as anyone can remember. It is separated from the Banks by only a narrow channel, called Back Sound. Looking from there, the newcomers to the Island could look towards, and on clear days, even see the glistening sand hills that still stood amid the places they or their parents had left behind.

Among the things that had not been transplanted were the graves and headstones of their deceased relatives. Those cemeteries were maintained for several generations after the living community had been displaced. Sadly, with each subsequent storm, the old graves became less and less identifiable, and all but a handful hidden amid the hills and cedar trees of Wade's Shore are now lost forever.

The Education of an Island Boy

But there was a more pragmatic reason for clustering on the Island's south shoreline. Because of proximity, as the Landing runs directly adjacent to Shackleford Banks and the two places are separated only by a channel called "Back Sound," the newcomers could easily work the same marshes and bays that they and their forebearers had harvested for generations. At least one other reason, nearly as practical as the shorter distance, made the south shore more attractive than the other side of this very narrow island. Seasonal winds — from the south in the spring and summer and from the north in the fall and winter — were always on the minds of people who had to make do as they could with heat and cold as much with their wits as with their physical resources. At or near the Landing, the strong southwesters of late summer were a welcomed respite from the dog-day heat and humidity that prevails all along the Southeastern coastline of the United States. In winter, the many trees and lush vegetation that covered the Island provided a barrier and protection from the chilly north winds from late October to mid-March.

Within just a few years after the beginning of their migration, most of the little homes were stacked, sometimes literally, between the Landing and an inland path that had been cut generations before from Shell Point to Red Hill. That path was called the "Old Road" and was supposed to mark the centerline of the Island for its original settlers. But with the arrival of the newcomers, a newer road was blazed much closer to the south shoreline. That one eventually became the primary traffic artery for wagons and carts, and later for cars and trucks.

The Old Road is still called that and has long since been paved, but not until several decades after the newer one got its first coat of blacktop. Although it was not the island's main artery, for the newcomers, the Old Road was the inshore boundary line for most everyday activities. Meanwhile, the "native Islanders," the ones who were already here before the storms, were scattered much more widely across the whole Island than were these latest homesteaders. In the two centuries after Ebenezer Harker settled the Island in the early 18th century, his descendants and others who came here had lived and worked what were generally much larger plots spread throughout the Island's broader expanse.

From the Banks to the Island

Thus, it was on or close to the south shore, the Landing, that most of the Islanders made their homes, and that template had not changed when I came to know it. Looking back to the world I grew up in, the building patterns from one end of the Island to the other could be described as a series of conjoining circles that, in one way or another, were connected to every other circle on the Island. From Shell Point at the east to Rush Point at the west, the entire community was divided into neighborhoods, and those neighborhoods were subdivided into extended families. Moving east to west, it began with the Yeomanses at the East'ard and extended all the way to the Brookses at the West'ard - with Yeomanses, Roses, Gaskills, Lewises, Joneses, Wades, Nelsons, Brookses, Chadwicks, Fulchers, Davises, Fulfords, Johnsons, Scotts, Gillikins, Lawrences, Hamiltons, Dixons, Styrons, Russells, Moores, Hancocks, and some others in between. Beyond that there were several clusters of Guthries and Willises, and especially the latter. The Willises, most of whom had come from the Banks, were so numerous that they were represented in every neighborhood, and most families.

Further, from one end to the other, every home could have been identified with both one of those neighborhoods, as well as one or more of those extended families. Even within the latter, there lay still smaller circles that were the nuclear families, usually housed under a single roof but still nestled within a larger family grouping and one of the many neighborhoods that filled the whole Island.

This close identification with families and neighborhoods sometimes created tension, especially when new couples were deciding where to settle and start their families, as a choice of one neighborhood over the other was sometimes viewed as a preference among sets of relatives rather than as a mere choice of a spot to build a home. But that was rare and an exception since by then every Islander, no matter their immediate family, shared lots of relatives with the same or different last name, and even more with similar DNA.

As time passed, the south shore enclaves continued to grow, primarily by subdividing the land already claimed by each family for three or more generations. Multi-acre plots were divided and carved up time after time. By the mid-1960s, most homes sat on

The Education of an Island Boy

plots of a quarter acre or even less, and sometimes much less, with boundaries that resembled randomly shaped patterns much more than the squares or rectangles of more typical land development.

By the midpoint of the century, and extending into the early part of the 1960s, the Island's population settlement had reached a critical mass. Quite simply, there was hardly any uncleared land left on the south shore at the same time as a generation of "baby boomers" were coming of age and wanting a place of their own. It became increasingly apparent that any new homesites would have to spread farther inland to allow any space for continued growth. Fortunately, that was made possible when, in the early sixties, two of the Island's longest standing and original families came to the rescue with plans that opened most of the rest of the Island to new homes and neighborhoods.

The Davises and Fulfords had lived on Harkers Island for the better part of two centuries when the departure from Diamond City and the other Banks communities began. Cousins Earl Davis (1902-1988) and Owen Fulford (1909-2007), both great-great-great grandsons of Ebenezer Harker, had separately inherited undeveloped acreage more than half a century after that initial influx of newcomers from the Banks. By the sixties, both began to formally develop and offer for sale that acreage into planned subdivisions, with well-measured plots and roads instead of paths. This was just in time for my generation and those who came along even after the baby boomers.

Earl Davis

As might have been expected, some wondered aloud why and how just two men, and cousins at that, had come to own such a large portion of the Island. A rudimentary knowledge of the Island's early history would have explained what the skeptics considered an anomaly, but most didn't care enough to find out. They seemed content to occasionally ask loaded questions or mutter some often-repeated lines alluding to the space exploration that was a hallmark of that decade. "Owen and Earl own the world. And watch out soon; they'll own the moon."

By the early seventies, Owen and Earl were not only selling, but also financing the sale of primarily half-acre plots in developments that soon reached across the Island to the Bay, as most of the north side of the Island was called, and that stretched from the east end of the Island to its westernmost points. Within two decades, the number of homes on the Island had more than doubled. Perhaps more important than the increase in available lots, at least for me, was that it was timed precisely right to allow at least one more generation of Harkers Islanders to remain close to their families and the livelihoods that had sustained them for so many years.

Because little of that land had been cleared of dense forest and vegetation, the roar of bulldozers and tractors was commonplace for several years as it echoed from the bay-side woods. Not a small portion of the clearing work was done by hand with axes and a tool for removing smaller brush called a "weed swiper." As Earl Davis was my uncle, having married my mother's oldest sister, Lillian, and whom all the family called "Big Sister," I was among those recruited to help with the most rudimentary work. In truth, I was more "allowed" than recruited, as it was quite a favor for Uncle Earl to hire me on. There were lots of others who

Owen Fulford

were older and stronger than me. But taking full advantage of whatever rights of nepotism I could claim, I spent a large part of two summers helping to "clear up" the unsettled section of the Island that would eventually be my grown-up home place.

Neighborhoods of Kinfolks

By the 50s when I arrived on the scene, and especially by the 60s when I came of age, domestic patterns for Harkers Island families had lost much, if not most, of the purely maritime nature that typified the lifestyle and routines of daily living known by my grandparents on either side of Back Sound. A glimpse inside the homes of most families on the Island of my youth would have revealed similar patterns and relationships to those that most Americans saw each evening on their newly acquired black-and-white television sets. Most households were some admittedly rustic versions of what was seen on "Father Knows Best" or "Leave it to Beaver."

This was true even as the home itself was much more primitive, and the furnishings and appliances evidenced a setting that was both coastal and rural —as well as one that was decades behind in economic and living standards. Families were both nuclear and extended and often included not just the parents and children but sometimes grandparents, aunts, uncles, and cousins. There were a few single-parent families, many resulting from romances that had started and ended with soldiers and sailors who passed through the Island during and after World War II. Most involved a mother raising her child or children with her parents and in their home.

Our house was situated amid a dozen similar-sized and shaped dwellings belonging to the "Charlie Hancock crowd." That enclave was surrounded by three other extended-family groups, the Willises (Rennie 1884-1940), Guthries (Willie 1898-1966), and Moores (Aaron 1897-1970), to whom we were blood-related in at least one way, and often two or more. Each extended family was an acknowledged part of the bigger neighborhood.

My mental snapshot of that neighborhood circa 1962 would show a group of about forty houses, give or take only a couple. They stretched from the south shore of the Island on Back Sound northward at least halfway across the Island to the Old Road and toward Westmouth Bay. On the south border, it ran east to west from the homes belonging to Hardin Guthrie (1869-1951) and his children to the homesteads of the families of brothers Rennie and Danky Willis (1891-1952).

On its northern end, the neighborhood was flanked by the families of Willie Guthrie and Aaron Moore to the east, and the assembled Hancock and Moore children and grandchildren to the west. In between, every home housed at least one of these four primary family names. Many had two, and some even three of those surnames represented.

As for the scores of cousins who were the grandchildren of those patriarchs, our relationships were sometimes so convoluted that we just knew we were "kin," even if we could not explain precisely how. During summer and whenever school was out, groups of children, especially young boys, would roam that neighborhood in packs — playing games, interacting with family pets, or picking and enjoying apples, pears, figs, briar berries, or wild grapes. Eventually, most of us could identify the inhabitants of every single home. If children were living there, we usually were as familiar with the inside of the houses as we were with the exteriors.

Brothers, Sisters, Cousins, and a World at War

For a century and a half, surnames all over the Island, and before that at the Banks, had remained almost totally static. The families that moved down the coast from the Tidewater area of Virginia might not have come as a group or at the same time, but by the middle of the 19th century, they had settled down and together. Except for an occasional venture up Core Sound towards Marshallberg, Davis, or Sea Level, or across the channel to Beaufort or Salter Path, the men and boys, as well as the women and girls of Harkers Island, found wives and husbands among the same family groups as had their parents and grandparents for as long as they could remember.

Then came World War II. Or, more precisely, then came the soldiers, sailors, and marines that were stationed all along the lower Outer Banks, and especially near Cape Lookout. They were there to protect against incursions from enemy submarines and surface ships. Only a few of the newcomers lived on the Island as most were housed in barracks at the Cape, Fort Macon on Bogue Banks directly west of Shackleford Banks, or farther north up the Sound. But Harkers Island, with its "show house" (movie theater), community center (Carl's Store), and several cafes and general stores, soon became their preferred evening and weekend hangout.

The Education of an Island Boy

There, they could find dozens of young men, who, like them, were looking for a diversion from the military service that had interrupted their lives and left them far removed from their own families and friends, and especially their girlfriends. By the time the last of them left for home after the war, several were accompanied by wives they had met and courted while serving near the Island. Others left behind wives or girlfriends, and sons and daughters, who were unwilling to say goodbye to their Island families, but who kept the surnames of war-time lovers for themselves and their children.

Livingston Brooks
CSWM&HC Collection

Even before the attack on Pearl Harbor in December of 1941, men and boys from the Island had volunteered and were serving in the Navy and Coast Guard. The first Gold Star, symbolizing a family member lost in action, hung in Carteret County, of which Harkers Island is a part, was at the Island home of Gordon (1888-1942) and Nettie Brooks (1893-1985). Their son, Livingston (1918-1942), lost his life in January of 1942 while serving on a Coast Guard Cutter in the North Atlantic. His ship, the USCG Alexander Hamilton, was sunk by a torpedo from a German U-boat as the Hamilton escorted other ships near the coast of Iceland. After the draft was enacted with the Selective Service Act of 1942, hardly a neighborhood or family was left untouched by a tearful goodbye to a son, brother, or cousin who was drafted or enlisted to serve in the armed forces of the United States at war.

Then, after the long war finally was over, those young men who were fortunate enough to make it home found an Island that had been changed while they were gone, even if not quite as profoundly as the lives of the soldiers and sailors who just a few years earlier had been obliged to leave their Island homes.

From the Banks to the Island

Though all of this occurred in the decade before I was born, its consequences were felt everywhere in the world I grew up in, and among the families and neighbors that made up my world. Three homes grouped closely together in a small enclave of our neighborhood epitomized how the war affected the people and influenced life on the Island for decades to come. In the northeast corner of our neighborhood was the home of Willie (1898-1966) and Carrie Moore Guthrie (1903-1985). Just to the south, less than a hundred feet away but across the Old Road that mainly remained a dirt trail, was the home of Aaron (1897-1970) and Annie Guthrie Moore (1901-1972). The two houses were connected by more than a property line and a path. Aaron Moore was Carrie Guthrie's brother, and Annie Moore was Willie Guthrie's sister. One house farther south and up the path towards the Landing was the home of Vannie (1894-1962) and Lula (1897-1969) Guthrie. Vannie was Willie and Annie's brother.

By the time the last shots were fired in Europe and Asia and the last soldier and sailor left his barracks near the Cape, four sons from those three houses had served either in Europe or in East Asia. Just as significantly, four daughters from two of those houses had been married and started families with soldiers or sailors stationed in our area. Within a few years, all but one of those husbands had gone back to his native home, and two of the three had left behind their Island wives and children.

As those children grew older, kids on the Island became familiar with new family names. In our neighborhood, those names were Irvine, Craver, and Beamon. Elsewhere on the Island, many more became just as commonplace. By the time a generation had passed, and the baby boomers started their own families, the younger Islanders assumed that these names had been here all along—just like the Lewises, Guthries, Moores, and even the Willises.

Life at the Landing

Typical of the time and place, most adult women were both wives and mothers and worked only in the home. Add to that their assumed role of helping their husbands as watermen, and it was usually more than enough to keep them busy. But busy as they were, they remained actively involved with each other and with the lives of the bevy of children within a radius close to their homes and families. Men and fathers had a broader reach that usually extended throughout the neighborhood and beyond. Because of that, at least as a group, their influence on everyday life was more easily visible, even if less profound than that of their wives. My mother was at the center of everything in our home and around Hancock Landing. But, collectively, at least, my father and the men who lived and worked beside him, many of them older than even he, were much more a part of my boyhood experience, and thus of my lasting memory.

This should not imply that the women didn't congregate outside their homes. They did, especially in their churches. Another memorable gathering place for women was in the sound on hot late summer afternoons. I don't recall how the occasions might have been organized, but it was not unusual for the neighborhood women to sometimes come and join their children as we were swimming. Still wearing their long skirts and dresses (frocks), they would walk out to where the water was waist-deep and then kneel so that only their heads and shoulders were above the surface.

Usually, in a large circle, depending on how many were there at a given time, the women would escape the "dog day" heat while visiting with their friends and family. Eventually, en masse, they would head back towards the shore where they and we would wash off the salt with hoses that spouted well-water so cold it usually left you shivering.

Children swimming together at the Landing was frequent but usually only from late May until mid-September. The gathering of older women at the shore was so much the exception that it stands out in my memory. On the other hand, groupings of men working together in the water or at its edge were a vital part of every day in the world that I remember. Our fathers, grandfathers, uncles, and cousins usually had already spent their day working somewhere in the water or preparing to spend their evening trawling or channel-netting for shrimp. Especially in the mid-summer heat, most commercial fishing was done at dusk or dawn. Clamming on the shoals off Shackleford was one of the few exceptions. Other than that, the grown-up men spent their daylight hours preparing or repairing their boats, nets, and rigging for the hard work ahead of them.

Hancock Landing in the 1980's. The old net houses were soon demolished, and the shore was cleared of debris.

Since most of this was done at or near the Landing, where we children spent most of our time, we were around our fathers and their friends as much, or even more so, than our mothers between May and September. It was in this setting that I came to know, love, and appreciate the "old men" who were at the center of the neighborhood that gave shape to my world. They told the stories that gave meaning to the lessons I was learning. They practiced and taught the skills that allowed me to appreciate how arduous the life of a waterman could be. And most of all, they helped me to understand that I was part of something bigger than myself or even my family. They never used those precise words, but they didn't have to. They lived out their part in a way that I would never forget.

Of all the things I miss about that way of living, that dynamic relationship of men and fathers with boys and sons may be among the most profound. As I compare it with the lifestyles that have taken their place, I sense that something important, even vital, has been lost. The lives of my children serve as an example of the contrast. Outside of our home, interaction with them, and now with my grandchildren, most often has been and is in the context of "their" (my children's) world. Like other parents and grandparents, I attend their ball games and recitals, awards ceremonies and graduations, and even their parties and parades. I see them as they go about their routines and rituals, and if I am involved enough, I can have some influence on what and how they learn from those experiences.

That stands in sharp contrast to the world of my youth, which evidenced a pattern almost totally the opposite. I got to know my parents, especially my father and other men in our neighborhood, in a setting entirely their own. I watched and learned as they prepared for and worked in the water, maintained their houses and boats, and especially as they gathered to share life stories and experiences.

I was lucky! Those interactions were exponentially more intimate and formative than what today's prevailing model will allow. Certainly, the change has been less dramatic for mothers, or at least for those fortunate few with the privilege of staying home with their children. For fathers, the role reversal has been as stark as it has been irresistible — for them and for their children — and especially for their sons.

I am sure I have had as many contemporary friends and associates as my father, likely even more. My children and grandkids know them only by name and a few anecdotal accounts they might have overheard through the years. But for me and my generation of Island boys, our fathers and their friends were not just spectators as we played games and learned to play and work. They were our teachers and mentors who helped us sense that we were part of something wonderfully special that was more than we could see with our own eyes or hear with our own ears. And, as we watched and heard them, we came to appreciate even more how they became who they were, and, just as importantly, who we were and how we might carry on those traditions.

Carl Lewis's home and store which sat directly across from the Methodist Church at the midpoint of the island. The store was a gathering place for locals and visitors for an entire generation.

The Education of an Island Boy

Above: Harkers Island Elementary School 2nd Grade class of 1950

Below: Harkers Island Elementary School 1925

2

A New Home and Way of Life

People moved slowly then. They ambled across the square, shuffled in and out of the stores around it, took their time about everything. A day was twenty-four hours long but seemed longer. There was no hurry, for there was nowhere to go, ... nothing to see outside the boundaries of Maycomb County.
Harper Lee, "To Kill a Mockingbird"

> *They have the very greenest trees,*
> *And skies as bright as flame*
> *But what I liked the best in Mira.*
> *Is everybody knew my name.*
> "Mira," from the Musical "Carnival"

Tradition!

Harkers Island was not classified as a town, and still isn't — at least not an incorporated one — but we did have some of the stores, shops, and services that were found in most small towns of the rural south, and some that were unique to our life as a coastal community remote from so much of the world. According to the 1960 census, the Island had 1,362 permanent residents — up from 1,244 ten years earlier — living in 446 houses. By 1970, the population had reached 1,639 people living in 602 separate homes. Those numbers actually were relatively large when compared to the other townships in Down East Carteret County. But our jointly shared history and the still largely isolated nature of our home place helped to make us unique even among neighboring communities just a few miles away as the "seagull flies." Those factors combined to give our little community an aura and "traditions" as real as what Tevya the milkman tried to explain and celebrate in "Fiddler on the Roof."

Shell Point

There are place names on the Island that everyone knows and remembers communally, as if they were genetically implanted: Academy Field, the Sand Hole, Red Hill, and the Bay among them, and each one because the name describes not just a natural or physical landmark, but also a set of shared experiences. None of these is more a part of the community consciousness than the place called "Shell Point." Once there, looking to the south, one finds an unobstructed view of both where the Cape Lookout lighthouse still is and where Diamond City used to be. It is the easternmost point on the Island and where it gives way to Core Sound, then Core Banks, and ultimately to the broad expanse of the Atlantic Ocean so that the next inhabited land mass anyone could see — if they could see that far — would be on the coast of Portugal.

A point of admittedly extraneous information that I nonetheless find interesting is this: A straight line westward from Shell Point on Harkers Island following that line of latitude 34.68 N reaches the Pacific Ocean at Surf Beach, CA. The straight-line distance is 2,481 miles, and the Google Maps suggested route for driving is 2,860 miles. Now you know!

But most Islanders of my youth never were thinking that far away, and few of us thought about anything east of Shell Point itself. It was as if it was on that very spot that the world began anew every day, and just going there was a private way of being part of that renewal. So, starting with the first cars that came to the Island in the "Roaring Twenties," there developed a ritual, often a daily one, of driving to Shell Point, turning at the disjointed cul-de-sac circle that marks the end of the road, and then heading back to where you came from. That was it – just driving or riding to Shell Point. There was something therapeutic about the way the rest of the world and

A New Home and Way of Life

its troubles seemed to come into a more reasonable focus once you were there, and especially once you turned your back to face westward with the serenity and seclusion of Shell Point at your back.

If someone was heading out for no apparent reason, so you felt like asking where they were going, and they responded with a simple "Shell Point," you understood that response with no further explanation needed. Saying "I'm going to Shell Point" meant that you just wanted to retreat for a while and get your bearings — nothing big or to worry about. You just needed to be "hugged by your heritage" for a few moments before whatever came next. I've tried and done it many times. Somehow, it always seemed to work back then. Sometimes, it still does.

Shell Point, at the end of the road on Harkers Island.
This photo was taken in the 1960's.
CSWM&HC Collection

The spot is called Shell Point because of the massive mound of seashells that once was piled high from the shoreline and far out into Core Sound. Longstanding tradition says that the shells had been piled there over generations by native Americans, supposedly trying to build a bridge from the Island to Core Banks. I am told that geologists have viewed them more likely to have been shell mounds, sometimes called "shell middens," which occur naturally and are common in many coastal areas, including all along the southeastern coast. Nearly all of the mound at Shell Point was gone by the time I can remember, although on low tide you could see remnants of the pile that headed out to the eastward. My brother Tommy, only seventeen years older than me, can vividly recall that the shell pile extended more than five hundred feet toward Core Banks. And, most likely, it went even farther than that. According to him, "On days when the water was clear, you could see them stretched out still farther on the bottom and under the water."

As to where the shells went, as dirt paths began to be replaced with paved roads, the shells of Shell Point were appropriated by the state and county to be used as the underlayment for asphalt and blacktop. According to an article published in a local paper by my aunt, Lillian Davis, as early as the 1920s, the state carried shells by barge from Shell Point to Hyde, Pamlico, and Onslow counties for use in building roads. She added that "... In the process of removing the shells, many Indian relics were found, [including] tomahawks, stone knives, arrowheads, spearheads, clay pipes, pottery, and even a large skeleton ..." (Carteret County News-Times, 19 February 1981)

A few years later, in 1926, the "new road" on Harkers Island became our first hard-surfaced street, with its bottom layer taken entirely from the Shell Point mounds. One of my father's oft-told stories was that as a young man, his earliest driving experience was with a truck used to haul shells from Shell Point and then dumped along the path that had become the main Harkers Island road. Consequently, whenever someone travels down Island Drive on the Island, they are driving or riding atop shells that initially came from Shell Point.

According to my father's story, his co-worker in the hauling shell project was Henry Davis (1911-1979), the son of Cleveland Davis (1886-1941), and like my grandfather, Charlie, one of the patriarchs of the Island at that time. My father maintained that much of the original mound remained even after their project was completed. So, as time passed even more shells were transported elsewhere in the county for similar purposes. That venture continued until late into the 1940s, as evidenced by Tommy's recollections. My father explained that his father and Cleveland had contracted with the county to move the shells. His anecdotes were mostly about how the shells would puncture the tires on the truck they were using, and that he and Henry would sometimes have to remove tires and patch tubes several times in one journey to and from the Point. Even with all the delays, their job was eventually completed, and when it was, the shells at Shell Point became just a memory.

Academy Field

There was another place nearly as much a part of our consciousness as Shell Point, even though the name recalled a structure long gone and that only a few Islanders could remember ever seeing. That spot was and is called "Academy Field." It lies on the south shore, two-thirds of the way from the Bridge to Shell Point and is directly across from the Island's elementary school. It took its name from "Jenny Bell's Academy" (est. 1864), a primary school established near the close of the Civil War by the Northern Methodist Church. Her school, and hundreds of others just like it, were an attempt by Yankee evangelists to help reconstruct the defeated South into a more civilized and egalitarian society in the decades that followed the War.

Long after Jenny Bell (1817-1894) left the Island for the last time to return to her native New England, her schoolhouse remained a central point and meeting place for the Island community. Both before and after the exodus from Shackleford Banks, which more than quadrupled the Island's population at the close of the 19th century, that small building was the closest thing to a community center to be found. The land title for the academy remained with the Northern Methodist Church after the school's closure.

Still, the church shared its use freely with other fledgling congregations that arose after the arrival of the refugees from the Banks, including even the Mormons for a short time when their missionaries first visited in 1898. As the Island developed with numerous stores, churches, and even a motion picture theater, Jenny Bell's building fell into disrepair due to age and neglect. It was finally demolished sometime before the Northern and Southern Methodists were consolidated into one congregation in 1939.

However, the approximately fifteen-acre plot surrounding it remained a community gathering place until the end of the last century. Blessed with some of the largest and most sprawling oaks on the Island, it was an ideal setting for picnics and camp meetings. Several times each summer, hundreds of people would line the shoreline there to watch the impromptu boat races that were a part of the usual Memorial, Independence, and Labor Day celebrations. The brush surrounding the trees was often cut enough that it was sometimes used as a ball field and as a clearing for traveling carnivals or circuses.

Once, in the mid-1960s, it was the site of a regional Boy Scout camporee I was lucky enough to be a part of. On that occasion, the entire plot was covered with tents, huts, and open campfires. Even when left entirely vacant, the vista it provided served another particular purpose for students at the Island school that lay just across the road to the north. Indeed, one of the best things about being assigned to the classrooms on the south side of the Island schoolhouse was that you could look to that field, and then beyond it, to see the Lighthouse at the Cape while sitting at your desk and filling out worksheets.

By the decade of the 80s, new owners had allowed the brush to grow so tall and the pine trees to sprout even higher that Academy Field became a new-growth forest, and even the path to the shore was hidden from everyone except the most ardent hikers. Still, more than a century after Jenny Bell and her supporters gave up on their plan to reshape the culture of a small section of coastal North Carolina, the school she established remains a part of the consciousness, if not the memory, of every Harkers Islander.

Red Hill

At the opposite end of the Island from Shell Point at the East'ard was Red Hill at the West'ard. The latter is the highest spot on

A New Home and Way of Life

Harkers Island. "Hill" might seem a strange moniker for a location less than twenty feet above sea level, but relative to the land around it, it was a hill — or at least the closest thing to a hill we had. The "red" part of the name came from how the sands on the shoreline dunes glistened in the afternoon and evening sun when viewed from the waters to the south of the Island, especially when coming up "Turkle Reef" channel from Wade's Shore. Those shining dunes were the landmarks we used to stay safely in the deep water between "Middle Marsh" and the "Cockle Shoals."

Red Hill was home to the largest grove of native oak trees on the Island. Rising more than a hundred feet in the air, the mid-day sun shining through the tops of the trees still can create a marvelous light show that is so picturesque and serene as to evoke a supernal, even a religious setting. In a few places, thick vines at the feet of the tall trees created such a jungle that it was a favorite place for childhood adventures and games. Wild grapes and briar berries were there for the picking. There was even a monkey living among the thickets for a while. No kidding, but how that came to be is another story altogether!

The people who lived under those oak trees; the Guthries, Lewises, Yeomanses, and especially the Willises, gave Red Hill its true character. Tom Lewis (1884-1963), Stacy Guthrie (1882-1974), Luther Yeomans (1886-1960), along with Maxwell Willis (1912-1974) and "Tookie" Willis (1918-1980), were all larger-than-life characters, and anyone who remembers them has tales of them to tell. Except for Maxwell, who never married but who helped to start and then ran the local REA (Rural Electrification Administration), they each left large families with an abundance of stories that preserve their legacies.

But it was perhaps the humblest of the people on Red Hill who carved out the largest part of my memories for that special place — one so indelible that it has often been a frame of reference for me in sharing life lessons. Sometimes, thankfully not all that often, when my children would bemoan the things they "didn't have," I would reply in wistful frustration, "I wish that just for five minutes I could take you to Boo's and let you see how some people had to live!" Then, just as fast, I would regain my bearings enough to know

The Education of an Island Boy

Louie Larson "Boo" Willis with friend and neighbor Margie Davis.
From the CSWM&HC Collection

that even if they could see it in a picture, they still could not fully grasp the image that colored my mind.

When I was a boy, at the top of Red Hill, there was an old wind-bleached and battered shack that was the home of "Boo" (1883-1971) and his wife Mary Anne (1894-1971). Boo's real name was Louie Larson Willis, one given to him by his father Isaac (1848-1900) in memory of my great-grandfather who had been his boyhood friend. But very few people knew that, as Boo was the only name they had ever heard him called by anyone other than his family. His family knew him as "Poppy." He and Mary Anne (Guthrie) were the parents of three children: a son Johnny "Boo" (1914-2002), and daughters Nita (1910-1986) and Fammie Lee (1920-2015). The two girls eventually lived in houses on the same plot of land that was home to their parents.

Nita's son, Carl William (1927-2004), married my oldest sister, Ella Dee, and since I was so close in age to their son and my nephew, Jonathan, I often was with him when he made his way to the west'ard to visit his Grandma Nita. What I remember most was the times we spent next door to her in and around the home of Jonathan's great-grandfather, Boo.

If the Island that I knew growing up was two or more generations behind the rest of the world in social and economic changes, then

Mary Ann Willis and her daughter Nita
CSWM&HC Collection

A New Home and Way of Life

the little world of Boo and Mary Ann harkened back at least another generation further. Their house may once have been painted, but by the time I played hide 'n seek in his side yard, nothing could be seen but the bare wooden sheathing and the vertical orange lines that formed below rusting iron nails. The roof was covered with wooden shingles, and the foundation was an open breezeway, hardly a foot off the ground, and held up by thinly scattered piers made from pine, poplar, or cedar.

The hand pump on the back porch was the family's only water source, and a small wooden shed, no larger than five feet square, was the family's privy, or "outhouse" in our vernacular. There was a small porch and a stoop by the front and back doors; one had a rusting metal glider chair, and the other a wooden swing hanging from sisal rope.

Their home had three rooms: a combined kitchen, dining room, and sitting room separated by a thin partition from two small bedrooms at the other end. Other than the kitchen table and beds, their only furnishings were two wicker chairs in the den and a framed picture depicting "Ben Hur's" chariot race that hung on the wall. Inside, that part of the clapboard floorboards not covered by cracked linoleum was so worn that it had a shimmer from the thousands of footsteps that had sanded them smooth over more than half a century of shuffling. Staring at the walls, you could see beams of sunlight peeking through the cracks that, in the late afternoon, seemed to shift and dance as the sheathing boards shifted from the outside wind or the movements inside.

In winter, the house was warmed by a tin heater. On cold mornings, it bellowed smoke through a metal flue that stuck out through the wall as it burned the scrap wood scavenged from among the oaks and cedars. It was told that during one especially cold spell when wood alone was unable to keep the house heated, Boo traded off a corner of the land the house sat on for a fifty-pound bucket of coal. The home was soon much warmer, but when Mary Anne discovered how the fuel had been purchased, she "ran her husband into the yard."

My childhood and lifelong friend, Karen Willis Amspacher, who was Boo's great niece and lived less than a stone's throw away through the oak grove, has memories of that setting that are just as stark as mine. "I remember them both ... Uncle Boo and Aunt Mary Ann ... remember going in that side door off the porch that faced the East'ard and Uncle Boo's overalls. Their yard was pure white sand, and Aunt Mary Ann raked it all the time. You could see the rake tracks in the sand as if it had been swept with a broom. Her kitchen had plastic curtains under the sink for doors ... Cabinets were just shelves with jelly glasses to drink out of. Don't remember much about the living room except it being small and dark ... the house sagged noticeably in the middle, but it bothered no one. That, my friends, was Red Hill ..."

The home was not just at the very top of Red Hill. It was at the inside angle of the sharpest curve anywhere on the Island roads. Sitting at the juncture of two relatively long straight stretches, heading either south from the Bridge or west from Shell Point, the bend in the road caught so many drivers by surprise that it came to be known as "Dead Man's Curve." On several occasions, Boo and Mary Ann were awakened at various times between sundown and dawn to the sounds of screeching tires and the collision of metal into the trunk of an oak tree.

Eventually, they grew weary of the excitement and feared one of the cars might get through the trees and into their home. Not willing to move from where both of them had spent their entire lives, they instead decided to "pivot" their house on its foundation so that it was several feet farther from the road, and behind a somewhat larger and more protective grove of hardwoods.

To dwell on the primitive and humble circumstances of his surroundings would be to do the couple, especially Boo, a disservice. In all my time with and around him, I never heard the old man — he seemed like the oldest man in the world to me — even hint at anything that could be considered a grievance. On the contrary, he seemed grateful, kind, gentle, and patient, almost at fault.

Boo was smaller, even shorter, than his wife. And if he was the epitome of meekness, Mary Anne could sometimes be entirely the opposite. She was often loud and boisterous and was sometimes given to rushes of anger and emotion. Those outbursts were

A New Home and Way of Life

usually directed at her family, and most often at her husband. But Boo seemed never to respond with anything other than submission, as if he accepted that whatever were her problems, they were at least partially because of his doing.

Once while oystering at Middle Marsh on a summer afternoon, Boo and his small sailskiff were caught in a violent storm of rain and wind that swept in from the westward. Knowing he could not outrun the thunder and lightning, he wrapped himself in the sail and lay in the bottom of the boat, hoping to weather the storm. But despite his efforts, the lighting hit the mast, splitting it into pieces, and some of the electrical charges streamed into Boo and caused him to lose consciousness for several hours.

It was well after midnight before he regained his senses and strength enough to point his skiff toward Red Hill. When he finally reached his home, he was greeted not with joy and relief but by the angry questions of a wife who seemed more frustrated and hungry than worried about what might have happened. As was always the case, he apologized and promised to head out again as soon as the sun was up the following day. Through all that, and the endless frustrations that his life presented, Boo was never heard complaining. He accepted her fits of anger, the drudgery of his work in the water, and the poverty of his surroundings, as his assigned lot in life, and that there was little if anything he could do to change it.

The physical harshness he knew as a waterman showed in Boo's form and shape, even if not in his demeanor. He seemed even older than his years. He bent forward as he walked, and his steps were more a shuffle than a pace. Watching him closely as he sat and told stories, we couldn't help but notice a steady shake in his hands, and he sometimes struggled to hear and understand our young voices. Still, he pressed on and seemed never to change in any way from one occasion to the next.

Once, while sitting on the sun-bleached planks of his small porch, talking to Jonathan, his great-grandson asked if the old man ever thought about dying, and if that thought caused him any worry. "Oh, no!" he responded with a gentle smile and a beam in his eyes. "Well, of course, I think about it, but it don't worry me none. You

The Education of an Island Boy

see, I figure with what I've had to go through and put up with these past sixty years, any where's I go is gonna be a whole lot better than this!"

The Sand Hole and The Bay

The north side of the Island was dominated by two well-distinguished landscapes; at the west end was the "Sand Hole," and from where that ended all the way to Shell Point at the east end was what we called "The Bay." The former was a high and hilly area of sand dunes covered with yaupon bushes scattered among short and misshapen oak trees. The sand was almost snow white and so fine that there was no ground cover other than the bushes, oak leaves, and fallen branches, except for large and frequent patches of something akin to Spanish Moss that lay on the ground rather than hanging from tree limbs.

The ground itself was different from that found elsewhere on the Island, and the only spot like it I can think of is at Wade's Shore near the west end of Shackleford Banks. In a few spots, there was marsh grass and rushes that sprang up in and around the numerous ponds that sat between the sand hills. There were no homes or buildings of any kind, so it eventually evolved into a community playground or park and was often the site of picnics and games, including some baseball. But there was only one open spot large enough for games involving groups and even that was too small once the players approached anything close to puberty. Mostly the Sand Hole was just that — sand hills with bushes and oaks, and pathways cut by several generations of visitors and explorers.

As for "The Bay," it was a two-mile-long stretch of salt marshes that were bordered by thick woods and a few scattered homes to the south and a narrow strip of sandy beach to the north that separated it from the tidal waters of the Straits Channel. It was a gathering spot for all kinds of shorebirds and waterfowl, and it was where most boys of my age learned to hunt and trap. It was not until the late 1960s that several ditches and canals were cut that drained most of the marshes and eventually turned what once had been a natural estuary into several different housing developments.

A New Home and Way of Life

At a spot near the point where the Sand Hole and the Bay come together, there was a large grassy field that once was a pasture for grazing cattle. It was just to the north of the Old Road and was far enough inland from the Bay that it was plenty dry to be turned into a baseball diamond every spring. That was where I got to know many of the other boys on the Island who were not from my neighborhood and where I learned much about the game which has been one of my life-long passions. It was also there that I learned some things about life and other people that I have never forgotten.

At the Sand Hole with daughters Alyson and Leah in 1986

Annis & Mississippi

Geographically, Harkers Island is part of the South — even the "Deep South." But to the extent that such applies to race relations, the Harkers Island of my youth was a world apart from the tobacco and cotton crescent that stretched from the Tidewater area of Virginia to the piney woods of eastern Texas. Racial stereotypes and attitudes may have been as deep-seated here as in Beaufort, New Bern, or Raleigh, but on the Island, there was a distinction that was also very much a difference.

The Education of an Island Boy

It was as simple as it was historical. The economic patterns of the antebellum period kept the Banks communities in general, and Harkers Island in particular, apart from the plantation culture that dominated social relations elsewhere in North Carolina before and after the Civil War. In short, the absence of those plantations also meant the absence of the African American communities that sprang up in and around them. The demographic patterns established before the war continued, and even hardened in the following decades.

In some communities, Harkers Island included, there were virtually no Black families at all. An exception that proved the rule was next door to our house. In the home of Tom Martin Guthrie (1872-1952) and his wife Evoline (Brooks 1872-1940) lived an old woman who was what was then called a "colored lady," named Annis Pigott (1853-1952). She had spent her entire life living with white families and was as much a stranger to the harsher aspects of the racial barriers that prevailed in inland communities as anyone and everyone else on the Island. Annis died an old and "wrinkled" woman before I could remember. Her appearance was said to be more typical of her gender and age than her race. In fact, according to my mother, she did not know that her neighbor was Black until Annis was one day visited by her brother from "town," whose color revealed both his race and that of his sister.

Her death certificate indicates that she was approaching one hundred years old when she passed in 1952. If accurate, it means that she would have come of age even before the outbreak of the Civil War, and, just as importantly, lived most of her life during the turbulent times of Reconstruction and Jim Crow segregation. Tracking her on the census data from the late 19th century until she shows up near Hancock Landing in 1950 indicates that her home was always on the Banks or in one of the other Core Sound communities. Hopefully, that distinction shielded her from the more stereotypical images of what life was like for a domestic African American woman of that era.

After Annis died a few months before I was born, the nearest Black families to Harkers Island were at North River near Beaufort. Except for Saturday trips to Beaufort or Morehead City, I lived nearly my entire life as a child without interacting with anyone of

A New Home and Way of Life

another race or color. The Island that I knew was about as "lily white" as one could ever imagine. But when I was about eight years old and growing into an intense love for baseball – watching it, playing it, reading, and talking about it – I came to know the first African American man I can remember. His name was James Archie, but no one called him that. Instead, he was known to everyone simply as "Mississippi," after the state he called home.

Annis Pigott (1848-1952) on far left of picture of the Cleveland Davis extended family. (taken abt. 1930)

He was an itinerant laborer who worked in the fish house of Henry Davis, the same as who had been my father's coworker in the shelling of the Harkers Island roads in the 1930s. Mississippi lived in a small one-room frame building at the foot of the dock that serviced the offshore wharf and building. That smaller structure at the shore had been built as a market for Henry's oldest son, Wayne. It was no more than ten feet square and had no facilities other than a cot to sleep on and a drop-down wooden window that, when lowered, served as a countertop when the market was opened for business. Mississippi loaded fish into boxes and the boxes onto and off the carts that ran on a one-hundred-foot-long makeshift railway that extended to and from the two docks — one out on the water for loading from boats and the other at the shore for loading onto trucks. Initially, he was with a crew that manned a larger fish house

The Education of an Island Boy

further up Core Sound at Atlantic. Wayne drove a truck that carried packed fish boxes to the larger facility to be loaded for shipment to their final destination. During his frequent visits, Wayne formed a friendship with Mississippi and invited him to come work for his father. During his time on the Island, he ate at the Davis family table and was treated as a part of their family.

With a large round face, closely cropped hair, and a deep bass voice, he could have been cast as a character in the popular Broadway play of the era, "Showboat." It's not hard to imagine him entertaining himself while sweating on the docks by belting out a chorus of "Old Man River." But it was his sinewy physique, from his neck and shoulders down through his arms and chest and to his hips and calves, that made him well-suited for lifting boxes of fish, shrimp, and clams that weighed well over a hundred pounds. He would jerk them with a hook, or even his bare hands, and hoist them above his head as he stacked them on the cart or onto the truck. All the while, he was singing, whistling, or constantly talking to anyone who could hear him.

Those same strong arms that lifted the fish boxes could do wonders with a 36-inch baseball bat. In what some have called Baseball's Golden Age, and the heyday of Willie Mays and Hank Aaron, who were from his neighboring state of Alabama, this man called "Mississippi" became our very own Negro League All-Star. And with this one, we actually could watch him play rather than just read about him in "The Sporting News" or hear about him on the radio.

Fishhouse work was mainly in the early morning and late evening when boats came in with their catch. During the day, Mississippi usually had time to come with Wayne, or Wayne's cousin "Corn Cobb" (Stacy Davis 1939-2021), to the baseball field we had fashioned on vacant pastureland mentioned previously that was directly behind the home of Johnnie Willis (1909-1986). It was the property of a retired Methodist preacher, Carl Johnson (1892-1966). Because cattle once grazed there, after a national nominating convention held in 1964 at San Francisco's "Cow Palace," some of us started calling our field "Johnson's Cow Palace." We even posted a handmade sign to that effect. But that was just a tiny and insignificant part of my experiences there. One of the things I recall most of all about "baseball summers" in the mid-1960s is that no matter where we were in our games, when Mississippi arrived, or even when word came that he was on his way, the excitement was palpable, and we quickly reconfigured our teams to make sure he had a place.

Our field had been fashioned to dimensions meant for lanky young boys still filling out their bodies. Those distances proved woefully inadequate when Mississippi came to the plate. He would hit the ball so hard that infielders always moved back several steps to protect themselves for those few occasions when he hit anything other than towering fly balls that had to be retrieved from deep in the pines and yaupon bushes that were our fences. Since we had only one ball, usually taped and dirty, searching for and finding it in the green thickets of early summer was not always easy. But that distraction was well worth the trouble due to the happy excitement of watching this enormous "colored man" hit the ball farther than we had ever witnessed.

Just as when he was working on the dock, he was as jovial and happy as anyone you could imagine. He laughed just as loud and hard as he played and worked. Unlike Annis, given his age and background, he must have known firsthand the sting of the racial prejudices that were the norm of that era. But he never let on even the faintest sensitivity that he was in any way different or apart from the rest of us, either at the fish house or on the ball field. Perhaps it was for that reason that we eventually came to feel the same way — that he was just another bigger and stronger one of us. After an initial consciousness of his distinctive color, at least to those of us in our finite group, that difference inevitably gave way to an appreciation of his person, his character, and his talents. Eventually, he went from being Mississippi the "colored man" to Mississippi the hard worker, the ball player, and the friend.

After that one magical summer, he was off to another fish house in some other coastal community somewhere along the Atlantic or Gulf coasts. As far as I can tell, no one from the Island has ever heard from or of him again. But he remains part of the memory of at least one young boy who still marvels at recalling the sound and image of a hulking Black man hitting a misshaped dark brown baseball wrapped with athletic tape.

I'm glad I had that lesson as early and as profoundly as I did. It made me a better person then, especially in those later years after integration when I would come to sit among, play beside, be taught by, work together, and be friends with African American men and women in every aspect of my life. The life lessons I had first learned — including those at Henry's Dock and at Johnson's Cow Palace — have served me well and often.

More Than Just a Store

Throughout the fifties and into the early sixties, every Saturday morning was marked by the purring sound of a big diesel engine accompanied by puffs of dark smoke and the smell of fumes very different from what we were used to when riding in boats or standing near cars and trucks. These announced for everyone along the roadway the early morning arrival on the Island of the "Town Bus." It loaded passengers all along the main road wherever there was someone waiting in a group or flagging for a stop.

Once all pickups had been made, the bus headed for Front Street in Beaufort, where it would drop off a load of would-be customers in the thriving commercial district of the county seat. A few hours later the same bus would head back to the Island to pick up a second group of would-be shoppers and to unload back home anyone returning from the earlier trip. The driver of the bus was Lloyd Guthrie (1916-1969), who was himself an Islander, and who knew all his riders by name, and exactly where each one needed to be dropped off. Later that same afternoon the bus would return for a final trip and to deposit its riders back at the Island after their day in "town."

Most of those who couldn't or wouldn't use the bus might make that same trip using a family car or one borrowed from a friend. And there remained a few, including my family at times, who completely avoided the twenty-mile circuitous land route to Beaufort. They relied instead on the time-tested option of using the family boat for the shorter, if less convenient, trip along the sound to a large waterfront pier that fronted the same shops and were bounded by paved streets and intersections on the opposite side. One drawback of these water excursions was that there often were more boats wanting to dock along the pier than spaces available at

A New Home and Way of Life

the wharf. That required that they be "stacked," sometimes several vessels deep, out into the waterway. As a result, making your way to and from the dock itself involved maneuvering across the gunwales of two or more randomly sized and shaped watercraft to reach the landing platforms. That was always a balancing act, and especially so when carting sacks of groceries or dry goods. It was, however, an exciting adventure for small children who were carried in the father's or mother's arms. I still can recall that sensation.

Bus, car, and boat trips for buying in town generally were reserved for larger shopping ventures. The everyday incidentals needed for daily living by Islanders were purchased, charged, or bartered for, at more than a dozen of the smaller establishments that could be found nearer their homes on an intermittent line that stretched along Harkers Island's main road from one end to the other.

Beyond the schoolhouse, the theater, the churches, and the REA office that served the whole Island, every neighborhood had a store, some more than one. In ours, we had three; four if you add in Miss Georgie's café (Georgia Hamilton, 1904-1997). Most were so limited in size and scope that they might not even be counted as real stores today. But small as they were, they were vital to our community. All were open Monday through Saturday and closed on Sundays. Most were ready for business on or before 7:00 in the morning, but only a few were open after the sun went down in the evening. None of them sold beer or any alcohol products until late in the 1970s. All were roadside operations with a front door less than twenty feet from the pavement. Only a few of them had spaces for parking as it was assumed that their primary clientele was all within easy walking distance.

Some may have had a few unique specialty items or services, but all of them were obliged to have the basic offering of soft drinks (just "drinks" to us), bread, eggs, sugar, canned milk, canned beans, bologna, candy and gum, pickles in a jar, sweet cakes and nabs, potato chips, and peanuts, and at least some coffee and tobacco products. Even the gas and service stations had to offer drinks, potato chips, peanuts, and cakes.

The Education of an Island Boy

Soft drinks and sometimes cold cuts, typically bologna in a roll and hot dogs in a package, were kept in a refrigerated chest with a sliding door. There was, either on the chest itself or fastened to the counter, an opener for removing the bottle caps (we most often called them "ale stoppers") that were collected and then used to fill potholes near the road. Everything else was kept on shelves that lined the wall or on the counter that separated the shoppers from the one whose name was on the sign above the door. The entire inventory was open to view, and if you didn't see it, it wasn't available. I can't imagine that anything was financed by the store owners — they had to pay for their stuff before they could show it or sell it. But there was a regular group of drummers, or vendors, stopping by to take orders for store supplies and merchandise. It was said that the salesmen acquired the name "drummers" because their visits were a way of "drumming" up business.

Sales were cash-n-carry, or at least were intended to be. But all stores had "informal" charge accounts that were supposed to be paid up every week, or every two weeks if someone was lucky enough to have a real job with a regular paycheck. There was, on the Island, an expression for using credit to buy things, from small items like candy to major purchases like a car or even a house, that I'm unsure was used anywhere else. It was "run in debt," as in, "Did you pay cash for that, or did you run in debt for it?" I don't recall that I have ever heard that phrase used except here and in places nearby, but I can assure you that it was part of the vernacular of everyone I knew growing up.

With some credit customers, weeks sometimes stretched into months and even years. I recall being there one morning and overhearing as a patron who carried a long overdue account explained to Edith Lewis at "Edith's Store" that because in her church she had "been saved and forgiven of her sins and her debts, she no longer felt obliged to pay on her account." "That's good for you," Edith responded with her signature raspy voice, "but how am I supposed to pay the drummer when he wants his money?"

Taken together, the various stores served to make the Island a self-sustaining community for well over half a century. Trips to "town" were reserved for those very few things, mainly clothing and large hardware items, that were unavailable on a local shelf. As

A New Home and Way of Life

explained above, a bus company from Beaufort sent a full-size carrier to the Island every Saturday morning that ferried shoppers to "town" and then brought them back late Saturday afternoon. Mail-order catalogs were used as frequently as online shopping is used today. Thus, it was that many Islanders, including my father, were able to get along nicely even though he did not own an automobile until late in his life.

Counting and naming the stores is a moving target since many of the stores of the 40s and 50s had closed by the time I became aware, and others sprang up in the early 60s, spurred by the relative prosperity of those years. The listing that follows is based on my own personal recollections and experiences.

Coming onto the Island by car, about half a mile from the bridge on the right, was Claude's store (Claude Brooks, 1913-1990). His was loaded with all kinds of stuff, including groceries and some basic hardware. It was known for having the coldest drinks — with maybe even a sliver of ice at the cap. Claude stayed in his store till late in the evening, sometimes until after midnight, and was a place to go if you were late from work on the mainland or in the water.

Also, at the west'ard, right at the bend of Red Hill, Luther Yeomans (1886-1960) had one of the larger stores. Made of concrete blocks, with a high ceiling and big shelves, it closed its doors shortly after the time I came along, but for locals, the building remains until today a landmark when giving directions in that vicinity. Fammie Lee Willis (1920-2015) had a small shop just past Luther's that was known for her ice cream cones, even as late as when I had children of my own. But Clarence's store (Clarence Willis 1914-1992), halfway between Red Hill and our house, was a focal point of that neighborhood for several generations. His wife, Lois, had a kitchen and cooked, but more importantly, Clarence had snow cones — we called them snowballs — in at least ten assorted flavors.

Once past the three stores in our neighborhood (I will tell you about them later), there was Carl's store. Owned by Carl Lewis (1906-1982), it was, in its day, the largest and most multi-faceted business on the Island and was the primary outlet for the basic supplies used by fishermen and boat builders. In addition to groceries and dry goods, it even had a bowling alley with hand-

The Education of an Island Boy

placed pins. My brother Mike could make enough money setting up those pins for a few hours in the afternoon to pay for his admission to a movie that evening.

At the ferry dock intersection, there were three more stores and the "showhouse" (movie theater) on the southeast corner. One of the Island's landmark places, Cleveland's (Davis 1886-1941) store, had been on the south end of the road and next to the original post office, but all that was left by the time I came along was the fish house still run by his son, Henry (1911-1978). Yet, at the crossroads, there were three shops that peddled general merchandise. Henry ran one of those (NW corner) that was later expanded into a Richfield gas station run by Fate Jones Jr. (1922-1991). Garfield's (Emory 1911-1972) store (NE Corner) eventually became the full-service gas station of R. J. Chadwick (1918-1993) and Perry Guthrie (1936-2002), and that later was just E. B.'s (Elijah B. Gillikin 1939-2010).

Charlie Davis Store in the 1930's
CSWM&HC Collection

But it was Fillmore's (Lawrence 1914-2001) store at the southwest corner that was a true gathering place in my youth, especially for young boys and men. There were two pool tables in the back, two gas pumps out front, and a heavy-set and friendly man behind the counter who had the inside scoop on everything that was going on from Red Hill to Shell Point. Groups of a dozen or more would be loitering in and around his tables, on his drink boxes, or leaning against his front facade. On Friday and Saturday nights, if anything was happening on the Island, more than likely, it was happening there. Just past the theater was the post office, at least until I was a teenager, and then a store run and owned by Billy Best (1932-

1998). It could be said that this little patch of businesses was the closest we had to a real "downtown."

Billy's store was adjacent to where Charlie (1868-1938) Davis's store had once been. The latter was one of the first and largest businesses on the Island, but it eventually closed after the proprietor grew too old to run it any longer. In fact, Billy started out in the same building Charlie Davis had used, but he later built a new one of his own, leveling the old one and using that space as a parking area. It should be noted that none of the stores, other than Billy's, ever had a designated parking area beyond their immediate road front. Few families even had cars, and until they did there were better uses for the spaces that later became an absolute necessity.

Billy and Dawn Best
Billy owned and ran the first real grocery store on the Island.

With his new building completed, early in the 1960's, Billy's became the Island's first true grocery store. Billy had apprenticed with a grocer in Beaufort before marrying an Island girl, Dawn Willis (1933-2020), and moving here more than a decade earlier. His new store had freezers as well as refrigerators, and even a butcher shop in the back. Billy worked the counter all day long, and well into the evening. It could be said that he was the one man who knew of, and about, every single person on the Island — and even many of the visitors.

Not far past Billy's and on the same side of the road was Donnie's store (Yeomans 1909-1968). Directly beside it, was a café run by his wife, Myrtle (Rose 1911-1998). Because the two buildings were joined, and had a connecting door, Donnie's place and Myrtle's were considered as one and the same. The hamburgers and milkshakes that were always on the menu at the latter, and the special smells that emanated from her windows, meant that you were always hungry any time you passed by, even if in an automobile.

The final store at the East'ard was run by Tommie Lewis (1898-1984), and was almost all the way to Shell Point. It closed before I came to know very much of it. My only memories are of the long aisles that I walked down when I spent a morning there with my father. As Tax Lister for the Island, he would camp out in the various stores on Saturday mornings each January to give locals a place to declare their property. Occasionally he would take me with him. Tommie's store was the farthest east I ever remember going for that purpose.

One of the neighborhood stores on the Island in the 1950's.
CSWM&HC Collection

Three Stores within an Earshot

All these local shops played some part in creating the community environment in which I grew up. But it was the three stores that sat between the REA building to the west and Georgie's cafe to the east that were a genuine part of our neighborhood. Collectively, they were the "shopping mall" of my youth. All were on the north

A New Home and Way of Life

side of the road but were near enough to our house that you could hear conversations there while sitting on my Mama's front porch.

Dallas's (Guthrie 1915-1954) store, just a little to the west, was a wood frame building with one long wooden counter that stretched the entire length of the room — twenty-five feet. There were doors at both ends and a pair of windows at the front on either side of the door. Except in the cold of winter, the main door remained open all the time, with just a screen door to check the entrance. Along with his wife, "Little" Ollie (Willis 1918-2008), and his son, Dallas Daniel (Dack 1942-2014), "Big Dallas" served up only the very basic staples of Island life and did it as both family and friend. Especially when "Dack," sat behind the counter, neighborhood boys would gather there sometimes by the dozen. Among the less-than-usual items that Dallas carried was one especially important to me and several others — baseball cards.

Headed east from our house, less than fifty yards, was Edith's (Lewis 1910-1980) store. It earlier had been run by her cousin, Raymond (Guthrie 1916-1987), but by the time I came along it belonged to her and her husband, Mart (Lewis 1910-1972). It was a rectangular building, painted white and made of cinder blocks, which was no more than 12 X 24 feet in dimension. When Mama sent me "to the store" for something, unless she told me otherwise, I knew she meant that I should be headed to Edith's. Her inventory was the same as Dallas's, but her building was smaller and thus more compact. It was here that we gathered to meet the school bus every morning, and where we were dropped off by the same bus each afternoon.

The final store imprinted on my memory as a boy was that of my cousin, Norman Hancock (1920-2008), the third of Uncle Louie's four sons. It sat directly across the road from our house and in the very same location where my grandfather Charlie had run a store for more than half a century. Norman's home was directly beside it to the west and less than twenty feet distant. When Ole' Pa died, Norman eventually demolished the old building and opened what he at first called "The Hobby Shop." The main portion of the structure was made from concrete blocks and had a concrete floor, but there was a small wooden shed attached to the back. For a while, he sold hunting and fishing supplies, including decoys and

The Education of an Island Boy

Norman's Store with neighborhood friends: Sno'ball Gaskill, Mike Hancock, Neal Willis, Norman Hancock (Owner), and Carl William Willis.

ammunition, along with rods, reels, and tackle. He even had a franchise for Chrysler powerboats and motors. But after a few years, he gave up on the sporting business and reverted to the general staples that were the lifeblood of every other Island store. By then, it was called just "Norman's," and like the others, offered just the standard fare of basic staples and hardware, plus a snowball machine that rivaled Clarence's for its variety of flavors.

At Dallas's, Edith's, and Norman's, the people of my small world would gather not just to shop but to talk. It was in the talking and listening that people kept in touch and remained as much friends as they were family and neighbors. Stories heard there were relayed around the dinner table or on the porch. Later they made their way to the fish house, or the net spread, or the long-haul set. Then the same stories bounced back again, maybe with some different or added details, to the circle of chairs that sat around the heater or in front of the counter in the store. The vitality of the stories added a similar energy to the lives they described and told of. It can be said that these little stores offered much more than just bread and beans, and a few other staples of life. They conveyed the very fabric of what made us a community — our shared experiences!

Prince and the Fudgesicles

There is a story, one of which I am a witness, that gives evidence of just how closely these three stores were woven into the fabric of our neighborhood. It's also a window to the inherent humanity of

A New Home and Way of Life

Calvin Willis (1912-1978), my daddy's cousin and closest friend, and an everyday part of our family's life.

Late in his life, Calvin adopted a dog, a beagle and "sooner" mix named Prince, who had belonged to his nephew, Peter. Peter was just then starting to work and go courting, so eventually, he found less and less time for his pet. Calvin, on the other hand, who lived just two houses away, and since most water work was done in the early evening or just before daybreak, had plenty of time every day to shower attention on what had become a "neighborhood dog." After a while, Prince was more than that to Calvin, who had never married and had no children of his own. He was Calvin's "baby." Soon Prince was seen everywhere Calvin went, sometimes even in his boat, and was usually under his feet or around his legs. As time went on, Calvin and Prince would go to the neighborhood stores together. It was there that a routine evolved wherein Calvin would buy a malted ice cream, called a "fudgesicle," and holding the stick in his hand, would feed it to Prince as his dog licked on the bar as it melted — literally in his mouth.

Prince grew to love fudgesicles so much that when Calvin was out fishing, the dog would hang around the only places where his favorite treat had ever turned up — the neighborhood stores. Everyone knew why he was there, and they soon began to tell Calvin about how often Prince would come by the store, alone, whenever Calvin was gone. Soon there developed an agreement between Calvin and the storekeepers, namely Dallas and Dack at Dallas's store, Norman at Norman's store, and Mart, Edith's husband, at Edith's store.

The terms were as follows; if Prince came by the store and hung around as if waiting for his treat, whoever was behind the counter was to prepare a fudgesicle for Prince and hold it down and out long enough for Prince to enjoy it. Each store would keep a tally of how many fudgesicles they had provided, and every Friday evening, after the fishermen were paid for their weekly catch, Calvin would settle with them for any debts that Prince might have rung up during the preceding week. Thus, it happened that Prince became known as the only dog on the Island to have a charge account of his own — and at three different stores.

Barbershop Lessons

By the latter half of the 1960s, the Island got its first beauty salons. But long before that, there were barbershops, and each one had its own character and ambience. Some were family endeavors, like the one that my daddy's Uncle Danky ran from inside his home. But at least three barbers had dedicated shops that included the distinctive barber pole beside the front door.

Starling Lewis (1898-1972) had a business next door to his home and beside his brother Carl's store. Before Paul Wade (1941-2020) opened his shop across from the post office in the mid-1960s, Starling's was the closest to our house. He also offered the cheapest price, 75¢ when I was a boy. He was my father's cousin, and sometimes Daddy would take my brother, Telford, and me there on a Saturday evening. Within less than an hour, we would be headed home, with our "ears lowered." But what I remember most of all was a very sore and stiff neck. Starling's way of cutting hair was to force your head down almost to a 90° angle, while he pressed his clippers up and down your neck and around your ears. By the time he finished and had whisked away the towel from around your shoulders, you could hardly stand or walk upright. Eventually, Teff and I would plead with our father not to make us "go to Starling's no more."

Mainly for that reason, after that and until Paul Wade's opened, getting a haircut meant going to "Louie's." Louie Guthrie's (1904-1983) was another of Daddy's cousins, and his barbershop was a small wooden hut, no more than two hundred square feet, that was past our church but before the schoolhouse — just beyond Myrtle's café. Because of everything that a barbershop was at that time, Louie's was another nerve center of the community. Especially on Saturday mornings, a line would

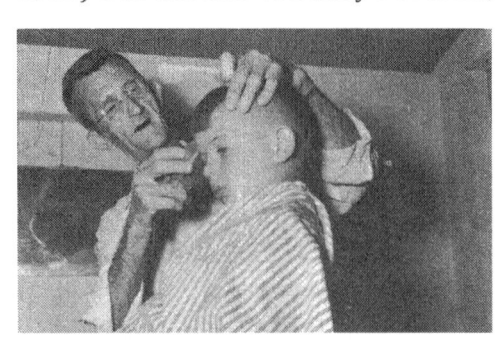

Louie Guthrie cutting the hair of Island boy, Leland Yeomans.
CSWM&HC Collection

A New Home and Way of Life

form that often extended outside the door. Indeed, my brother Ralph was sometimes able to finance his own haircut by selling his place in the waiting line to others who preferred "paying" to "waiting."

There were at least two things about getting a haircut at Louie's that those who went there have never forgotten. The first is a lasting mental image of a large, framed picture hung on the wall behind the barber's chair and over a mirror. It depicted a ghoulish scene of a ghost chasing a frightened farm boy down a country road. Ask anyone who ever went there, and they will be able to describe it in vivid detail. The second was listening as the older men, especially Louie, expounded on the issues of the day. Beyond his unique insight, drawn from daily conversations that within a few weeks would have included most of the men of the community, there was the barber's special voice pattern that resulted from a life-long speech impediment. The more excited he became, the longer it took him to express his point. But rather than a distraction, his stumbling words were as endearing as they were either humorous or insightful.

By the time I became a teenager, and the Beatles had ushered in a seismic change in how boys and young men wore their hair, Louie had closed his business. Paul Wade, a much younger man from nearby Williston who had married an Island girl, opened a new and thoroughly modern shop less than a quarter mile to the west of our house. It would be there that succeeding generations of sons, brothers, and husbands would be groomed for the next half-century.

But all these many years removed from waiting and listening while getting a haircut at Louie's, I still remember warmly what it was like to be there and to learn from him and his patrons some lessons that a young boy of those years might learn only from the company of older boys and men. As elsewhere, getting a haircut at a barbershop, especially a first haircut, was an early rite of passage to maturity. Eventually, as a boy grew older, he could go to get a haircut without his dad or a bigger brother with him, yet another step towards the gates of real manhood. That's when the barbershop became as much an educational as a grooming experience. Sitting on the metal chairs of Louie's Barbershop, with

The Education of an Island Boy

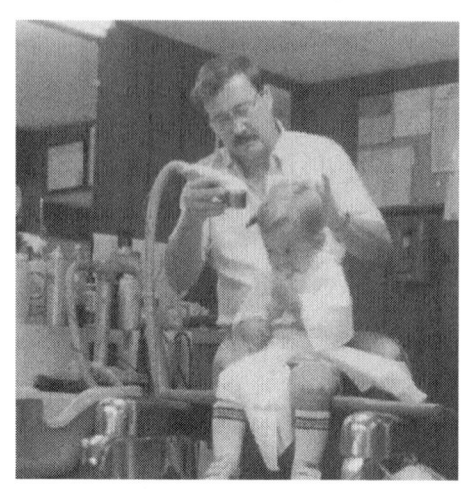

Paul Wade cutting Joel Hancock Jr.'s hair about 1985.

a vinyl-padded seat that could be raised or lowered, and armrests made of metal tubing, I learned some of life's most memorable, if not profound lessons — and sometimes with words and expressions that would have made my mother cringe.

Politics, sports, and even religion were explained in terms that exposed me to a vernacular I had not heard on my father's front porch. But it was the interactions of men and women and other personal relationships I heard described there, discussed in ways that, even at that early age, I knew I'd best not share when I got home. I also learned about who on the Island was most honored and respected, disliked, or even feared. I gleaned from detailed, often humorous stories whom I could trust, and, just as importantly, whom I should avoid.

It also was there that I came to sense that most Island stories, no matter their topic, ended with a punchline, or some memorable phrase that weeks, years, or even generations later could be related and understood without ever having to tell "the rest of the story." Some of them cannot be repeated here, but time has softened their edges in my memory so that I recall them now with as much fondness as I once did with amusement.

When I later took my own sons to Paul Wade's, long after both Starling's and Louie's were left only to memory, there was still a sense that my boys had reached a milestone in their lives and, thus in mine. By then, the Island was less communal than it had been a generation earlier, and as a result, the conversation was much more circumspect. But there remained a sense that they had just made their first visit to a place where a boy could start to learn more of what it was like to be a man.

"Lying Willie"

One of the storytellers I came to know best while waiting in line at Louie's Barbershop was an old man whom everyone called "Lying Willie" (Willie Burney Guthrie 1902-1968). As might be assumed, there was a reason for the name. He would have been well into his sixties by the time I got to hear his stories. He lived in the same neighborhood as Louie's shop and was a distant cousin. He often stopped by to visit and to share with others the exciting events he had seen or heard of — if only in his own mind. Beyond that, I don't ever remember seeing him take his place in the barber's chair. Wearing ragged overhauls and worn-out canvas shoes, he would

"Lying" Willie Guthrie- one of the Island's best storytellers.
CSWM&HC Collection

discourse on the issues of the day. Pausing only for a chronic cough that sometimes had him bending over in his chair, he always, always, made his point by recounting something fantastic.

Willie was as mild-mannered and gentle a person as I ever knew and was just one of the many men and boys who shared their tales with the group who waited in line for a haircut. Yet his stood out from all the others for two reasons. First, they were so outlandish that there was hardly any way that they could ever be true. Lots of folks told stories that might have been a stretch or an exaggeration, but with Willie's yarns, each twist and turn of the plot made them more and more bizarre.

The second reason why Willie's stories were so unique was even more significant. They were told without his ever betraying their implausibility. Willie rattled off his accounts with the same demeanor as if he were describing something as real as the rising of the tide or the setting of the sun. His stark and sullen expression never changed, even when he delivered the final punch line that rendered his tale as totally unbelievable. Then, with only the hint

The Education of an Island Boy

of a smile that must have hidden a bulging internal belly laugh, he would move on to the next story. Usually, that one would turn out to be just as incredible as the one that preceded it. "It may have been a lie, but it was told for the truth," someone would say as he recounted one of Willie's many yarns, no matter how outlandish. Usually, it was the former.

Reflecting on his stories through the prism of more than half a century, I have determined they all had a common strain and message. Willie's tales always seemed to be about how a poor and simple man can, with enough imagination and ingenuity, turn unexpected things to his advantage. Just one example can illustrate these qualities even though there were several dozen more in the same vein told for the same purpose.

According to Willie, one spring day, he was sitting on a marsh in Banks Bay several hundred yards off the north shore of Shackleford Banks, and directly across from his home near the Landing. He was hoping that a loon might fly by close enough that he could venture a shot. After several hours of waiting without a single sighting, Willie was about ready to head home. Just then, he caught sight of a loon flying along the shoreline of Bell's Island and towards the horse pen on the shore of Diamond City. The bird was so close to the shoreline and so far from Willie's perch that he knew he would never be able to reach it with the small birdshot he had loaded in his shotgun. But rather than give up on his chance to carry home something for supper, Willie quickly came up with a plan.

In the blink of an eye and in rapid succession, he pulled out his pocketknife, broke off the blade, peeled open a gun shell, and poured out the shot. He then placed his knife blade in the shell and sealed it before loading it into the barrel of his gun. With hardly a second to spare, he took aim at the loon that was now directly between him and the waterline. Still thinking, he waited for the precise moment that the bird came in line with an oyster rock that was just off the shore, and at the exact instant, he pulled the trigger. Then, according to Willie, the knife blade he had used to replace his birdshot sliced cleanly through the neck of the loon, killing it instantly, and before smashing onto the exposed rock where it opened a half a peck of oysters and finally lodging into a stray piece of driftwood! By using his head as well as his talents, rather than going home empty handed he had both meat and shellfish to share with his family.

That was what Willie, and his stories were like. Even if you didn't believe them, because you had been so entertained, you had something to keep and share with your friends.

The Island "Showhouse"

Jimmy Styron (1881-1945) was one of my father's closest friends despite the nearly three-decade difference in their ages. Beyond that, what I know most about him, based on the stories I heard as a child, is that he loved the actress Marlene Dietrich. More to the point, he loved the characters portrayed by the German starlet who was a queen of American cinema throughout the decades of the thirties and forties. Jimmy waited anxiously for her movies to come to the local theater, and when they did arrive, he usually was there to watch.

For one Saturday night feature, Jimmy Styron with several of his friends, including my father, enjoyed a Marlene Dietrich movie together, leaving their wives and children at home. Such male bonding was common among married men and fathers of that era. This evening, they sat together and watched as the character played by one of their favorite actors came to an untimely end in the film's finale. Jimmy was visibly upset as he walked home to the west'ard after the movie along with his friends. My father recalled that, "He just kept looking down, shaking his head and asking, 'Why did she have to die?'"

Daddy and the others assumed that Jimmy's depressed mood would wane as the night drew on, but this time their friend carried the movie with him well into the evening. The next morning word reached my father that when his friend got home, still fretting about the movie's outcome, and needing an outlet for his disappointment, Jimmy Styron systematically pulled out his family's plates, bowls, and saucers, and then "broke every dish in his house!"

The Education of an Island Boy

This is just one of the dramas in which the small rectangular-shaped wood frame cinema on Harkers Island played a starring role. If the Island ever had a "downtown," a "business section," or a "main street," it was at the crossroads of what are now the Island and Old Ferry Dock Roads. Tucked into the southeast corner of the intersection it shared with three other businesses, the theater was at the center of social and cultural life for the whole Island. It was known officially as the "Charity Theater." We seldom, if ever, called it that. Sometimes it was just the "theater," but most often it was dubbed the "showhouse."

It got its official name from an early civic organization on the Island, the "Charitable Brotherhood." The group was organized soon after the arrival of the newcomers from the Banks at the turn of the century as an ad-hoc support group for members and their families. One of its services was to collect an assessment from subscribers to support a member's family at his passing. But its most lasting contribution was the building of a lodge that later became a theater, where the people of the Island could watch the parade of movies that film producers began to turn out by the hundreds in the decade of the 1920s.

Before there was the internet, cable, broadcast television, or even a radio in every home, there was the "silver screen" as Hollywood movies entered their golden age. For more than half a century that stretched from the "roaring" twenties to the mid-seventies, it was on movie screens, both inside and outdoors, that most Americans found their entertainment, and with that, a sense of national community. Newsreels, cartoons, and feature-length dramas from New York and Hollywood provided a common cultural experience for anyone who could afford the cost of admission. Despite its relative isolation on what was sometimes described as "the edge of civilization," Harkers Island was no different from other small towns and villages when it came to the movies.

Admission was still only 25¢ through the mid-sixties. Soft drinks, candy bars, and popcorn all cost a dime, and a pickle, dill or sour, could be had for only a nickel. A center seating section of perhaps as many as eight seats and twenty rows was flanked by "couple's seats" on both sides. Many a first date was had in those side seats, and the arms of both boys and men began to rest around the shoulder beside them not long after the lights went down. Because everyone there knew everyone else, and the setting was so intimate, it was not unusual to overhear comments and conversations among the patrons throughout the show.

Tandem projectors concealed behind a raised balcony were run by teenage boys who found a way to combine an evening at the showhouse with a part-time job. My brother, Ralph, was one of those, and the experience left him with a love of movies that spanned a lifetime. He eventually acquired a collection of both Beta and VHS tapes that filled several large boxes and was accessed daily as he picked out his preferred evening entertainment.

As a concession to work schedules and the lack of weeknight patrons, normally there were only three showings a week. One title would run on Thursday and Friday evenings, and another would be highlighted on Saturday night. This meant that during most weeks we had access to two feature films, even if it was months and sometimes years after they had been shown in larger towns on the mainland. But that never mattered to us, as the "showhouse" experience of being part of the crowd was many times more important than the movie itself.

The advent of cable television and then VCRs eventually led to the demise of many small-town movie theaters, including the one on the Island. By the late 1980s, it had become an arcade room and, a

The Charity Theater, called the "Showhouse" on Harkers Island, about 1960.
CSWM&HC Collection

decade later, sat both empty and abandoned. It eventually fell into disrepair and was destroyed in a fire of unknown origin. But even after a home was built on the spot, most Islanders are still prone to describe that area and even give directions referring to "where the showhouse used to be."

Several generations after Jimmy Styron walked out of the front door so incensed that he took out his frustration on plates and saucers, many others can still recall the wonderful experience of going out to a movie when and where "everybody knew your name."

A New Home and Way of Life

My sister Lillian beside a soldier visiting the Island during World War II.

The Education of an Island Boy

My father, Charlie William Hancock, standing on the path to the Landing that ran beside our house. Behind him is the home of Tom Martin Guthrie on the left, and of my grandfather, Ol' Pa on the right.

3

Ol' Pa's Neighborhood and Bertha's Legacy

The old life has swept before me like a panorama; the old days have trooped by in their old glory, again; the old faces have looked out of the mists of the past; old footsteps have sounded in my listening ears; old hands have clasped mine, old voices have greeted me, and the songs I loved ages and ages ago have come wailing down the centuries!
Mark Twain, "Letter to Will Bowen" 1870

The Path to the Landing

From the south-facing upstairs window that adorned the small bungalow my father had built on land provided for him by his father, I could look out and see the home of the man everyone I knew called Ol' Pa. He was my grandfather. And it was his place, sitting on the shoreline at the Landing and just two houses away, that was the center-point of our whole world.

Thirteen years before my leaving home for college in August of 1970, on a warm Indian Summer's afternoon late in September of 1957, a long line of people had followed the same route I would later walk when saying goodbye to my father as I headed out for college at East Carolina University. There was also a long black hearse in that entourage. In my mind's eye, I can still see clearly how it carried Ol' Pa's body towards his house at the Landing. It had large letters on the side showing the name of the funeral home that sent it, but I was too young to read them, and I knew that what really mattered was what it carried inside.

It was a dirt path, more shell and sea sand as dirt, and it was bisected by a long row of jointed grass that could survive and even thrive between the tire tracks on either side. It was no more than two hundred feet from the paved road to Ol' Pa's house, where his body was to lie until his burial the next morning. Our house was where the path met the Island's main road. Next to it was the home of my Uncle Louie, whom the family knew as Big Buddy, and finally, the big white house that Ol' Pa had built for Aggie, my grandmother, and his first wife when finally, they moved here from the Banks in December of 1900. For almost its entire length, the path was lined with wild pink roses and honeysuckle vines, woven among the pickets and wire mesh fences on both sides. The roses had no aroma, but the scent of honeysuckle filled the air from early April until well into autumn.

There was hardly a bend in that path then and now, although it wasn't really straight — shifting just a little from due south to the southeast as it approached the shore — but not so much as to notice unless you were trying to look from one end of it to the other. And it sloped downward just a little, no more than a couple of feet, as it approached the old house and the shoreline where it ended. But it dipped just enough to give little boys like me a boost when we were running or riding our bikes and wanted the help of gravity in acceleration.

Charlie Hancock home was located on the southern shoreline and was severely damaged during Hurricane Donna in 1960.

At the corner between our house and Big Buddy's, there was a small oak tree, one we would later call "Denny's tree," after my nephew fell from one of the limbs and broke an arm while trying to retrieve a baseball lodged in a bough. But that would be a few years later. And there was another larger oak about midway down the path that shaded both Big Buddy's side porch on the westward side and Tom Martin Guthrie's side porch on the eastward. A few yards further, and just inside Big Buddy's fence, was a persimmon tree that hung all the way over the path. The fruit from the tree was so numerous in late summer that you couldn't walk barefooted to the Landing without having a hot, juicy persimmon squashed between your toes.

Then, just where Big Buddy's fence ended and Ol' Pa's place began, a grove of silver maples extended to the shoreline. The same roses and honeysuckle that covered the fences were also there, and the teeming vegetation was so thick that that whole portion of the yard was all but

Big Buddy's home in the 1980's. The home of my uncle, Louie Hancock. It sat directly south of our house and between our home and the home of Ol' Pa.

impenetrable. Yet it was a large and tall oak tree that had been and remained the main landmark of the site since long before Ol' Pa even thought about building right beside it. My daddy once told me that when Ol' Pa's house was being built, the workers would shade under its branches while they rested from their labors. More than half a century later, it still dominated the landscape so that its stature dwarfed the silver maples that ran from its roots to the shoreline.

That giant old oak and the big white house that sat just to its southwest had marked a gathering place for more than three generations of Hancocks and their relatives, especially the Willises, Guthries, and Moores. Together, within sight of both the oak and the roof of Ol' Pa's house, they had established a neighborhood of homes and families that were so closely connected by blood and the everyday routines of life that most of us didn't even bother to acknowledge what our blood relation really was.

All of us, especially the young ones, just knew that somehow, we were kin to everyone else, and what affected one of us mattered to all of us. And for as long as anyone living could remember, nothing and no one else mattered more than Ol' Pa. Throughout that day and evening, and into the next morning, lots of people trailed down that same path to Ol' Pa's house. Sometime after supper, I went down the path too.

I had turned five years old just two months before Ol' Pa died. He would have been eighty-nine had he lived until that December. In some ways, he seemed even older, much as if he had been around forever, because, for most of us, he had. And even to a five-year-old, his slow pace and hesitating voice suggested that the world, even his world, had long since passed him by. I might not have anticipated it then, but more than half a century later, I still feel his influence and an obligation to preserve his legacy.

Our Neighborhood

At the time of his passing, it must have seemed that Ol' Pa and his house had been there forever. Yet some of the Island's oldest residents might still have considered him one of the "newcomers from the Banks." Only since the turn of the last century was his home place and the land around it referred to as "Hancock Landing." Before that, he and most of his family and neighbors had lived at Shackleford Banks --- barely more than two miles to the south across Back Sound. But by the time I came along half a century later, his presence and influence were felt by everyone.

The actual footprint of the neighborhood surrounding Hancock Landing was less than a hundred acres. But as I grew up, the expanse of that little world grew with me — and did so exponentially. From my mama's yard I soon had free sway to it all, and when I was no older than ten, or even younger, the whole Island was my oyster — no pun intended. By the time I was a teenager, the Banks and the Cape had been added to both my playground and my classroom. Harkers Island was small enough that even as a child, I never knew the feeling of being away from home — because the whole Island was my home. Yet it was just large enough, in space and population, that there was always someone and something new to know and discover.

Until the pace of changes in modern life began to accelerate at the midpoint of the last century, the Island and the life I came to know were only slightly different from the ones known by my grandparents, parents, and older siblings. But there were some changes, and essentially it was a world and way of life that they had helped shape. In the half-century since the departure from the Banks, the generations of my parents and grandparents had transformed a sparsely settled collection of families on a secluded island into a thriving community of connected neighborhoods. Given the timing of my birth, I had a front-row seat to watch and be a part of what came next.

Becoming Ol' Pa

At his birth in 1869, just four years after the end of the Civil War, he was named Charles Sterling Hancock. On the surviving documents that mention him, his name shows simply as Charlie Hancock. He came of age as the "Reconstruction" that followed the war gave way to the "Redemption" that soon returned to white southerners the social, political, and economic privileges they had known before the fighting began. On the Outer Banks, those changes, even the War itself, were and had been far less of a disruption than they were just a few miles inland.

The watermen who lived in the shadow of Cape Lookout had owned no slaves. For that reason and several others, the day-to-day living patterns before, during, and after the war were little changed. But by the time Charlie Hancock was called Ol' Pa, his life as a boy on and around Shackleford Banks would have been all but unrecognizable to his parents.

Soon after he married my grandmother and started a family, the shore-based whaling industry that had sustained his ancestors for the past century suddenly began to disappear. Then, two major hurricanes, one in 1896 and the other more powerful in 1899, forced him to abandon his home and property on the Banks almost

The Education of an Island Boy

entirely. A few years later, horseless carriages would begin to maneuver along the dirt paths that ran close by his new homeplace at Harkers Island. Just a few years later, he was aroused from his sleep one morning by the sound of a seaplane coming to rest near the shoreline that fronted his home. He would race his friends and court his first wife in a small sailskiff as his ancestors had done for centuries, but a little more than two decades later, he would transport her body to her childhood home place for burial in a boat powered by a gasoline engine.

While the Civil War had barely been noticed by his parents, World War I would cause him to say sad farewells to young men he had known since their births. Having hardly any formal education, and trained only as a fisherman, he eventually fashioned a construction company of his own, only to see it quickly vanish after a failed venture hundreds of miles away in the North Carolina mountains. Near the end of his life, his own grandchildren were called upon to fight in yet another World War. And in what he considered most miraculous of all, he sat in his son's living room and listened to men and women talking in faraway places on something called a radio.

As Charlie approached the end of his life, he might have imagined that he had seen it all. He felt he had ridden those waves of change at the crest, always retaining his role as the head of his "crowd" and a leader in his community. Through it all, nearly a century of change and disruption, from the time he emerged from childhood he was never dependent on anyone or anything other than

Charles Sterling (Charlie) Hancock, my grandfather, as a young man, and long before I knew him as Ol' Pa.

himself to sustain his family. He might have considered that his proudest achievement.

He was not a big man, especially after age had bent and shrunk him. Like Ernest Hemingway's "Old Man," everything about him was old — except his eyes that still sparkled like jewels and continued to evidence the vitality that had marked his younger years. But until the end, he still carried the suggestion of the "Patriarch" that he had been and still was. It was said that in his prime, he could "suck the air out of a room" with his commanding presence and aura of authority. But that was not how I knew him in the short while that he was still around me, and when my impressions were formed. My images of him then were less daunting and sprang mostly from my childhood senses of him and his surroundings. These were drawn in large part from the daily jaunts my father would make down the path to his house, carrying me in his arm or pulling me by his side, that always ended as we walked through a kitchen door and into the sitting room where Ol' Pa would be found half reclining in his high back chair.

My grandfather, Charlie Hancock or "Ol' Pa" as he was called near the end of his life.

Occasionally, not all the time or even usually, he would ask me to sit on his lap, and he would wrap the little mass of his once-strong arms around my shoulders as he pulled me to him so he could "smell my neck." As he did, I could smell him too: the starch in his shirts, the cigars in his pocket, and even the chewing tobacco he spit out each time before he walked into the house.

But this evening, after the undertakers had positioned his coffin in front of the westward wall of the living room that faced the shoreline and the Sound, as well as the Banks that had once been his home, this evening, everything was different. By the time we got there, Daddy and Mama along with me and my brother Teff, the whole house was crowded with well-wishers who had come to say goodbye to Ol' Pa for the last time. There were some who hardly knew him but who knew his crowd, or his second wife, Carrie, who was seated beside the casket to be consoled by those who passed by it.

As was usually the case, except in mid-winter, the house doors and windows were opened, and the southwest breezes of late summer blew the curtains aside. You could hear the water as it lapped no more than twenty feet from his south-side porch. If it had been another occasion or earlier that same day, you might have heard men and boys at the Landing talking, walking, working on the dock, unloading their boats, or just planning how they would spend that evening or the next day. But not this day or this evening. Ol' Pa had died, and everybody stopped to show and pay their respects. Most had never known a life he had not been a part of, or even the focus. Some of them must have wondered how that life would change as it continued.

My step-grandmother Carrie (Murphy 1879-1957), my uncle Sterling (1916-1996), my aunt Mary Louise (1915-1998), and her daughter, Marian Lloyd, still lived in the house with Ol' Pa. Aunt Ellen (1918-2018), Ol' Pa and Carrie's youngest daughter, sat quietly in a corner. But, as was often the case, Uncle Sterling was talking loudly to the people who were there. Aunt Mary Louise was crying, sometimes out loud. My daddy was stoic, as was his norm. He walked up to the casket, holding me with one hand and my brother with the other. Mama was beside us. We looked in and down, with Daddy lifting me up for just a few seconds so I could see over the side of the casket, and then we moved on.

Daddy said just a few words to some of the people who were there and within no more than half an hour after having left our back porch, we were back at our house. By outward appearances, everything was just as it had been before, but somehow, we knew, even those of us too young to understand how or why, that nothing would ever be quite the same again.

I regret that I don't personally remember more about Ol' Pa than I do, as my recollections are mostly of those walks down the path with Daddy to Ol' Pa's house each evening after Daddy came home from work and finished supper. But Ol' Pa's mystique and influence would remain a part of our sensitivities for many years to come — and still has not completely vanished. Amid everything that happened and went on around him, he was always the center of attention. Everyone seemed to look at him, waiting for a nod of approval before going ahead with whatever might be next. Though I was only five years old, I was made to understand that I lived in a world he had fashioned and still colored. The turn of the 20th Century ushered in changes for the families of both sets of my grandparents that were far more profound than adjusting their calendars to mark the new epoch. The lives known for generations on Shackleford Banks and at the Cape were about to change to a degree not experienced since their ancestors settled near Cape Lookout more than a century earlier. My grandfather moved his family from Diamond City on Shackleford Banks to Harkers Island on Christmas Day of 1900. Like his neighbors, his move was driven by the great hurricane of 1899 that left Diamond City in ruins. It was little more than a ghost town within less than a decade.

At about the same time, or maybe a few months earlier, the parents of my maternal grandmother, Bertha Willis, had made the same short journey. Those two, Charlie and Bertha, together created concentric family and social circles, and fashioned the world I came to know. Both were strong-willed and intelligent and were to have many children of their own. Just one generation after leaving the Banks with their lives disrupted, each would stand at the head of large extended families. And even today, more than a century after both passed, their influence is felt by the legions of their descendants — and perhaps by none more deeply than me.

Ol' Pa's Crowd

When Ol' Pa arrived at the Island with my grandmother Agnes (1872-1913) and their children, he set up his family in a large two-story house directly beside his mother-in-law's home. It was near the midpoint of the Island's south shore, overlooking Back Sound with a clear view of the Banks. He positioned the house far enough from the shoreline that my father often spoke of playing baseball on the grassy lawn that sat between the family's two-story south-facing porch and where the grass gave way to sea sand.

The Education of an Island Boy

Agnes Bell Larson, my paternal grandmother, died long before I came along and when my father was only four years old.

From that same spot, he eventually laid claim to and purchased a swath of land several hundred feet wide that extended all the way from the south shore of the Island to the marshes of Oak Hammock on the Island's north side. He likely felt he had reserved enough land to last his children and theirs for generations. By the time he died in the mid-1950s, it was obvious that he had been mistaken. The numbers of his children, his grandchildren, and then his great-grandchildren, expanded so quickly that they used up the land faster than he could have envisioned. As he was laid to rest in the family burial plot, nearly all the acreage he had claimed already was cleared and covered with houses.

As they moved into their new home, my grandmother Agnes, called Aggie by family and friends, worried less about the distant future than the immediate need to secure a place to raise her growing nest of small children. By then she already had three, and three more eventually would join them. Aggie's real father had died before he could celebrate her first birthday. Along with her sister, Lilly, who was two years older and who had been blind from birth, they had only the stories of their mother to remind them of the Norwegian sailor who had come to America as a stowaway on a ship from Europe. Despite the advances in genealogical records and research of the last few decades, no more is known

My father's maternal aunt, Lilly Larson, or "Blind Lilly" as she was known by family.

about the lineage of Louie Larson (1835-1873), my father's maternal grandfather, than the small bits my great-grandmother related to my father when he was still a young boy.

Louie had lived for thirty-eight years, and what his descendants know about his entire life can be summed up in a few sentences that leave as much to the imagination as they talk about who he was, and what he might have become. Sometime before 1869, he arrived somewhere on the southeast coast of the U. S. and made his way to Wilmington, NC, along with a Swedish friend, Charles Clawson (1838-c.1910), with whom he had crossed the Atlantic. The two immigrants made friends with a young fisherman and would-be entrepreneur from Harkers Island, who soon brought them home with him to meet his family. While here, Charles met and married a young girl from nearby Beaufort and eventually had his own store that took his name. That building, as well as the name, is still used by a local restaurant on the spot where the old store once did business.

At about the same time, Louie met my great-grandmother, Emeline Brooks (1853-1923), several of whose ancestors had married into the Harker family from whom the Island takes its name. Louie and Emeline were married in 1869 and settled on a several-acre plot on the northwest end of the Island, a spot that to this day is known as Harker's Point. Louie provided for his family by running a grist mill that ground the corn brought to him from local gardens and farms on the mainland across the Straits Channel. But before he could establish enough presence to preserve a full picture of where and who he had come from, he was gone, the victim of any of a hundred diseases grouped together as "natural causes" in 19th-century postmortems.

My great-grandfather, Louie Larson, a Norwegian stowaway, died shortly after marrying my great-grandmother, Emeline Brooks.

Family lore maintains that he named his daughters Lilly (1870-1942) and my grandmother Agnes after his mother and sister, respectively. But these names were likely anglicized, either by him or by his family after he died. Other than these morsels, all that remains of Louie is a gravestone with his own anglicized name, the grindstone that had been used in his mill and that still serves as a yard ornament for the plot's current owners, a small photograph kept by my great grandmother and passed on to her children, and a short letter he sent to her from Wilmington before they finally were married and his move to the Island was made permanent. The affection Aggie had and maintained for her father, despite having been too young at his passing even to remember him, was evident when she later gave birth to children of her own. No doubt, because of the memories, mementos, and stories held onto by her mother, Emeline, Louie Larson would remain a driving influence for the infant daughter he left behind. Aggie chose to name her first son, Louie, and her first daughter, Louisa. She then named her second daughter Lourena and as she herself was named after her father's mother, she gave that same name, Agnes, to her third daughter.

Ten years after her father's passing in February of 1881, Aggie's mother, Emeline, was remarried to Calvin Farr Willis (1856-1923). From then on, she and her girls were mainstays at the south shore homestead that encompassed those few acres that would be my childhood world, even though I was still seventy-plus years from coming onto the scene. While living there, Aggie met and married my grandfather, Charlie, who eventually became Ol' Pa.

Aggie and Charlie's first home had been at Diamond City on the Banks, where the Hancocks had homesteaded well over a century before and where Charlie had grown up. It was understood that they had migrated down the Banks from the Tidewater area of Virginia. Hancocks were listed among the settlers there as early as 1619 and numbered among the "Berkeley Hundred" victims of the Powhatan War and Massacre of 1622 that nearly snuffed out the Virginia settlement and colony. My sixth great-grandfather, William Hancock Jr., was born in Norfolk, VA, in 1674 but was married in Carteret County in 1712.

Records show that he died in Bath, NC, around 1730. But his son, Hector (b. 1712), spent all of his life in Carteret County, and from Hector's grandson Calvin (b. 1775) through his son Joseph (b. 1738), on down to the end of the 19th century, all of my Hancock grandparents (James b. 1806 & William, "Billy" b. 1840) show up on the census records of Shackleford Banks.

Like most of the other families who then lived on the lower Outer Banks, the Hancocks made their living in and on the water. And for the last few decades of the nineteenth century, especially at Diamond City and on Shackleford Banks, working the water meant one thing more than any other — whaling. According to family tradition, all the Hancocks had been whalers. But whaling to the Bankers was not the deep-sea sagas depicted in the stories of Herman Melville and shown in the paintings of the New England naturalists. Whaling was shore-based for the crews of Diamond City, and crews were limited to the number of men who could fit into a small skiff or dory. Whales were spotted by lookouts placed atop the large sand dunes that covered the ocean side of Shackleford Banks. From their perches, they could see far out into Onslow Bay, where the Atlantic Ocean's shore juts sharply eastward to form Lookout Bight. Wright and Sperm whales moving north in the early spring would maneuver close to the beach and move so slowly that within a matter of minutes of being spotted, whaling crews would be on their chase.

Whaling was seasonal and carried on mostly in the months of February, March, and April. For the remainder of the year, whalers of the springtime were the mere fishermen, or "proggers," that by searching — what they called progging — amid the marshes and tideland eked out little more than sustenance from the sound to the north and the continental shelf to the south and east. As with any acquired skill, some whalers were more proficient than others, and none was more celebrated than Ol' Pa's daddy, and my great-grandfather, Billy Hancock (1840-1914). Stories abound of Billy's many escapades while finding, catching, or bringing in whales. One of my sisters displayed a harpoon that had belonged to him over the fireplace mantle of her den until her recent passing. It was then donated to a local museum where it remains on exhibit.

The Education of an Island Boy

Billy married Mary Wallace Rose (1843-1881) in 1864 and with her had six children before her passing in 1881. He would outlive her by thirty-three years. My grandfather, Charlie, was the third of their children. He and three of his siblings survived until the midpoint of the next century. Within a year of losing his first wife, Billy remarried Rhoda Willis (b. 1852), who was twelve years younger and by her had one son (Harvey 1891-1950) who likewise lived into his seventies.

My great-grandfather Billy Hancock was one of the last known whalers on Shackleford Banks.

Having been born in 1840, Billy was old enough to have experienced the Civil War and its direct aftermath, neither of which were as disruptive on the Banks as they were on the mainland. After Union forces assumed control of the entire Outer Banks very early in the conflict, Confederate raiders made several attempts to disable the new and nearby Cape Lookout lighthouse after it was commissioned in 1859. But they were never wholly successful. Soon after General Sherman's Federal troops restored Union control early in 1865, efforts began to repair the structure and its powerful Fresnel lenses. By 1867 it was back in service, and by 1870 the lighthouse had been restored to its intended glory, and life in its shadow was back to normal.

His whaling adventures were just a small part of the legends that sprung up around and about Billy Hancock. Even more than whaling, his super-human swiftness as a runner was considered his most remarkable ability. I vividly recall the excitement I felt as my father told me stories of his grandfather's vaunted speed. By then, throwing harpoons into the back of a giant mammal while perched in a skiff was just a fantasy. But imagining being able to outrun your friends or chase down wild animals, was among every young boy's dreams. My brother and I sat with bated breath as

Daddy would weave his tales about how his grandfather used his special talent.

There was the time he was recruited to cut the last foundation post from the old Cape Lookout Lighthouse (1812-1859) that was no longer operable and had been partially destroyed during the war. It was assumed that he was the only man anywhere who was fast enough to remove the final pole balancing the old tower and still escape to safety. The older structure had been decommissioned when the new one came online, but it remained in place within 100 yards of the newer one for several decades. When the crew charged with its demolition began a search for someone to perform the final task in the felling, they looked no farther than the man everyone claimed was the "fastest man on the Banks." It is said that although Billy tripped while scurrying away, he was still able to crawl fast enough to avoid the falling debris. As one storyteller once put it, "We don't know exactly how fast he could run, but he could crawl at twenty-five miles per hour!"

Other stories tell of his routinely running down the feral horses that roamed the Banks, and of being quick enough to get to the windward of a feeding duck, and then be able to catch it as it arose and instinctively set off in the direction of the wind. But my father's favorite story was of when Billy was recruited to play "Cat" — an early version of baseball — for the Diamond City team against a squad from Beaufort.

The town group sported a player who was thought to be the fastest man in the whole county. Sam Windsor (1825 -1880) was a former slave who had made a name for himself as a ballplayer in the days before Jim Crow laws and post-war traditions prevented games from being played between the races. He would later move to Shackleford Banks, where to this day, a clump of cedar trees and yaupon bushes are still known as Sam Windsor's Lump.

In Cat, to make an out, a runner had to be touched with the ball while it was still in the hand of the fielder. Thus, fielders had to catch the ball and then try to tag the hitter before he could reach the base. According to the legend, no one had ever been able to run down Sam Windsor — no one, that is until Billy Hancock caught him on his very first at-bat against the team from the Banks. My

The Education of an Island Boy

father's voice would rise, and his cheeks would grow flush as he tried to act out for those who were listening how Billy held back his hand and the ball until the very last moment to decoy the over-confident runner.

Finally, he would throw out his own clenched hand to demonstrate how his grandfather had gleefully outstretched his arm with the ball to "soak" (put out) the runner just before he reached the base.

My own grandfather later would bring the twice-widowed Billy with him when he moved his family off the Banks after the 1899 storm. His youngest son, my father, was born in 1909 and was too young to have more than a few memories of his grandfather, who died in 1914. But my father's brother, my uncle Louie, seventeen years older than my father, told another story about Billy that was not nearly so happy or gleeful as the ones about his whaling and running.

My uncle, Louie Hancock, "Big Buddy" to everyone in our neighborhood.

Rather, Louie would tell, sometimes with a choked voice, how Billy would stand on the south shore of Harkers Island and look longingly across Back Sound to the Banks and where he lived all but the last few years of his life. "Ah Lord!" he would exclaim over and over as he waved his hands towards what had been the community of Diamond City and the setting for all his happy memories. Louie would relate that on one occasion, after his grandfather had gotten "really old and feeble-minded," Billy started to walk out into the water and headed for the Banks, determined to return at least once more.

When his son and grandson noticed what was happening, they set out after him in a skiff where they reached him just before the shallow shoals gave way to a much deeper channel. There, they grabbed hold to restrain him and lifted him into their small boat. As they did, Billy plaintively explained to his son and grandson that he "just wanted to go home again!"

"He would cuss us," Louie recalled, "and then begged us why we wouldn't let him just go back to Diamond City. That was all he wanted. He would ask us what he had ever done to us so we wouldn't let him go home just one more time?"

By then, Diamond City was just a memory, having been washed away by the great August storm of 1899. There quite literally was no home for Billy to go to. Though it was less than five miles away across the Sound, and the yellow hue of its sand hills still could be seen on the horizon, Diamond City was, for Billy, as far away as "Old England" had been to his forbearers three centuries earlier when they landed in Virginia.

On the other hand, the population of Harkers Island had mushroomed from less than one hundred in 1890 to nearly a thousand residents by 1901. Diamond City and Shackleford Banks had been completely dismantled, loaded on skiffs, carried across Back Sound, and rebuilt. As the Harkers Island I would later know began to take shape, Billy's son and my grandfather, Charlie Hancock, became both a "mover and a shaker" and one of its leading citizens.

Old Pa's house sat majestically at the end of the path to the Landing where the dirt, grass, trees, and bushes gave way to beach sand at the high-water mark. The gable end on its southern façade, along with the high chimneys that emanated from just inside the east and west walls, were so large and distinctive that they were an obvious landmark used by everyone in the family when making their way back home from a day on the water. By then, the house was more than half a century old, yet it retained most of its original elegance despite the wear of the constant winds that battered it from every side depending on the season.

The north-side and inland portion of the house was a one-story structure made up of a combined kitchen and dining area and a small den, along with covered porches on both the eastward and westward sides. This was also the home's main entrance. Situated between it and the shoreline was a two-story section of similar size that sat perpendicular to the other. The downstairs had a bedroom on the east end and a large living area on the west end that held a long sofa and a pair of high-backed chairs. But its focus was an upright piano that was played often and loudly by my aunts Mary Louise and Ellen.

Between those rooms was a stairway that led to two upstairs bedrooms with large windows that opened onto an expansive view of Back Sound and across to the Banks and the Cape. When opened, they allowed the southwest breezes of summer to flow freely, so much so that Aunt Ellen claimed not to recall ever having slept without a blanket, even in the hottest part of summer.

At the midpoint of the south-facing wall, doorways on both levels opened to a two-story porch framed with large square pillars and waist-high banisters. The porches, bedrooms, and den were close enough to the tideline that you could easily hear even the slightest ripples of waves as they washed ashore no more than thirty feet from the red-brick foundation. The foundation itself was hardly visible as it was shielded by thick vines of pink wild roses that bloomed from early spring until well into the cold of winter.

Having left behind most of his commercial fishing days when he moved to his new home, Ol' Pa's stature in the community soon grew even larger than his homeplace. He was what later generations would call an entrepreneur. He dabbled in lots of different business ventures, large and small, and generally turned a profit in everything he touched. He had a boat and was a fisherman like all his neighbors, but he was never dependent on fishing to make a living. Still, it would be a generation or more before he and others broke their final bonds to the Banks. At first and for another twenty years or more, he kept a cabin there that housed his nets and other fishing equipment, along with a small herd of livestock — horses, cattle, and sheep — until as late as 1940.

Back on Harkers Island, he also ran several general stores, took in lodgers, sold or traded livestock, and if nothing else was pressing, would find something or anything to do to "make an extra dollar." One story frequently told was of how, if he had nothing else gainful to do on a given morning, he might sail a small skiff back to the Banks. Once there, he would rope a colt or calf from among the livestock that still roamed there freely, put it in his boat, and then hobble it. From there, he would head to Beaufort, where he would unload his cargo from the skiff and reload it on a train bound for New Bern, some forty miles inland. New Bern had been the state's colonial capital and was several times larger than Beaufort, with a bustling commercial district. After offloading his cargo, he would offer it for sale on the busiest corner he could find. Inevitably, it was said, he would come back home with at least ten dollars, and one more story to tell.

On another occasion, while at the Banks and herding some of the horses and cattle that he claimed for his own, he was branding a new calf and seemingly oblivious to what else went on around him, a stray bull emerged from among the cedar and yaupon bushes where it took aim at him and rushed in his direction. Finally noticing that he was in danger, Ol' Pa took off for a thicket of trees, hoping to shield himself from the approaching menace. But the trees were a hundred yards away, and it was by no means certain that he could make it in time to save himself. My father, who was then just a small boy, was playing near the very trees toward which Ol' Pa was hurrying but could do nothing but watch.

He later explained what happened next. His older brother, Louie ("Big Buddy" 1892-1987), who had been toiling not far away, took off after the bull at the same moment the bull had taken aim at Ol' Pa. My father's clearest recollection is that as the chase unfolded, he nervously screamed at the top of his voice, "Run, Papa, run!" and "Come, Buddy, come!" Thankfully, Big Buddy had some of the same swiftness afoot that his grandfather, Billy, had once enjoyed. According to my father, Big Buddy reached the bull and grabbed his tail in time to slow and divert him before he could overtake Ol' Pa. Once in the thicket, all of them agreed to never herd cattle again until all the bulls had been accounted for!

Ol' Pa was also known for his sailing ability and would frequently join in impromptu races with the many other sail skiffs that lined the south shore of Harkers Island by then. My father could remember that one of his father's most prized heirlooms was a winner's cup he earned in an annual sailboat race from Davis

Island (about 20 miles north) to Shell Point on the east end of Harkers Island.

Not all his sailing ventures were successful, as he once challenged some dories (round-bottomed skiffs) sailing westward in the Island channel to a race from the Island to the Beaufort Bar. In a favorable wind, the smoother bottoms of the dories made them swifter than the flat-bottomed skiffs used by most of the local sailors. But favorable winds were the exception rather than the rule for vessels that had a stated destination and an appointed time, and often had to "tack their way" around or into a constant breeze. In this environment, the deeper skegs and centerboards of the flat-bottomed skiffs were far better able to negotiate the many turns needed to maneuver through the marshes, shoals, and channels that separated the Island from the town, as Beaufort was usually called. Facing a strong southwester, Ol' Pa knew he could easily outrun that day's competition despite their having much larger sails and a crew to man them. But fate turned against him once he made his way to Wade's Shore and the wide channel that headed straight to the Bar.

The wind suddenly shifted to the northeast, where it billowed out the sails of the dory in the very direction they were headed. That was all the advantage needed by the crew of the dory to overtake the sailskiff that, until that moment, had them in its wake. Less than half a mile from the breaking waves that marked the entrance into the Bar, the dory seemed to "fly past him" as the crew shouted hoots and jeers to the erstwhile leader. After that, he never challenged anyone else to a boat race.

No one who knew Ol' Pa could remember seeing him actually "working." Rather, he always had someone else doing his work for him. In later life, these were always his grandsons. Even then he was selective as to which ones and how many he drafted for a specific task. He was careful never to have more boys than needed because the extras always did more harm than good when working on a job. One of his favorite maxims was, "If you've got one boy, then you've got a boy. If you've got two boys, you've got half a boy. If you've got three boys — well, then you ain't got nothing!"

Using his wiles rather than his hands or his back, Ol' Pa always seemed to have plenty of money for the things he needed or wanted. His large home with ample furnishings, along with his businesses and other holdings, including the undeveloped acreage he owned elsewhere on the Island, proved his success as a provider. My father, his son and namesake, used to quote Ol' Pa as boasting that he could be left penniless and naked on a Saturday evening, and put on a shoal in the Island channel, but with Aggie by his side, he would have a suit of clothes and money in his pocket by Sunday morning.

Life After Aggie

But Aggie would not always be there. Early in the spring of 1913, when my father was barely old enough to remember, forty-year-old Aggie fell sick with an intestinal or stomach disorder that her doctor called Pellagra, resulting in her severe dehydration. A common treatment for such illnesses at that time was to withhold liquids to help preclude further nausea or diarrhea. Later medical knowledge would reveal that in cases such as hers, the treatment as administered made the illness worse. Within just a few days, she had succumbed. My father's memories of what must have been a traumatic experience were sketchy at best.

He recalled that some of the neighborhood women took him to their homes while his mother was bedridden, and how her casket was loaded on a small boat to be carried around the west end of the Island to Harker's Point, where her own father, Louie Larsen, had been buried before she herself could have remembered. Most poignant of all was his recollection of standing by the graveside of the casket which held his mother. As it was lowered into the freshly dug hole, the pit had already begun to fill with the groundwater that was always only a few feet below the surface everywhere on the Island. In his childhood memory, he was worried about what the water would do to his mother once it had covered her completely.

Five of Aggie's six children were still living at home. Her oldest son, Louie, had married Rebecca Francis (France) Guthrie (1895-1941) a few months before. Her oldest daughter, Louisa (1895-1979), would marry Clem Gaskill (1887-1927) just six weeks after her

Children of Charlie and Agnes Hancock: Charlie William, Helen, Lurena, Louisa, and Louie. Agnes, their sister, died in 1965.

mother's passing, and Lourena (1898-1984) married Terrell Scott (1896-1971) two years later. But the remaining children, twelve-year-old Agnes (1901-1965) and nine-year-old Helen (1904-1997), along with my four-year-old father, still required more attention than a grieving, and soon courting, father could afford them. Only six months later, the elder Charlie was remarried to Carrie Murphy (1879-1969) of the nearby Davis Shore community, who soon set up house where Aggie had only recently left. Carrie was a widow and brought with her two children of her own, daughters Georgie (1902-1983) and Mollie (1906-1987), who still required most of their mother's attention.

So it was that Aggie's mother, my great-grandmother Emeline, soon stepped in to fill the void. The young Charlie soon began spending most of his time in her house, which was next door to his own. Before long, he was daily surrounded by a rapidly expanding group of cousins, Emeline's other grandchildren, who lived either with her or in the house next door. As he later told of his childhood, my father spoke of Emeline as if she had been his real mother.

As for Ol' Pa, his entrepreneurial days reached their climax during the boom years that followed World War I. He joined up with Willard Davis from Davis Shore and started a construction company that, in short order, became one of the largest in the county. Their completed projects included the still extant sea wall on the Beaufort waterfront, school buildings at Harkers Island and Davis, and several bridges built to connect the various fishing communities of eastern Carteret County. Soon, he had an office on Front Street in Beaufort, that my father remembered as having a "large desk with a padded chair," where he entertained clients and gave directions to his employees.

This was after he had remarried and moved the new family, including my father, now eleven years old, into a large two-story home near the heart of the lively seaport town that Beaufort had been for more than two centuries. Before he knew what had happened, my father was enrolled as a student at a grammar school maintained by St. Paul's Episcopal Church and was obliged to dress up in starched shirts and knickers every morning. Having spent his first ten years as footloose and free as a young boy could ever be while on the Island, it didn't take long for the younger Charlie to decide he had already had enough of his new surroundings.

Eventually, he was determined to return to the Island and what he considered home. Early one Saturday morning he packed up his belongings, stole away while no one else noticed, and hopped a ride on the mailboat that carried him back to Harkers Island. Louie, his older brother, granted him haven, even after Ol' Pa had come to "find him and bring him back!" Repeated pleas and the assurances of my uncle Louie finally convinced their father that it would be all right for him to stay on the Island, at least for a while.

My father's personal quandary was solved when the financial boom my grandfather had enjoyed eventually turned into a bust. His company looked to expand and had the winning bid to construct a new school in Morganton, NC, four hundred miles west and in the foothills of the Great Smoky Mountains. Working there, his crews found rock instead of dirt as they prepared the foundation. The company went bankrupt within a few months, and the office closed. Ol' Pa had used his property on Harkers Island as collateral to finance the venture, so he ended up losing most of the land he had owned on the Island, including the old homeplace of his first in-laws, Louie Larson and Emeline, at Harker's Point.

Only the big house he had built for Aggie and the adjoining acreage remained in his possession. So, he returned to that home on the Island and went back to the life he had known before becoming a big-time contractor. Not long after that, he reopened his store and

The Education of an Island Boy

resumed the many-faceted little jobs that had sustained him before and would again for the remainder of his life.

Eventually Ol' Pa's influence in the community and with his family went far beyond his land and his money. He was like one of those old post-Civil War Southern gentlemen portrayed in the novels of William Faulkner and others who held sway over every aspect of life for his extended family. He was a political boss who could deliver the votes not just of his kinsmen but many others who depended on him. He was a church leader and helped hire and fire preachers. He was a community organizer and head of the local school board, charitable organizations, and any impromptu group that arose or was needed.

One of my father's earliest memories, which had to have been when he was no more than six years old, was going by sailskiff with Ol' Pa to a political gathering. The featured guest and speaker that day was none other than William Jennings Bryan, then serving as Secretary of State in the first Wilson administration. Bryan was an acclaimed orator, former presidential candidate, and future prosecutor of John Scopes in the infamous "Monkey Trial" of 1925. He served only a little more than two years and had resigned by June of 1915. But my father vividly recounted the pageantry and excitement that accompanied Bryan's appearance on the front steps of the Beaufort courthouse, and that his father was one of those privileged to shake hands with "The Great Commoner," as he was known to many.

Politics of the kind that prevailed in the "Solid South" were an important part of Ol' Pa's life and living. Along with several others he had been one of the "bosses" that influenced elections on the Island, and it was his prerogative to hand out rewards and patronage to loyal supporters. He served as a Justice of the Peace or magistrate, tax lister, and registrar at various times. The latter position allowed him to keep close tabs on the political leanings of all the Island voters. Ol' Pa's family, and eventually their spouses and children, took their marching orders from him for most things and were considered part of the "Charlie Hancock crowd." When he went fishing, his crowd worked his boat and shared his earnings. His home was their gathering place; his party and candidate were their party and candidate; and his church was their church.

"Ol' Pa" with some of his grandsons: Ralph Hancock, with Bill Hancock in front of him, Creston, "Sno'ball" Gaskill with Tommy Hancock in front of him, and Louie Hallas Hancock on the end.

As it related to politics, work, and business, none of his family was more faithful and truer to that legacy than my father. Especially in politics and even after the Democrats and Republicans traded places as the majority party in the South after the Civil Rights Act of 1964, Daddy never wavered in his allegiance to the one that he continued to call "the party of Franklin Roosevelt." But when it came to matters of church and religion — well that was a little more complicated. That final credo of my grandfather caused some sparks to fly when his youngest son, my father, who was still a month short of his nineteenth birthday, married one of Bertha Lewis' daughters, my mother Margarette, on the last day of 1927.

Bertha's Legacy

Like my grandfather Charlie, my maternal grandmother, Bertha Willis Lewis (1886-1932), was born at Diamond City on the Banks.

Bertha Willis Lewis, my maternal grandmother, standing in the back left. Her mother, Margaret Meekins Lewis is sitting beside her father, Joseph Wallace Willis. Little girl is her sister, Mary James, and little boy is her brother, Telford. Standing beside her is Bertha's best friend, Edie. Margaret and Joe had buried three children by the time this photo was taken.

And like so many others who had lived there, she relocated to Harkers Island with her family after the 1899 storm. As her life ended two decades before my birth, I have no personal recollections of her — of her appearance, behavior, or personality. All I know is what was conveyed to me by my mother and aunts and several of her contemporaries who survived until I was old enough to be around them at the Sunday church meetings, where they frequently reminded me that I was an heir to her legacy. From their assembled descriptions, it was evident that in her youth she was considered to be physically attractive, with long flowing hair and a physical vitality that would serve her well as she matured into a matriarch of a family that was considered large even for her time. As she matured into middle age, her appearance inevitably evidenced the effects of seven full-term pregnancies that included two sets of twins. But it seems her energy and vitality never diminished.

Her parents, Joseph Wallace Willis (1854-1929) and Margaret Meekins Lewis (1861-1946) were prominent personalities on the

Banks, as they would be on the Island. Joe Wallace was known for his eccentricity as much as for his often-awkward appearance. Margaret, called Aunt Marg by everyone, including her own grandchildren, was recognized as being the community midwife who, before she died, would help in the delivery of several hundred babies at Diamond City and later at Harkers Island.

Joe Wallace was short and stout. He sported a long flowing beard, and not always a clean one. He spoke often and loudly and was known for saying and doing the strangest things. Case in point: He once painted his boat two colors, one on the left and another on the right. His reasoning, he explained, was that the contrasting colors allowed Aunt Marg to look far into the distance and be able to tell if his boat was coming home or still going out, based on which color glared in the sun. Likewise, when asked by a salesman visiting the Island how many children he had, he answered that he claimed to have three, but many people said that one of them really belonged to Charlie Hancock!

It is not difficult to imagine how that tidbit was received by Aunt Marg when she soon thereafter was told what had been said. Her anger may have been somewhat assuaged by the well-known fact that a great deal of community gossip held that my paternal grandfather was the father of at least one child born to my maternal great-grandmother. In fact, it was so well accepted that it was shared by the time I came along, often with a sigh and a grin, among most of her descendants.

By then, it was recognized by most people that my mother's Uncle Telford looked so much like her father-in-law that it would have been difficult to deny that there was at least some biological connection. But whatever that connection may have been, it was far enough in the past that it proved no real concern by the time both families relocated to the Island.

In 1906, not long after leaving Diamond City and arriving at Harkers Island, Bertha married Richard Lewis (1886-1960), a soon-to-be dredge boat captain from the nearby community of Lennoxville that lay just to the west of Harkers Island across several shoals and a small winding channel. Dick, as he was known, was never certain as to who was his own father, at least not

The Education of an Island Boy

officially. His mother, Charlotte (1865-1919), had three children, including him and two sisters, but was never married. She maintained throughout her life that the father of each of her children was a highly successful local doctor who was much revered throughout the county.

She was six years his senior and served as his family's seamstress and housemaid. In addition to being a physician, he was also a successful businessman whose ventures included heading a local dredging company. In fact, Dick would confide to his children that the same doctor later provided him with the financing he needed to get started in the dredging business, where he eventually became a captain. When Charlotte died in 1919, her death certificate was signed by the same doctor she alleged to have been the father of her children.

Richard Lewis, my maternal grandfather

Charlotte was much loved by her new daughter-in-law, and, most especially by the large group of granddaughters that Dick and Bertha soon presented. My mother would often explain that her favorite month of every year was August. That was because when she was a girl, her grandma Charlotte would spend that month with them and help her mother sew new clothes for the girls to wear for the upcoming school year.

Immediately after marrying, Bertha began having daughters, a total that eventually reached nine, although only seven grew to maturity. My mother, Margarette (1912-1997), was the third of those. Grandpa Dick, as later he was known, was so successful in the dredging business that he was able to provide his large family a comfortable standard of living and a spacious home at the west end of the Island and at the foot of what was called Red Hill.

Captain Dick's work responsibilities caused him to be gone for extended durations, usually several months or more, without returning home. It was said, not entirely in jest, that he came home only often and long enough to father another child. When he came home, his long absences made him very remote from his children. My mother would sometimes lament that she could not recall that he ever kissed or told her that he loved her.

She related how on one occasion when her father had announced by letter that he would be arriving home on a certain date, she and her twin sister, Helen, made a pact that "this time they were going to run up and hug him, and kiss him on his cheek." But despite their pledge, she lamented, when he presented himself to his children, his attitude was so aloof that neither of the twins nor any of their sisters could muster the courage to ask for a sign of his affection.

Although my maternal grandfather survived until I was eight years old, I recall being in his company only once, and that was less than a year before his passing in 1960. My Aunt Lillian, his oldest daughter, pulled up in front of our house one summer with a gray-haired and still handsome older man sitting beside her. As the two of them made their way towards our porch, my mother stepped out onto the steps and while calling Telford and me to her side, she announced that the man we did not recognize was her father. I rushed to her side as my mother and grandfather extended greetings as if they were business partners renewing an old friendship. There were no embraces or expressions of affection as Mama and her company took seats on the porch.

What I remember most of all was that I expected my grandfather, whom I had never met before, would in some way acknowledge me and my brother Telford. I was often in the company of older people, including men, some related and most not, and all of them would regularly greet me and even offer an embracing gesture of some sort. But this time and with this old man it was different. I vividly recall that not only did he not speak to me or reach out to touch us, but he never looked in my direction, even as Mama introduced my brother and me as two of his grandchildren. Instead, the three adults, my mother, grandfather, and aunt, chatted for a short while and then the latter two got back in the car and headed towards the home of another of his daughters. That was the one and only time I ever saw him.

The Education of an Island Boy

Whatever may have been his shortcomings as a nurturer, there was no disputing Captain Dick's ability and willingness to provide financially for his wife and children. The comfortable lifestyle his profession afforded his family allowed that often, and for extended occasions, Bertha was able to take in orphans or other children who, for whatever reason, could no longer be cared for by their parents. At various times, she had in her home as many children who belonged to others as she did of her own. And, eventually, one of those would become the son she always had wanted.

The children of my maternal grandparents, Richard and Bertha Lewis.
L-R My aunts Lillian & Helen, my mother Margarette, my aunts Bertha Gray, Louise, Rosalie, & Ruth, and my uncle Richard (Dick). As often was the case with large families during this time, two daughters, Ella Dee and Lucille, had died in infancy.

My mother told the story of how, on at least one occasion, the issue of "the strays" that Bertha had taken in became a source of contention between her and her often absent husband. Late in her life, after all her own children had been born, Bertha found out that one of Captain Dick's sisters, Jenny (1895-1958), was expecting an illegitimate child.

The shame that then accompanied such an event was so profound that many women, especially younger ones, looked for someone willing to accept the baby as their own. This would spare both the mother and the baby from some of the humiliation which at that time was an anticipated consequence of giving birth and raising a child out of wedlock.

Responding to what she knew was a delicate situation for her husband's sister and mother, Bertha let it be known that she would be willing to take the baby as her own. Eventually, one morning early in the fall of 1928, Bertha went out on her porch to speak to one of her husband's relatives who moments before had arrived at the Island in a sailskiff from Lennoxville. A short while later she followed him to the Landing and boarded his skiff where the two headed back towards the town. Just before sundown, she landed back home carrying a beautiful dark-haired and brown-eyed newborn baby boy nestled snugly in her arms.

With its arrival, she finally had a son to be loved and spoiled by her and seven older sisters. She even named the boy Richard, after his uncle whom he would grow up believing to be his father. Captain Dick likely was aware of the child's true identity, even before the new baby was born. And he was probably sensitive to the situation, given the circumstances of his own birth and childhood. Perhaps that made him even more discreet than he otherwise might have been about the child's identity once he arrived home and met his newborn "son."

My grandmother, Bertha Lewis, before her passing in 1932 from injuries sustained in a car wreck

Shortly after his arrival back home, neighbors came by to visit and to see the son who had joined the family.

The Education of an Island Boy

One of them commented out loud about how many other indigent children there seemed to be on the Island at that time, at the dawn of the Great Depression. Probably quite innocently, and maybe even with a touch of pride, he suggested they might all be brought to Bertha, and "she would find a place for them."

For some reason, Bertha took exception to her husband's remarks. Maybe it was something he had said in private, or maybe something he had not said when told that the baby had come to stay. Standing up, and obviously perturbed, she spoke directly to Captain Dick, asking, "Do you want me to tell you whose baby that is?" After moments of chilly silence, the dredge boat captain calmly stood up and walked out of the room without answering his wife's question. After that, the subject of "Baby Dick's" identity, or why he had ended up as part of Bertha's home, never came up again — at least not in a public setting.

Even with a house full of children, regardless of their relationship, Bertha and Dick's family remained relatively well off, especially when compared with their neighbors. So, if making a living and sustaining a family had been the overriding influence in Grandpa Charlie's life, it was far less than that for Grandma Bertha. For her, the defining moment of her life was a religious epiphany that occurred when she was twelve. She maintained that she was healed of crippling arthritis by Mormon Elders (missionaries) who had arrived at Diamond City shortly before the storm of 1899. As a result of that experience, she, along with her parents and siblings, became among the earliest members of The Church of Jesus Christ of Latter-day Saints in eastern North Carolina.

But Bertha was more than just a member or a follower. She was a real convert and a living emblem of the power of her new faith. With all her heart and soul, she embraced the responsibility of conveying that conviction to her children, and anyone else who would listen to her story. Such a message was not well-received by everyone, or even most, of the profoundly traditional religious folk that lived around her at Harkers Island. She was well known in the community, and even loved by her friends, but in general, their affection was despite her religious faith, rather than because of it.

Though Captain Dick usually was away from home attending to his work responsibilities, my grandmother's house was often a hive of activity. Much of that activity revolved around Bertha's church associations. Members and missionaries gathered there for meetings, and Bertha was deeply involved with various church responsibilities. That involvement would continue unabated until Bertha's untimely passing in 1932 when she was just forty-six years old. She was accompanying her daughter Helen (1912-2000), my mother's sister, to begin studying to be a nurse at a school in Washington, NC when their vehicle was involved in an accident. Though it was obvious that she had been shaken up by the crash, her injuries did not appear to be life-threatening, and she was transported home rather than to a hospital. She at first seemed to be recovering. But unexpectedly, less than a week after the incident, she suffered what was deemed to be a heart attack and died in her sleep.

My maternal grandfather, Richard, "Dick" Lewis

My grandfather, Captain Dick, would survive his wife and my grandmother by three decades. He remarried a year later and permanently relocated to the Tidewater area of Virginia where his dredging company was headquartered. His new family eventually included two more daughters and a son. As a result of my grandfather's near-total exodus from the island, his five children still living at home were, in effect, left to fend for themselves.

Twenty-year-old Helen was called "Hessie" by her family and was my mother's twin. She assumed the responsibility of maintaining the home and caring for her younger siblings, including four sisters and Dick, the four-year-old namesake of his adoptive father. Just a few years after his new marriage, Captain Dick proceeded to sell all his property on the Island, including the house, and the younger children were obliged to live with their older and married siblings until they themselves became independent.

A Part Of — but Apart From

Despite Bertha's early passing, she had lived long enough to instill in her children, including my mother, a keen awareness that though they were a part of the Island community, they were also something of a breed apart because of their "peculiar" religious faith. As they eventually mothered families of their own, they and their posterity would become, and remain, a major part of the Mormon community that sprang up on the Island.

The home of Richard and Bertha Lewis, my maternal grandparents. Here she mothered nine daughters and an adopted son.

From as far back as I can remember, Sunday services for the Harkers Island congregation of The Church of Jesus Christ of Latter-day Saints have been de facto reunions for the descendants of Bertha Lewis. At first, it was just her children and then her grandchildren who greeted and gathered in their chosen corner before sitting together in their favorite pews. By now the weekly gathering of her lineage extends back as much as four additional generations. Indeed, one entire section of the sanctuary can trace at least a portion of their spiritual roots as well as their physical DNA through her line. To that extent, the range of her influence has matched and even exceeded that of Ol' Pa.

It would take a while longer before that part of my grandmother's legacy would become self-evident. Whether my father anticipated or even suspected as much in the fall of 1927 is doubtful. In fact, religious concerns might have been among the last things on his mind when he met, and immediately fell in love with, one of Bertha's daughters in the fall of 1927.

Part of the descendancy of Bertha and Richard Lewis assembled for a Family Reunion to celebrate what would have been Bertha's 100th birthday in 1986.

The Education of an Island Boy

My parents, Margarette and Charlie Hancock
Photo was taken on an Easter Sunday morning before attending church

4

Charlie and Margarette

"How can we live without our lives? How will we know it's us without our past?"
John Steinbeck, "The Grapes of Wrath"

Most Islanders of the generations before mine had humble aspirations when it came to a career and profession. It was assumed that they could and would make a living just like their ancestors had done for as long as anyone could remember. But despite what might have been viewed as a lack of ambition in some circles removed from their unique culture, there was a strong work ethic for many of them. This included doing all that was necessary to provide for a family without having to depend on others. No one had epitomized this attitude more than my grandfather, Charlie Hancock. Ol' Pa's most frequent advice to his children and anyone else who would listen was that they should always be "doin' something." "That was," he said, "the only way to make sure that you will ever 'mount to anything!"

He was likewise adamant in his admonitions about having a nest egg of savings for tough times that he knew by experience would someday come. To his crewmen, who included not just his sons and grandsons but many others of his extended family and friends, he had more specific advice. Every time he passed out weekly shares for what had been caught and sold, along with cash and coins, he

The Education of an Island Boy

would include this advice: "Remember now," he would say with an emphasis that betrayed the fact that he had repeated the same maxim so often that not one of them could possibly have forgotten it, "there are twelve months in the year, and you've got to eat in every one of 'em."

My father had dropped out of school after the seventh grade and shortly before his thirteenth birthday. The kinds of learning that were acquired in a classroom, he assumed, were intended primarily to prepare one for making a living. In his mind, nothing else he would garner at the schoolhouse on Harkers Island was going to improve his status in that regard. In fact, any further delay in entering the workforce would leave him behind most of his friends in getting started in the only career he or they ever had imagined. He rightly assumed that he already could make as much money "working the water" as if he were to wait until he was older. Within a few years after "quitting school" he had acquired a small boat with a gasoline engine as well as a skiff to pull behind it. He was now, at least in his own mind, a full-fledged "Harkers Island Waterman."

Though he was not yet nineteen, he knew he was ready to get married, and he was actively looking to find the right girl when he met my mama late in the fall of 1927. She was from "Red Hill" at the west end of the Island, nearly a mile from where the Hancocks had gathered — and had been three years behind his class at school.

Charlie William Hancock shortly before asking for Margarette Lewis's hand in marriage.

And, like my father, she too had decided that she had been exposed to quite enough book learning after completing the seventh grade. They had made their first real acquaintance when my mother, two years later and still not quite fifteen years old, visited with her grade school friend and fellow church member, Edith Guthrie. Edith's parents lived directly diagonal to Ol' Pa's home, with the northside boughs of "Ol' Pa's Oak" serving as an informal boundary line. Edith's mother, Evoline, was one of Grandma Bertha's closest friends dating all the way back to before their families had left the Banks.

Sparks began to fly as soon as their first meeting, and within weeks my father had decided she was the one he had been looking and waiting for. And it was obvious to him and to her, and even to their friends, that my mother was in complete agreement with the plans he had in mind. There was one obstacle in the way, however, and it had the potential to be a big one. Although it was not uncommon for someone of her age to be married, Mama was not yet legally old enough to make that decision for herself. In North Carolina, the minimum age of consent was sixteen years old. She had turned fifteen only a few weeks earlier in late November. So, it was going to be necessary for one of her parents to sign a consent form showing their concurrence.

Margarette at age 17. She and Charlie William had already welcomed Ralph, their first of ten children, into their family.

Mama first asked for her mother's blessing and permission but was disappointed in the response. But Grandma Bertha did volunteer that although she would not offer her signature of approval, neither would she interfere if Mama could convince her father to agree with their plans. It was mutually decided that the task of convincing Captain Dick would be left to the prospective groom.

Getting my grandfather's signature, or even his tacit approval, was not going to be easy or simple. For one thing, his would-be father-in-law was not scheduled to be home again until late in December. Further, even if he could be reached, there was no guarantee that he would approve of their intentions. When Captain Dick finally arrived home just in time for Christmas, my father determined to stiffen his shoulders and confront him directly about their plans.

Soon after Christmas, Daddy sought him out and asked for permission to marry his daughter.

Captain Dick's initial answer was a resounding "No," but after a few days of repeated pleas from my mother, and another meeting with my father, he finally threw up his hands and relented — but only partially. "I ain't gonna sign no papers saying Margarette can get married. She's still too young for that. But if that's what she wants and you can get somebody else to sign it for me, I won't stand in your way," he declared.

As far as Daddy was concerned, that was all the consent and approval he needed because he knew just whom to call upon for help to make that happen. He went straight from Red Hill and my grandfather's living room back to his own neighborhood. There, even though it was a Saturday, he was able to convince his older cousin "Danky" (Danny Willis 1891-1952) to go with him and Mama on the mailboat, which also served as a passenger ferry, to Beaufort and to the office of the Register of Deeds.

The embarking and drop-off spot for the mailboat was less than half a mile east along the shore from Ol' Pa's house on a dock that ran out from the Landing at the store of Cleveland Davis. That small building sat amid a hodgepodge of stores and churches, the post office, and other gathering places that made it the hub and "downtown" of the community. Getting there would not be a problem. The trick was going to be getting to Beaufort and to the courthouse, and then back on the mailboat, in time to make the last departure for Harkers Island. That was scheduled for an hour before sundown each evening, which in late December meant before four o'clock in the afternoon.

Somehow, they made it work. Danky played well his part of pretending to be Mama's father. The clerk in the Deeds' office prepared the necessary license whereupon Danky signed on the dotted line just as if he had been Captain Dick himself. The three then hurried to catch the last ferry ride of the day back to the Island. Despite what had been agreed, Daddy was less than certain that Captain Dick would stick to his promise, and more than a little worried that Grandma Bertha might belatedly decide to get involved.

Charlie and Margarette

So, as soon as they got off the mailboat at Cleveland Davis's Landing, they went directly to the justice of the peace, Mart Guthrie (1872-1947), who lived just two doors down from Ol' Pa's house at the foot of Hancock Landing. The sun had already set, and it was dark by the time that Daddy and Mama, along with Danky who would now serve as a witness in his own person, knocked on Mart's door. They found the old man sitting at the table having supper with his family. After Daddy explained his purpose for being there, the justice of the peace asked if he could at least wait until after he had finished eating to perform the wedding ceremony.

"I can't wait," Daddy explained. "Something might happen. I'll pay you an extra five dollars (beyond the standard five-dollar fee) if you go ahead and do it right now." That was all the encouragement it would take.

"You stay right there," he said, as off he went to get his little black book, as well as to recruit his wife, Virginia (Willis 1869-1954), to be a second witness and to make it completely "legal." Within just a few minutes it was.

So, within less than an hour of having arrived back at Hancock Landing, my father and mother were legally married and ready to set out on their life together. According to Daddy, they walked up the path to Ol' Pa's store where he bought her a soft drink (Coca Cola), before escorting her across the road to the home of his oldest sister, Louisa (1895-1979). She was called Ezzer and was recently widowed and had three small children to raise on her own. Having always been like a second mother to my father — his own mother had died when he was only four years old — she was willing and happy to have him bring his new wife to live with her and her children.

Daddy and Mama spent their first night together just a few steps away from where they would be for the next seventy years. But awakening the next morning in the southeast bedroom they had little time to ponder or dream about what those years together might be like. Even though it was the first day of a new year, and a holiday for everyone else, they were awoken by the sound of someone rapping on their window exactly as the new year's first sunrise broke through the twilight sky.

Pulling the shade and raising the window, my father was startled to see his father, Ol' Pa, standing outside with an anxious, even a hurried and frustrated expression on his face. "I can't believe you are still in bed this time of day," he exclaimed to my father as he peered through the opening in the glass. "You ain't gonna 'mount to nothin' if you lay in bed this long!"

Making a Family of Their Own

My mother woke that morning into a world that must have seemed to her more than a little removed from what she had been accustomed to at Red Hill as one of Bertha's girls and Aunt Marg's extended family. She was now "smack dab" in the middle of Hancock Landing and Ol' Pa's crowd. Within less than a year they were able to move into their own new home that would be adjacent on the eastward side of Ezzer's house and less than twenty feet away.

Their newly constructed dwelling was a 24' X 26' bungalow-style structure built by a local carpenter and Daddy's maternal cousin, "Bud" Brooks (David Nelson Brooks 1874-1957). With my father as a daily helper, the final cost of construction was $750 for both labor and lumber. Ol' Pa had insisted that Daddy stop anything else he was doing to allow him to assist in the building because Bud was charging 50¢ for each hour of labor. Ol' Pa added, "Ain't nobody that can afford to spend that much for a carpenter." Daddy was able to pay for the whole project with his own cash as he had spent the previous several years saving every possible penny to avoid going into debt for what he anticipated (correctly) would be the single largest investment of his life.

A few weeks before their first child, Ralph, was born the following October, the couple was settled into their "honeymoon retreat." According to my father, they enjoyed those few weeks of being alone, but those months would be their last experience of staying in a home by themselves for the next forty-plus years.

All in all, they would share the next seventy years together on that same spot until my mother lost her life in an auto accident in 1997, shortly after her eighty-fifth birthday. Daddy remained there alone but attended daily by his children for another five years. During those years they experienced the births of ten children and raised nine to maturity. After my oldest brother Ralph was born in 1928, came my sisters Ella Dee and June in 1931 and 1933, my brothers Tommy and Bill in 1935 and 1937, my sister Lillian in 1939, and my brothers Michael, Denny, and Telford in 1942, 1944, and 1950, respectively. Denny succumbed to childhood leukemia less than a year after I, the last of their children, was born in 1952. Only June and I have survived until the time of this writing, but each of my siblings was and is so much a part of my life that this narrative might rightfully be considered a collective memory for all of them as well as for myself.

This is a rendering of our family home done by a friend, Susan Young McLeod, in 1990.

Their new home had been far from finished when they moved in. It was complete and furnished enough that it kept out the rain and the wind, but that was about as far along as their carpenter had left it. The interior walls were framed but not sheathed, and the floors were strips of "tongue and groove" pine that were so rough that they got splinters when walking barefoot. Eventually, it would have two downstairs bedrooms, a kitchen, and a living room. There was a hand pump over a porcelain sink, and the bedrooms had chamber pots that made use of an outside wooden "privy" that was partially hidden away in the southwest corner of the quarter-acre lot and shaded by several fig trees. Within a few years an upstairs attic with a ceiling of barely six feet was turned into a bedroom that was large enough for two full-sized beds. There was a narrow stairwell near the center of the house that was just wide enough for one person at a time to go up or down.

Shortly before I was born in 1952, Daddy added a small 8' X 16' den that was next to an even smaller 8' X 8' laundry room on the south end of the structure. The laundry room eventually was outfitted to become our first indoor bathroom — but that was ten years after I came along and more than a quarter century after the house was originally built.

Finally, shortly after the addition of the den and laundry, Daddy and the brothers, including me, built a back porch off the house's south end. We had gathered most of the lumber used in the construction from driftwood that had floated ashore on the ocean side of Shackleford Banks. Daddy waited for a day when the wind was blowing from the north to carry the lumber away from the beach and to his open boat as it circled just beyond the cresting waves breaking at the shoreline. I can still recall how excited and proud I was the day that he deposited me on the shore just to the south of where Diamond City once had been.

My charge was to gather and then put adrift anything that even remotely appeared to be usable in construction. There, the northerly wind would float the pieces out to where my father could retrieve them. For the next several hours I hauled and then floated off dozens of planks, posts, and sheets of plywood that had washed or otherwise discarded from the decks of tankers and cargo ships as they entered the Beaufort Bar coming from the east. Once the boat was loaded and so full that there was hardly room for me to find a place to sit, we headed home with enough lumber to finish the building project.

Yet, even after all the later additions to the original structure, it was the front porch of our house that became and would remain the central gathering place of the family — and later of the extended family. It stretched the full length of the north portal and fronted the Island's main road. Sitting on the porch swing, two rockers, half a dozen chairs, and the white-washed banisters, we would gather there with family and friends in numbers that often spilled over into the front yard. Just as important as the regulars who sat there were the countless friends and family who walked by each day and into the evening. There was a steady stream of passers-by, and every one of them would offer their regards as they passed.

Many of them even stopped by at least long enough to catch up on the latest news from our crowd. "Mama's porch," as we knew it, or "Margarette's porch," as most others called it, was like a small-town square by the way it served our neighborhood. With only a screen door between the porch and the house proper, that "pizer" (a local vernacular for the word "piazza") was a window to the outside world and a daily stage show that played out in plain view of and for our entire family.

A typical Sunday summer afternoon at my parent's home as family and friends would spill into the yard after the porch was too full to hold everyone.

The home of my parents was near the center of what eventually would be called Hancock Landing. Between that and the stately home of Ol' Pa to the south and at the shore sat the smaller but similarly designed home of my Uncle Louie. Just across the road and to the north was the home and family of another of Daddy's sisters, Lourena. Beyond those in every direction, there were more of my father's aunts, uncles, and cousins in a cadre of houses, each of which was within easy earshot of the neighboring homes on either side. Both literally and figuratively surrounded by the world my Grandfather Charlie had built, Mama was more than a little overwhelmed when first married. She was still less than sixteen years old, and within a few months, was carrying an unborn baby of her own.

Mama would later laugh as she told of sometimes walking out to the dirt road in front of where she now lived and looking down it through her tears, to the west and toward Red Hill and the home of her parents and six of her unmarried siblings. But even through her laughter we could still sense what had been her uneasiness, if not her uncertainty, for the new life that had enveloped her as she was expected to become a part of the Hancock family.

Frances Guthrie Hancock, Louie's wife

In most ways she eventually did that. She grew to be loved and accepted by Ezzer and Lourena, and especially by Big Buddy's wife, "France" (Rebecca Frances Guthrie 1895-1941). Mama's children were as much a part of Old Pa's work and play platoons as were any of their cousins. But there was one part of Mama's identity that did not change when she left the west'ard and Bertha's house. Margarette had been raised with an unshakeable faith in the stories her mother told of her own healing, and in the church that had sent the young missionaries who worked that miracle. With a fervor that grew more intense as her family enlarged and matured, her house would become a bastion like what her mother's had been of the Mormon faith and culture, and in the very center of the more traditional world my grandfather had fostered.

This division was not without its tensions, both inside the home and within the extended family. Daddy was constantly pulled between the expectations of his father and especially his sisters, and the equally firm commitment of his wife to the faith she had inherited from her mother. Usually, the tension was below the surface, but it sometimes boiled over and resulted in outright demands for orthodoxy from my father — and equally vehement defiance from my mother.

On several occasions, Daddy took my older brothers and sisters with him, usually out in the boat, at the very time he knew that my mother planned to carry them with her to church meetings. He also refused to give permission for my older siblings to be baptized into membership on their eighth birthday as is the custom and practice for believers in the Mormon faith. But by the time that I came along, most of that was a thing of the past. My brother Telford and I were baptized on our eighth birthdays, and by then, all our siblings were already officially members.

The major break in Daddy's objections, or at least in his will to enforce them, came with two events: one followed closely by the other. The first occurred when my sister June — the third of his children and his second daughter — at the age of thirteen demanded of my father that she be allowed to be baptized and he relented. The second, just a few weeks later, was when my oldest brother, Ralph, took his cue from June's example and, on his own, was baptized despite our father's wishes to the contrary. Ralph was old enough that Daddy's permission was no longer required.

But Ralph was not just my father's oldest son. He was, next to my mother, his closest friend and comrade. He was also seen as my grandfather's favorite among his scores of grandchildren, and the one who had spent most of his life near Ol' Pa's side and within his reach. When Ralph moved outwardly and openly to join and identify with Mama's faith, it seemed to signal to my father that the battle over religion within his own family was now over, and at least this time, Mama and Bertha had won out over him and Ol' Pa.

My parents' family gathered in our back yard in the Spring of 1950, shortly before the birth of my brother Telford. Back Row, L-R My mother Margarette, my father, Charlie, my sister Ella Dee, my brother Ralph holding my nephew Jonathan (Ella Dee's son) and my sister June. Front row L-R Our dog Shucks, my brother Tommy, my brothers Michael & Denny, and my sister Lillian (Sister). I didn't arrive until two years later.

Working Away from Home

Not long after my parents were married, my father accepted an invitation from his father-in-law to become part of Grandpa Dick's dredge boat crew that was then working near Petersburg, VA. My grandfather's offer was to give Daddy an exclusive franchise for ferrying men and supplies from the docks to his much larger dredge boat that housed the massive pumps and rigging. That was how my grandfather had made his start two decades earlier, and he encouraged my father that it would be possible for him to fashion a similar career in the same place and in the same way.

How that prospect was viewed by my mother was seldom discussed, but it was understood that she was by no means anxious that her marriage would follow the same pattern as her mother's. Despite her objections, he set out one spring morning in his small

Charlie and Margarette

gasoline-powered boat and headed north on a 200-mile journey up the inland sounds of North Carolina into the tidewaters of Virginia. There, he followed the James River inland and all the way to the harbors and docks of Petersburg and Richmond.

He never ventured to fully explain to me why he had been willing to attempt such an ambitious undertaking after never having been more than fifty miles from the Island in his entire life. Perhaps he had grown anxious about the responsibility of supporting a family by working the water. Or maybe he was enticed by the thought of having a steady income, a siren's song that eventually would lure more than a few fishermen's sons from the Island to mainland jobs.

Daddy's initial commitment required that he be gone for six weeks, and that might have seemed not so long to someone who had his whole life still ahead of him. So off he went, leaving Mama, who was expecting their second child, and his son, Ralph, who was still less than a year old. When he returned home after the first six weeks of his new job, he made it clear that his feelings had changed as to his interest in a dredging career. If his mind was not already completely made up, his decision was driven home for him when, as he greeted his family, Ralph ran from his grasp to the arms of Mama's uncle, Telford (Willis 1898-1949).

My father later related that at that very moment he made a vow never again to allow his children to feel more comfortable with some man other than him. He soon announced that he would not be going back north to work for the dredging company, or more specifically, that his intention was never again to do anything that took him away from his home and family after sundown. The rest of his life, he would boast or lament, depending on the occasion, that his first extended trip away from his family was also his last, and that if he had it to do over, he would have skipped that one as well!

Aside from that, there was one other time when my father toyed with the idea of taking on a job that would oblige him to spend more than an occasional day or night away from home. In the early summer of 1942, when my mother was not yet thirty years old, and soon after the outbreak of World War II, she awaited the birth of her seventh child. All but the first had been born at home under the watchful eyes and direction of Mama's midwife grandmother, "Aunt Marg." But Aunt Marg was now over eighty years old, and calling on her for the delivery was no longer viable. It was agreed that this time, Mama would have to go to the hospital in town (Beaufort).

Without insurance or a steady income, plans had to be made for how to pay for the doctor and several days in a hospital room. It was thought that the total cost would be close to one hundred dollars. Wartime concerns had caused the Navy to impose restrictions on fishing on the ocean side of the Banks, so there was little hope of earning that much on the water. But there was one sure way to make the money.

The Army had commissioned the building of a station at Ocracoke on Pamlico Sound that included a long wooden dock for servicing the boats that patrolled the nearby Banks and Inlet. Word had quickly spread that workers on the dock were paid a dollar an hour, far more than any of the laborers along the Sounds had ever even heard of. So early one Sunday morning, Daddy headed up along Core Sound towards Ocracoke, looking for a job working on that dock.

Sure enough, he was hired as soon as he presented himself to the foreman supervising the project. Working as much as twelve hours a day, seven days a week, he began to count both his earnings and how much longer he would have to stay there before he could go home with the money he would need. In less than two weeks he figured he had enough wages coming his way to gather his belongings and head back south down the Sound. But upon confronting his foreman, he was flabbergasted to learn that he would have to wait until the next payday, more than a week later, to collect his final earnings. Bitterly disappointed, he returned to his work with his sadness so evident that one of his coworkers asked him what was wrong.

When Daddy explained his situation, his friend commiserated with his predicament and then suggested a plan for how both could get their money immediately.

"The foreman is right about having to wait until payday," he conceded to my father, "but only if you quit before the project is finished."

"On the other hand," he asserted, "if they fire us, they will have to pay us right away and probably order us to get off their dock as quickly as possible. You just follow and do just like me, and we'll both be out of here before the day is over."

A few minutes later, the two had laid down their tools and sat down on the edge of that portion of the dock that was already completed, sometimes laying back as if to take a nap in the summer sun. When told to get back to work, they just ignored the order and continued to waste away their time as the other workers toiled on busily around them. Finally, the foreman gave the two malingerers exactly what they had wanted.

"Both of you are fired," he shouted so loudly that others could hear, and hopefully learn from the example. "Go straight to the paymaster and get your wages and don't let me see either of you on this dock ever again!"

Within less than an hour, Daddy was back in his boat with $115 in his pocket. Not long after sundown, he tied up at the Landing and ran up the path to let Mama know that he had the money they would need to allow her to have her new baby in a hospital. Four weeks later my brother, Mike, was born in Beaufort, and Daddy paid both the doctor and the hospital for their services before carrying his wife and his new baby home in the same boat he had used to get to and from Ocracoke.

That adventure at the north end of Pamlico Sound working on a government dock was one of only a few ways that our family was directly affected by the two great wars of the first half of the century. My father was only ten years old and too young to have been called up to fight when the United States entered World War I in 1917. His only recollection of the conflict was of knowing men who were drafted into the army or navy, and of their eventual return and stories.

The Education of an Island Boy

Yet, throughout the remainder of his life he made certain to remind his children of the approach of the "eleventh hour of the eleventh day of the eleventh month" so he and we would remember Armistice Day, later Veterans Day, that marked the end of fighting in Europe at 11:00 am on the eleventh day of November in 1918.

By the onset of World War II, more than two decades later in late 1941, he was too old for the military. And the oldest of his sons, my brother Ralph, was not yet seventeen years old when the war finally ended in September of 1945. Among the memories of the war years that were spoken of most often by my parents and older siblings was that all windows had to be covered at night so that no lighting could be visible from the outside. That requirement was to preclude the possibility that German warships operating off the coast could use those lights for targeting any coastal locations. They also remembered the wartime quotas on consumer goods, including candy and nylon hosiery, and that soldiers and sailors from nearby bases often frequented the Island's stores — and especially the local movie theater.

Despite not having served himself, Daddy did receive a special commendation letter and certificate from the US Navy for rescuing two Naval pilots whose plane went down in Pamlico Sound due to mechanical problems. In addition, I did have several older cousins who were drafted or enlisted and saw military action in both Europe and the Pacific. Eventually, in the late fifties and early sixties, three of my older brothers; Tommy, Bill, and Mike, all joined the United States Coast Guard, and the former two made it their careers. Then, my brother Telford, anticipating that he would be drafted at the height of the Vietnam War, enlisted in the Army in 1970 and remained a soldier until he retired two decades later.

My father was a couple of inches short of six feet tall. He had a slim build that remained the same throughout his life. His facial features were unlike those of his father and much more akin to the sharp cheekbones, nose, and chin evidenced in the one surviving photo of his mother. His hair was thick and brown until late in his life, and his darkened skin evidenced the many hours he had spent on the water and in the sun. He was strong and limber and could remain in a crouching squat for hours at a time while mending a net or sorting through items he had salvaged.

Charlie and Margarette

His eyes were bright blue and revealed his every emotion. In fact, he most often expressed his displeasure by pointedly asking his children, "Do you see my eyes?" We did, and we knew exactly what that meant! He loved to sing aloud and to tell tales that had been shared with him as a young boy about life on the Banks and the special people he had known and loved. For evening entertainment, and especially before we got our first television, was sitting around him, or in his lap, while he related those stories and sang the songs he had learned as a child.

To help in supporting the family, my father, Charlie Hancock, hosted fishing charters that went as far offshore as the Gulf Stream.

Beyond his wife and children, and his responsibility to provide for them, the other most important commitment of my father's life was in carrying on the tradition of his own father as a local operative for the Democratic party. Ole' Pa had been a loyal worker for the "party machine" before leaving the Banks. Once established on the Island, he became both voting registrar and tax lister for Harkers Island. By the early 1940s, he was getting too old to continue in both, so those patronage jobs were passed down to his son and my father. Daddy remained as loyal as his father to the local leaders and was deeply involved in marshaling local voters for every election.

The "Solid Democratic South" that had prevailed since the end of Reconstruction began to unravel in the 1960s as the national party gave its support to expanded civil rights for Black people and an end to racial segregation. My father openly cast his lot with the progressive wing of the party. That decision put him at odds with several local bosses and resulted in him being pushed out of his "tax lister" position in 1966. He remained voting registrar until he voluntarily stepped aside to make room for my sister Ella Dee to assume that position in 1976. He remained a "Yellow Dog Democrat" to the very end, casting his final vote in November of

The Education of an Island Boy

2000 for the Democratic nominee, just as he had in every election since 1932 when he first voted for Franklin Roosevelt.

My mother, Margarette, holding my four daughters: Joella, Aly, Leah, and Emily. She was always smiling and laughing at the children and grandchildren — as well as everyone else.

My mother was just over five feet tall, and in later years her figure evidenced the fact that she had carried and delivered ten children. Her hips appeared to have been fashioned specifically for carrying a child in one arm while doing her daily chores with the other. Her hair was dark and wavy, and her complexion was olive. Her bosom was not unlike a soft cushion or cradle in which she cuddled her children, even when they were taller and larger than herself. She expressed her affection openly and frequently and often reminded her children that we were the focus of her attention and the source of her greatest happiness.

Her face was a perpetual smile, and laughter was her response to every question and situation. Echoing Mark Twain's description of "Aunt Rachel" in "A True Story," "It was as easy for her to smile as it was for a bird to sing." Whenever any of us expressed even the slightest sadness or concern about our circumstances at present, she would commiserate for only a few moments before reassuring us that things were seldom as bad as they seemed and that, eventually, all would turn out well.

Other than for neighborhood and church activities and obligations, her life revolved entirely around family. She remained in close contact with her sisters and younger brother, even though we

Charlie and Margarette

didn't have a telephone. The ones who remained on the Island would assemble each Sunday at church, and often during the week on one or the other's front porch. A recurring topic of every such private gathering was recounting again the "healing and conversion" of their mother and reaffirming their faith in how and why it had occurred. Since there were always young ones around, her children wanted to make sure the story was ingrained in Bertha's grandchildren just as it had been in them.

Mama's home and yard were also where the neighborhood extended family often met to catch up or to wind down. Even though the porch had a swing and half a dozen or more rockers, chairs, and benches, there was never enough room for the younger ones of us to sit. That was not a problem as we always had plenty to do on the lawn and in the yard, down the path, or even by the roadside.

Her children and family were not just the primary focus of Mama's world, we were the ultimate source of her joy and happiness. She allowed us the freedom to make our own life decisions, and to leave and find our own places in the world when that time arrived, but with an understanding that where we had been raised would remain a home to us forever. When we, her children, later started families of our own, she sometimes stared at us with a broad smile as we interacted with them as parents. If ever we evidenced even the slightest frustration or weariness at tasks that might have appeared either mundane or arduous, she was always quick and eager to remind us that, in her special vernacular, "Don't you ever forget, you are eating your white bread right now!" Her point was that having children close and still dependent was the happiest and most worry-free time we could ever know as a parent.

That my parents were devoted to each other would be an understatement. There was never any confusion among them, or me and my siblings, about their relationship with each other and us. Perhaps because of having lost his own mother at such an early age, my father clung to his wife with an unflinching sense of loyalty and devotion. She was the undisputed centerpiece of his world, even as they were surrounded by children of their own. Later, he would call her "woman" as a show of affection, using "Margarette" only when around company.

At home and in public, she called him by both his given names, "Charlie William," perhaps to distinguish him from his father who lived within hearing distance of their back porch. Throughout their seventy years spent together, he would wrap her in his arms daily to let her know he was her champion and protector. Mama returned his affection in good measure but with an understanding that nothing and no one, not even her husband, could ever come between her and her children. As her mother had done with her, she made certain that we were always aware that we were safe, secure, and, most of all, loved.

The Last of Ten Children

According to my mama, the summer of 1952 when she was approaching forty years old, was one of the hottest she could ever remember. That was also when I was born. The extreme midsummer heat of that year was problematic throughout the South, especially in eastern North Carolina. A check of weather records on internet databases suggests that a large portion of the heat records for specific days of the calendar are from the year 1952. My mother always used that year as her standard of comparison when she wanted to point out just how awfully hot it might be. "It's just as hot as it was the summer Joel was born," she would lament as she fanned herself or later sat in front of a window-mounted air conditioner. And she wasn't the only one to say it. My sisters would often remind me of the hot and miserable conditions during the dog days of July that year when our mother was awaiting delivery of what would be her tenth and final baby.

My sister, June Marie Hancock, shortly before her marriage to Ronald Davis, her high school sweetheart.

My sister June was soon to be married, and she would describe how her fiancé, Ronald Davis, brought blocks of ice from Henry Davis's (1911-1975) fish house where he worked and put it in a wash pan in front of a fan to try to make my mama more comfortable. My sister, Ella Dee,

Charlie and Margarette

would wash my mama's face, arms, legs, and feet with cold washcloths to cool her some and rid her of the sweat that, they said, "ran off her nose."

It was a sweltering summer and would turn out to be a really hard year, but on the 28th of July, I was finally born under Dr. Luther Fulcher's (1910-1973) care at the recently built hospital in Morehead City. Only a few days later, my mama and the rest of the family were able to get on with the life they had carved out on this small and remote island.

Within a few more months my father would buy our family's very first television with which he and many of our neighbors could strain to see and hear the news and early TV shows broadcast by a station in Norfolk, VA, over two hundred miles to the north. They could also watch the World Series, which for more than a decade had always involved at least one team from New York. My father liked the Dodgers, but my mama always pulled for the underdogs, and one of my first memories is of her cheering for the Milwaukee Braves when they played and beat the Yankees in 1957.

My sister, Ella Dee Hancock, shortly after her marriage to Carl William Willis.

For never obvious reasons, my mother especially liked the "prize fights," as she called them, and came to idolize a heavyweight champion with North Carolina roots, Floyd Patterson. Harry Truman was still President, but he was not seeking another term. Indeed, both the Democrats and the Republicans had hoped to convince General Eisenhower to be their candidate that year, but he opted for the latter. The Democrats settled on Governor Adlai Stevenson of Illinois, and both candidates ran about as gentlemanly a campaign as the country would see for the next half-century.

And though our family was one of the first on the Island to join the television generation, we were among the last to get what many Americans had taken for granted as much as two decades earlier:

The Education of an Island Boy

an automobile. We had a boat, and usually more than one, but it would not be until after I was grown and gone that Daddy had the first automobile of his own. Eventually, my brothers would have cars, even while they still lived at home.

But my father never saw the need for one, at least not so long as he had a boat to take him to town (Beaufort) whenever he needed something bad enough. And he certainly was not ready to "run in debt" for something, even a car, as he was never certain that he would always be able to afford the monthly payment. Perhaps because of his Depression-era experiences, he never felt confident that he would have anything of monetary value for his tomorrows, at least not when it came to cash and currency.

The same hesitation that he had for purchasing an automobile applied to getting a telephone and the monthly billing that necessarily went along with it. Even after my brothers and sisters moved away, and most other families had at least a party-line connection, when it came to telephone communications, our only access was to the one that belonged to Clara Willis Yeomans (1924-2006), who was one of Daddy's first cousins.

Clara Mathelda Willis (center) with her daughter Olivia Jean. To her right is her father Daniel "Danky" Willis.
From the CSWM&HC Collection

I don't recall that my parents ever initiated a call, but on some rare occasions, Clara would send her daughter, Olivia Jean (1944-2011), to run to our house and let us know that someone was calling their house "person-to-person" for someone in our family. Other than that, handwritten letters remained the only means readily available to stay connected with our family and relations who were away from home. That wouldn't change until after I had graduated from college and my brothers and I pooled together to have a wall phone installed on the side of a kitchen cabinet that was adjacent to the threshold between the den and Mama's kitchen.

Charlie and Margarette

The fallout from the stalemate in Korea, which was laid at the feet of Truman and the Democrats, along with the fact that Eisenhower was such a beloved and respected war hero, all but determined the outcome of the 1952 Presidential election well before the votes were counted. But that didn't make the results any less unsettling to my parents. My brother, Tommy, once told me about coming down the stairs in our house the morning after the election. He noticed that as my mama bent over the potatoes, she was peeling at the kitchen sink, he could tell she was crying. "What's the matter, mama, what's wrong?" he asked her, hoping nothing awful had happened.

"Eisenhower won," my mama explained, as she continued cutting up the potatoes, "and now we've got to go back to the Depression!" That was what the Democrats had argued during the fall election. They had been in power without interruption since Roosevelt's electoral triumph over Hoover two decades earlier. My parents married on the last day of 1927, and already had three children by the time that Roosevelt took office and started his "New Deal." So, she was all too familiar with the hardships associated with the last Republican president, and worried at the prospect that those days might be returning.

As it turned out, my mama's fears of a return to the economic conditions of the "Great Depression" were unfounded. Some historians have judged the middle part of the 1950s as the "High-Water mark of the American Century." A later TV sitcom would call it simply "Happy Days." Segregation was still a blight on the nation's character, and a "Cold War" would continue to heighten, but the entire country was breathing a collective sigh of relief following the last "hot war" and the fall of the dictators. A combination of industrial and economic advances and the influx of returning soldiers who were ready to work hard spurred a national economic boom unlike the world had ever seen.

But the "good life" I would come to know on Harkers Island was not just the consequence of national peace and prosperity. It was much more the result of a happy coincidence of time and place, and of family, neighborhood, and community. Harkers Island was by then fifty years removed from a weather catastrophe that for its people was just as traumatic as Hurricane Katrina would be for

New Orleans and the southern Gulf Coast a century later. In the interim, it had become, at least to me, something like what Hannibal, Missouri, had been to a young Sam Clemens — a wonderful school and playground that has remained an inspiration and a backdrop for my life ever since.

It was not until I left the Island for the first extended time that I realized that by most economic standards I had been raised in poverty. Because my circumstances were so much like those of everyone I knew, I just assumed that this was how everybody lived their lives. Our house did not have an indoor bathroom (toilet) until I was in grade school, but as far as I can remember, most of my friends shared the same situation. It was no different for us than for the other families on the Island in that we lived by the old adage, "Fix it up, wear it out, make it do, or do without." Because of that, anything about our way of life that might have registered as less than standard was so widely experienced as not to be noticed by us — or at least not by me.

And despite the many other amenities that I might have missed out on, I can say for certain that I never knew what it was like to be hungry. I will grant that there were times that I might have wanted something different from what I was offered, but I am grateful to my parents, and especially to my father, that I never experienced the deprivation that I later heard others tell of. Again, I assumed that fried potatoes or baked beans, yeast rolls, and corn biscuits were a major part of everyone's diet, no matter where or how they lived. I guess I felt that we were better off than most since we so often had an abundance of shrimp, flounder, and other seafood for our evening menu.

I vividly recall my mama telling a story about how one afternoon as she cooked a pan of homemade light bread, one of our neighbors (Polly Guthrie, 1912-1989) came to our back porch door and asked if she could have "one of them biscuits you are cooking." In the days before air conditioning, open windows announced to everyone who passed by what was being prepared and when it was ready. Probably embarrassed that she hadn't noticed to offer food to someone who so often was needy, my mother was quick to provide several rolls along with a portion of butter. Mama would sometimes choke up as she related how Polly eagerly ate both the

Charlie and Margarette

morsels of bread she had been given, and, after thanking Mama profusely, added, "You know Margarette, being hungry hurts!"

The Loss of a Son and Brother

I was the last of ten children born to my parents, and by strict definition, I am a baby boomer. But my birth had nothing to do with the unique national demographic that would define an entire generation. Shortly after the arrival of child number eight, my brother Denny in 1944, Mama assumed that she had entered her "change of life" and that her family was complete. She was more than a little surprised when, more than six years later, my brother Telford came along. And then, two years later, and still with no indication that she was able to have any more children, I had been born.

Although I always have taken both pride and joy in explaining that I was part of a big family, the numbers had thinned out by the time I came along, at least within my Mama's house. My oldest brother, Ralph, had left home in 1948 for college, a family, and a career in the West. He had two children of his own before I came into the picture.

At about the same time as Ralph was leaving, my oldest sister, Ella Dee, got married and moved into a newly built and very small dwelling just a few hundred feet to the north of us on part of what remained of the land my grandfather, Ol' Pa, had claimed when he arrived from the Banks. That left June, Tommy, Bill, Sister (Lillian), Mike, Denny, and Teff in the 624-square-foot house where my parents raised their family. In short order after I was born, June got married, while Tommy and Bill joined the Coast Guard and soon too were married. Not very long after, Sister took a husband, and by the time I was in the second grade, Mike had started a family in a home that he himself had built.

But it was the early loss of Denny, child number eight and boy number five, that was the watershed moment in the story of my parents' family. Just a few months after my birth in 1952, my brother Denny, who was only eight years old, began showing signs of chronic fatigue and irritability. When his situation worsened, Mama took him to a doctor in Beaufort, who eventually began a series of tests that revealed a leukemia diagnosis. At first, my mother did not grasp the seriousness of that conclusion. According to her, no one in the family had ever heard of the illness before being told that Denny had it.

It was not until she mentioned the word "leukemia" to a Mormon missionary serving on the Island that she sensed the severity and gravity of her son's condition. The young elder had spent a year in medical school before beginning his mission and casually dropped by our home to say hello to a church member and her family. "When I told him that Denny had leukemia, there came a look in his eyes that shook me to the bones and broke my heart," she confided. "Only then did I realize that Denny might never get any better."

In the succeeding months, Denny's condition continued to grow worse. Several blood transfusions served to give him temporary bursts of energy, but within a few days after each, he would continue his downward spiral. Eventually, Mama and Denny went to Wilmington, where he was admitted as a patient at the Sidbury Children's Hospital. Treatment for childhood leukemia was still in its early stages at that time, and Mama remembered that several times she gave permission for Denny to try some experimental cures. None of them worked, and eventually, he was sent home, where he and the family were to await an inevitable outcome.

Like most infants in those days, I was nursed (breastfed) by my mother. Her departure for Wilmington, therefore, proved to be as physically uncomfortable for her as it was unsettling for her six-month-old child — me. It was left to my two oldest sisters, Ella Dee and June, to take care of me while Mama was away. Ella Dee was twenty-two years old and had a husband and five-year-old son of her own to care for. As the oldest of the girls, she was then and remained a second mother for Telford and for me. There would be times in the ensuing years when Mama would defer to her when making plans and decisions for us regarding school and church activities. June was two years younger than Ella Dee and was engaged to be married by the time Mama and Denny began their trips to Wilmington. She had been helping to provide for the family since she was in her mid-teens by working at a textile operation — what was called locally a "shirt factory" — in nearby Morehead City.

Charlie and Margarette

Daddy was either in Wilmington with Mama and Denny or working in the water daily to support the family. So, the two sisters toiled together to care for six younger siblings as they assumed responsibility for maintaining some sense of order and routine in Mama's absence. Their tasks were not always easy or simple. Tommy (18) and Bill (16), numbers four and five in the family birth order, were in a particularly competitive and rambunctious stage of male adolescence. Sister (Lillian-13) and Mike (11) were just entering their teenage years and had another set of needs that could not be ignored.

My brothers Denny, Mike, and Telford in a photograph taken about a year before Denny was diagnosed with leukemia. He was diagnosed in October of 1952 and was buried on his 9th birthday in March of 1953.

But the two oldest girls proved equal in every way to the task that confronted them. In the years that followed, they often pointed to those several weeks of stewardship for the rest of the family as having been their most formative time ever — not just for them but for the entire family in instilling a sense of familial loyalty and devotion that has marked our family ever after.

They often reminded me that one of their more difficult tasks during that period was the need to "walk the floor" at night, with a baby in their arms, trying to convince me to drink milk from a bottle. They even resorted to taking me to the home of another nursing mother to see if I might be satisfied by a substitute source for mother's milk, a "wet nurse" in the parlance of the time. It took several days, or even weeks, for me to accept the bottle routine, and not long after that, Mama and Denny were back home. Ever after Mama would tearfully describe to us how torn she had been while waiting in the hospital room with one son who needed her attention, while being biologically reminded every few hours that she had another son who still craved and demanded it.

Early in March of 1953, just a day before what would have been his ninth birthday, and long before I was old enough even to remember him, Denny's struggle with leukemia came to an end. Despite having known for a while what the outcome would be, the family had been unable to prepare for the financial obligations that awaited them as they sought to arrange for Denny's burial.

Knowing the situation, and wanting to help, Sheriff Gehrmann Holland (1905-1970) of Beaufort, and the nominal head of the Democratic party "machine" in the county, quickly came to the family's assistance and rescue. He negotiated, secured, and paid for a casket and the services of a mortuary in Beaufort. From that moment on for the remainder of their lives, the name and memory of Gehrmann Holland was hallowed to both of my parents.

Gehrmann Holland was the Carteret County Sheriff in the early '50s

Denny was buried the following day in a full-sized casket as there were no child-size ones readily available, and Mama's family began the process of coping with the most painful trial they would have to confront for the next forty years. Mama was often heard to explain in later years that her saving grace after the sorrow of losing her son was that she had two small children — Telford and me — who still required her attention and energy. "Every time I felt to wallow in my sorrow," she explained, "I was brought back to my senses by the fact that Teff and Joel still needed me so much!"

In the years that followed, Denny was spoken of and talked about so often by my parents and siblings that in some sense he was never gone, only suspended in an eternal childhood, with a sheepish smile and calm demeanor that looked down on us every day from his picture that hung on our living room wall. Soon, Ralph would name his second son, Dennis Dale, after our brother, and everybody in the family and the neighborhood often ran their fingers through my hair and would tell me that I looked just like Denny. "I don't know how it happened," Big Ollie (Olive Guthrie Willis 1902-1979) used to say, "but the Lord has given Margarette another son that looks just like the one she lost!"

Halcyon Days

So, life went on for Mama and Daddy and their family in their little house in the middle of what we knew as Ol' Pa's neighborhood and crowd. And, since all my brothers and sisters but Teff (Telford) were now out on their own, it was usually just the four of us, Mama and Daddy and Teff and me, in our house. I should add that this finite number applied only to sleeping arrangements, and even then, only when none of the others were visiting from their nearby homes.

During the day, especially in the warmer months, my siblings and their ever-growing number of children seemed always to be there. Mama's house, especially her front porch, along with the shore just down the path at Ol' Pa's landing, was a gathering place frequented regularly. Many, if not most, of the stories I

My mother Margarette holding me and my brother Telford shortly after the death of my brother Denny.

will share, were either witnessed or first heard of, in those very same places.

In the years that followed my birth and Denny's passing, life played out for me as if it were in slow motion to make sure I could savor and enjoy every moment. A lot happened, but it was with a rhythm and a flow that seemed to put everything in order and harmony. Growing up was fun, sometimes exciting, and always secure. I had parents and siblings who loved me and each other. There were bunches of aunts, uncles, nieces and nephews, and a seemingly endless number of cousins, who knew exactly who I was and could call me by name. To paraphrase the words of the young Jack Crabb in "Little Big Man," I wasn't just playing like I lived on an Island paradise. I was doing it!

But even with all the growing-up fun and excitement, among the happiest and most recurring of my childhood memories are of those days, halcyon days to me, of being surrounded by my immediate family. I especially recall with fondness those summer days when most or all my siblings were gathered somewhere between our own backyard and the Landing. Daddy and my older brothers would be working together on some building or fix-up project: hanging a net, tuning an engine, or maybe just painting or repairing the porch. Mama and my sisters were just as busy: cleaning the house, hanging out laundry on the clotheslines, or preparing a spread lunch for everyone who was there or coming.

As the youngest of the group except for my nieces and nephews, I perceived even then that I had landed in some very special vortex of time and space where both the clock and the calendar at once stood still in my consciousness, even as they raced all too fast towards a day when it all would be just a happy but fleeting memory.

In those first and formative years, most of what I still remember happened in a special place and around a special group of people. Among them were aunts, uncles, and older cousins whom I came to view not only as family but also as caretakers and teachers. Younger cousins, nieces, and nephews grew closer and closer with each passing year so that they became more like siblings than mere relatives. And just as an awareness of family increases with the passage of time, so does my appreciation of the neighborhood and community in which we all lived together.

My mother, Margarette, standing on the front porch of our home. She moved into this home just a few months after her wedding day and raised ten children with my father Charlie William. She lived here for her entire married life until her passing in 1997.
Photo courtesy of Mark Atwood

The expanse of my world eventually broadened to include the whole Island and even more as I matured and grew in understanding and stature. Looking back, those years of childhood and adolescence are an increasingly smaller percentage of the totality of my lifetime experience. But with the passing of time, those same years are an ever-expanding numerator in the numerical fraction that represents the shaping of my perspectives and my character.

The Education of an Island Boy

What My Parents Wanted, and Expected of Me

When it came to the hopes and dreams of my parents for their tenth child and seventh son, their ambitions were not the same — but thankfully, they were not mutually exclusive. For Daddy, his main concern was two-fold. His primary wish was the same as for all his children — that I never bring shame or disrespect to the family name his own parents and he had worked so hard to establish. And secondly, he expected that I would remain loyal to the political party he credited with having helped him to protect and provide for his family, as well as having rescued his country from the ravages of the Great Depression. My mother's fondest hopes were that I remain faithful to the religious faith that had guided her life and that of her mother, and that I grow up to have a happy family similar in size and affection to the one she had raised.

Their final ambition for me was one on which they both agreed. It was simply this: I should achieve their other goals while living in close proximity to them and my siblings—and the closer, the better. Anywhere on Harkers Island would suffice, but hopefully no farther than just on the other side of the bridge. On this final item, they agreed it had priority over all others.

Hopefully, I never gave either of them a reason to be disappointed in me for any of those very specific ambitions!

Charlie and Margarette

Me (left) with my nephew Jonathan Willis (middle) and my brother Telford (right). Even on Harkers Island, adolescents were not immune to teenage angst — as evidence in our expressions.

The Education of an Island Boy

Above: Harkers Island Elementary School in 1962.

Below: As a fifth grader sitting at the front of the row to the far left. As with other small schools, this was a fourth-fifth grade combination class taught by Clovadel B. Montgomery.

5

Livin', Learnin', and Playin'

We didn't realize we were making memories. We just knew we were having fun.
                                         "Winnie the Pooh"

All the summer world was bright and fresh, and the sun rose upon a tranquil world, and beamed down like a benediction.
                            Mark Twain, "Letter to Will Bowen"

I would be mistaken ever to undervalue the importance of the "traditional education" I experienced while growing up. The teachers and the school itself offered me and others everything and more that we would need to prepare ourselves for life both on and off the Island. There had been slow turnover in the staffing of the school over the years and so I had many of the same instructors who taught my older siblings and cousins. That continuity offered a familiarity that was not unlike what I knew at home and around my extended family. The building itself was only one year old when I started there and was surrounded by woods on three sides with an open view of Back Sound and the Cape Lookout lighthouse on the other side facing south. It was a beautiful and even a happy place to be.

Once the school day was over, and all day long during the summer break, the Island itself was a vast playground and even an amusement park. As I grew older, the Banks was added to that expanse. Boredom, for me and those I lived with and around, was unheard of. Each day of every new season was a new adventure. Looking back, life was as exciting as it was enjoyable. At least for me, just thinking of it even now serves to relieve some of the stresses brought on by advancing years and the changes those years have wrought.

HIS (Harkers Island School)

As mentioned earlier, by virtue of the year of my birth, I belong to the Baby Boom generation. I was part of another more localized boom, evidenced by the mushrooming size of the elementary school on the Island. By the time I finished there in 1966, it would have close to three hundred students in eight grades, the highest it has ever been before or since. Ours was the second generation born on the Island after the exodus from the Banks half a century earlier.

I entered the first grade in late August of 1958, for as of then, the Island had no kindergarten, either private or public. The first truly public school had been built in the second decade of the 20th century, nearly two decades after the mass exodus from the Banks to the Island. My grandfather, Ol' Pa, had been the general contractor in charge of its construction. Before that there had been Jenny Bell's Academy, situated on the site that still is referred to as Academy Field. It offered remedial classes during the last few decades before the turn of the century. But after its closure, the only other attempt at a community school was one that was sponsored and planned by The Church of Jesus Christ of Latter-day Saints in 1906.

The headmaster for that school was a visiting Mormon missionary from Utah, Elder William Petty (1877-1951), and classes were scheduled to start in late January of that year in the church's recently completed meeting house located near the midpoint of the Island. But a few days before the first students took their places, the church was torched by a mob that feared the growing influence on the Island of what they considered an "alien" faith. A few weeks later, Elder Petty and his companions were obliged to evacuate themselves from the Island because of threats to their safety.

It would be more than a decade before another school would open to students. That one was a much larger wood-frame building that eventually housed eleven grades — first through eleventh. The high school classes were moved to Smyrna in 1950, and in the early spring of 1956, the remaining grades were moved to a newly constructed masonry building that remains in use even today. I was a member of only the second class to spend all my elementary years at the newly constructed Harkers Island School. That was its official name, and the curtain that draped the stage in the dining hall showed the initials "HIS."

The friends who sat beside me in my classrooms for the next eight years were far more than mere classmates. We were or became - and still remain - as family. Some of them actually were first cousins. But had we been submitted to a modern DNA test it would have shown all of us to be cousins — ever how many times removed. Beyond that we didn't just know each other. We were to varying degrees acquainted with their parents, their siblings, and their other cousins, as well as their aunts and uncles, and often even their grandparents. In short, we knew what crowd or crowds each other belonged to.

Though the basic learning processes may have been fundamentally the same as now, there were a few things that were noticeably different. Extra-curricular activities and learning aids were at a minimum. The library was called that rather than a "media center." What we learned we learned either from our textbooks or from what our teachers taught us. The idea of computers for the classroom was still relegated to science fiction — and science fiction was not a part of the curriculum.

But we did learn, and most of us enjoyed it. Memorization was still an important part of the learning process. At various times we were required to memorize everything from the poetry of Robert Frost and Edgar Allen Poe to the periodic tables and the Pythagorean theorem. One of life's greatest accomplishments and pleasures was being able confidently to recite the multiplication tables —one through twelve.

Reading was portrayed as an adventure. It became my gateway to that vast world that lay beyond the bridge. My favorite pastime was thumbing through a set of World Books. In fact, to us, World Book and Encyclopedia meant the same thing, for they were the only encyclopedias available. Somewhere in that same school today, there may be even now a set of World Books that has my fingerprints on every page.

Spelling "bees" were still the primary form of intra-school competition. Students stayed in the same classroom with the same teacher throughout the school day and with the same age group, regardless of how they might have placed on a standardized achievement test. Group photos taken over the years of the classes revealed something about the school and the Island that was taken for granted, but seems unique, almost quaint in looking back. What is most striking about each group, year after year, is that there was hardly ever any change in the classes. With each succeeding year the class members were getting older and bigger, but the makeup of the group changed only in small increments. Most years showed that just a few classmates, never more than two or three, were "held back" to repeat the same grade for another year. This meant that those new faces were added to a new group while leaving their old one, but remaining part of the same student body they had belonged to since they started.

Occasionally there might be a new boy or girl to show up, usually from the family of a recently assigned pastor for one of the several congregations on the Island. But that sometimes also meant that his or her family was taking the place of someone else who had been transferred away. So, year after year, the units remained so static that the group that sat together for my eighth-grade photo was largely the same as the one that sat in smaller desks seven years earlier for a first-grade picture.

So, the core of that class, like all the others, was together for eight consecutive years. There is little wonder that we grew as close as family and have felt a special bond since. Most of us would remain on the Island to raise our own families. Our children grew up together as well, but by then, there was much more fluctuation in the school's demographic. Class sizes that had changed little for several decades eventually began to shrink as the Island ran out of affordable space for yet another generation of homes.

Livin', Learnin', and Playin'

The makeup of the classes was far less static than before, and in some years, there were no new faces to replace others who had moved on or away. Another characteristic of those yearly class photos that seems to stand out more and more over time is the family makeup of the individual students. In my eighth-grade class photo, all but three of the thirty-two students who posed together were living with both of their biological parents.

The fun and games of my elementary years, physical education we now call it, with few exceptions, had to be spontaneous or not at all. Until my final two years there, I cannot recall any organized outdoor recreation other than an occasional game of "ring around the roses," which involved a circle of children holding hands and singing the same verse over and over. In the primary grades, we lined up on Friday afternoons to be marched outside to an eight-foot-high metal slide, the shell of which remained evidence in the schoolyard for another thirty years. Once there, we proceeded in an orderly fashion up the ladder of steps and down the slide — and then around and to the back of the line. After no more than a few of these sequences, we proceeded to march back to class and that was our physical education for another week.

In the middle grades, we were allowed some more liberal outdoor time as I can recall playing in pickup games of baseball and touch football during recess. But my first experience with any really organized physical exercise arrived at our school when Mr. David Willis (1940-2011) from Morehead City came to our school as the seventh-grade teacher. He began to divide the upper-class boys, (the girls were completely someone else's responsibility) into several teams for intramural games and calisthenics. At about that same time, a large concrete slab, maybe 50 X 100 feet, was placed at the east end of the schoolyard. It was divided into two segments of equal size, and four wooden backboards and rims nailed at the top of elongated wooden posts were placed at opposite ends of each section. That was our "outdoor" gym and basketball court.

Finally, in what was an answer to the prayers of myself and several others, while I was in the eighth grade, there was organized a league of county-wide and school-sponsored basketball teams for seventh and eighth graders. One of the driving forces behind the idea was our school's new principal, Walker Gillikin (1936-2020),

The Education of an Island Boy

Walker Gillikin, lifelong educator and principal of Harkers Island School during my 8th grade year

Henry Allen Brooks, coach of my 8th grade basketball team at Harkers Island School, and lifelong friend.

who was from Otway but had married a Harkers Island girl and moved here after leaving another teaching assignment. He arranged for us to have physicals at the school administered by the "county doctor," a title given to a physician designated to work with underprivileged families and educational and civic organizations. For several of the boys on the team, it was the first time we could ever remember having experienced such an examination, especially one that involved "turning your head and coughing."

A full-season schedule was prepared wherein we played every other elementary school in the county. New uniforms were out of the question, but Mr. Gillikin arranged for us to salvage the discarded and oversized, yet still quite handsome— at least to us — uniforms of Smyrna High School. The consolidation of all the county's high schools the year before had rendered the outfits useless as there no longer was a team, or even a school, to be represented.

Henry Brooks (1934-2017), a former All-County performer at the erstwhile Harkers Island High School, agreed to be our coach, and we practiced and played in the only indoor gym on the Island, the one attached to the sanctuary of our church. To the surprise of many, but not to us, we had a successful year and won seven of the nine games we played. That preparation and experience paid some dividends later, as during my senior year at the new East Carteret High School, four members of that team were the varsity starters. Even then, the team's supporters loved to call us the "four Loons" in deference to the fact that some people from off the Island referred to locals as "loon eaters," as mentioned earlier.

Ridin' the School Bus

Another aspect of attending school on the Island has left lasting impressions, although it related to something outside the classroom walls. Nonetheless, it was a vital part of my grade school socialization. Like so many other aspects of growing up when and where I did, the setting and surroundings were as much a part of what happened as the characters and their stories.

Here is a simple example that illustrates that reminiscence. One bright and sunny fall afternoon in October of 1960, as I arrived home from school, I saw my mother waiting on the front porch. Even at a distance, I could tell she was excited. As soon as I came close enough to hear her, she started relating to me something she was anxiously waiting to tell.

"They won," she shouted, "the Pirates won! Their second baseman (Bill Mazeroski) hit a home run in the last inning, and the Pirates won!" She was letting me know that the Pittsburgh Pirates had defeated the New York Yankees in the seventh and final game of the World Series. She loved the Pirates, and because she did I did too, and she was excited to let me know that our team had won this time, especially against the Yankees.

She knew exactly when to expect me to come walking along the road, because that day, like every other day of my grade school experience, I had taken the bus both to and from school. For eight years, without an exception that I can remember, each morning, I walked one hundred feet or so from our front porch and across the road to the bus stop. My brother Teff and I would gather there with as many as a dozen others just like us and wait to be picked up by an orange-colored school bus driven by Miss Frankie (Emma

The Education of an Island Boy

Frances Lewis 1930-2014), a gracious lady who lived at Shell Point who would continue in that job for the next forty plus years.

With only one medium-sized bus to serve the two hundred plus student population, routing and scheduling had to be precise. Just like clockwork, at about 7:30 in the morning, the bus would pull to a stop, extend a brightly colored "stop" sign, and then open the door to let us get on. There were other stops both before and after, and they were spaced to allow neighborhood groups to gather for an economy of both time and cost. Even so, we would arrive at school no more than five minutes before the first bell rang, announcing the beginning of the school day.

A few of my classmates lived near enough to walk to school, and even fewer were dropped off by a family car, but most of us shared the experience of commuting each day on a school bus. Once inside, we were divided into classes, but at the bus stop and until we were let off, we were all, from first graders to eighth graders, packed together and part of the same special group.

In our neighborhood, we were picked up and later dropped off at Edith's store. It had a gas-powered heater that we gathered around on cold winter mornings, but most of the time, we amused ourselves outside as we waited for the bus. The store had #2 pencils that were 3¢ each, or two for a nickel, as well as both nickel and dime packs of paper. The pickings may have been small, but those were about the only two tools then used in a classroom, besides books and desks, and chalk for a chalkboard.

Some friendships and relationships that were unique in my childhood experience were forged at the bus stop and on the bus. Older kids, usually but not always girls, would take special care to make sure that the younger ones were seated and safe. Sometimes they would even ask about homework, or if you had your lunch money for the day. They would also protect the smaller and seemingly weaker children from the "bullies" that were, and probably always will be, a part of growing up. As the years progressed, we younger ones matured into the same roles and responsibilities. All these years later, I still recall with affection the special friends that I knew so intimately only on that bus.

Livin', Learnin', and Playin'

The dynamic of the bus stop and bus ride would change only a little when I started high school in the fall of 1966. Even then, I was never among the select few who traveled to school in a car. The daily routine of commuting started a little earlier and ended a little later, as the ride went from being less than one mile to more than ten. And, because of after-school practices for football, basketball, and baseball, I often had to find another way home in the evening.

My situation was no different from that of most of my contemporaries. Hard as it may be for today's students to imagine, there were nearly as many buses as cars in the parking lot of our high school. Most of us lived in a world where only parents had cars of their own, and not even all of them. My mother did not drive at all, and my father didn't own an automobile until after I had left for college. I took my driver's license exam in the same car that would ferry me to East Carolina University two years later, and that belonged to my brother-in-law. Even after I bought myself a 1959 Ford Fairlane that my sister and I painted glossy black with brushes to hide the rust, the 20¢ per gallon cost of gas alone made driving back and forth to school each day impractical.

So, the school bus remained my primary transportation until the very end of my school years at home. The main exception was on those days when I was too late making it to the stop and was obliged to resort to hitchhiking. Sometimes when "thumbing," I was able to beat the bus to where the main highway was joined by the narrow strip of road that accessed the campus. Unlike today, hitchhiking was considered an acceptable transportation alternative for adolescent males without their own cars, which meant almost all of us.

But typically, my school day began and ended on an orange bus packed with teenagers of both sexes who acted and sounded pretty much the same as me. On the day I graduated from East Carteret High School in the spring of 1970, I left home on Bus # 27

Mrs. Emma Wade, Principal of Harkers School during my first seven years.

181

The Education of an Island Boy

which picked me up at Edith's store, and I jumped out of the same bus at the very same location nine hours later.

During those "happy days" at Harkers Island Elementary, when the final bell of the school day rang, usually at 3:00 in the afternoon, the Principal, Miss Emma Wade (1909-1978), would announce that the "first bus" load could gather at the front door to leave. The "second (last) bus" crowd that included me would have to wait another half hour or so for the bus to return. We would then be packed back into our seats and backtrack the same route we had followed in the morning. After Miss Frankie put out the stop sign and opened the door, I would run across the road in front of the bus, where I would find my boyhood world just as I had left it, except on special occasions, such as when the Pirates beat the Yankees in the World Series.

The Bittersweet

Back to the classroom, where everything centered, there were some memories that might be labeled as "bittersweet." My most excruciating recollections are of those days when we were obliged to line up for the seemingly endless array of inoculations that the state inflicted on all public-school students of that era. Such precautions were heartily welcomed by our parents, many of whom had witnessed or even experienced the ravages of preventable diseases such as tetanus, diphtheria, measles, and even polio. Standing in line while watching your friends suffer was nearly as bad as the needle itself — but not quite!

Invariably, one of the nurses or parents who were helping to administer what seemed to us as mass torture, would try to calm our fears by saying, "It feels just like a mosquito bite." But who would stand in line for a mosquito bite? And besides, the sensation was much closer to that of a "yellow jacket sting" to me. And if that weren't punishment enough, the shots would stiffen your arm so much that you couldn't throw a baseball for a week.

Additionally, as late as the decade of the sixties, discipline with a paddle remained as much a part of education as did a pencil. Especially for us boys, a "paddling" now and then might be dreaded, but it positively could not be avoided. Speaking out of

Livin', Learnin', and Playin'

turn, using profanity, failing to turn in an assignment on time, and a host of other infractions were on the list of offenses that could result in "corporal punishment." By the seventh grade, it seemed like a daily occurrence. "Come to the front and bend across my desk!" was repeated seemingly as often as "get out your geography books."

After a while, a few of us developed calluses over the afflicted area that served to lessen, but not eliminate, the burning sting. The complete demise of "paddling" as a tool of discipline is one development that a part of me wholeheartedly applauds.

Another not-always-pleasant memory of those times is of the several operettas and plays that each class had to stage every year. Practicing and learning the lines was ok. But it was never easy to stand in front of a packed auditorium and recite those lines. And it was even worse when you had to sing them. Because I had been cast as a dwarf named "Squeaky" in a second-grade production of "Snow White," some of my friends continued to call me by that name for several years afterward.

But mostly, it was fun. We were living and learning in a school that sat within view of the bank of a tranquil sea. We were being taught by teachers who were genuinely concerned for us and for our futures. Each of them left an indelible imprint on the young boy they tried to help build into a young man. I can still hear Miss Rita Harris, undoubtedly the most influential teacher I ever had, telling me that no one other than myself could ever stand in the way of my becoming all I wanted to be.

Something else beyond our scholarly, social, and athletic skills resulted from the time we spent together at Harkers Island School. It was something that we took note of even as it happened, as it seemed to repeat itself every time a group of us left the Island together for any type of mainland excursion, whether it be academic, athletic, social, or even just a family outing. There developed a unique sensitivity relative to what was a stretch of "two-lane blacktop" we called simply "the Bridge." Specifically, this — it was always far better to cross it heading south than heading north.

Not Completely Detached ...

Miss Sudie Guthrie, my 6th grade teacher
CSWM&HC Collection

Amid all the happy and carefree recollections of my time as a student at Harkers Island School, there is one specific and more somber memory that has faded hardly at all over the years. It was one beautiful Indian Summer afternoon late in November of 1963, soon after recess, when our Principal, Miss Wade, came to the door and beckoned our six-grade teacher, Miss Sudie (Guthrie 1896-1991), to speak with her just outside the classroom. We could sense that something out of the ordinary was being discussed, both from the urgency in the gestures of Miss Wade as she summoned our teacher, and especially by the concern that was evidenced by Miss Sudie as she turned away and ambled back in while calling for our attention. In short order she stood at the front of the class, but her words were halting and much more measured than was usual. It appeared to us that she might even be holding back tears. Little could we have anticipated how much what she then announced would change us and our world in the years that followed.

Though we were coming of age on an Island, we were not completely isolated from what happened in the world around us. Important and often tumultuous events were taking place quickly in the 1960s and they were reflected even within the walls of our seemingly protected enclave. More than six decades later, I recall most of them as still images of how I first experienced them. Years of education in the social sciences continue to dim in comparison to the influence of those images upon my political and social conscience and consciousness.

In 1960 when I was in the third grade, John Kennedy, a Catholic, had run for President. Among the changes implicit in his candidacy was his hope to end forever any suggestion that a man or woman's political opportunities as an American citizen might be limited because of their religious beliefs. That effort caused shockwaves to run throughout our country, especially in the South. Not a few of

Livin', Learnin', and Playin'

those shockwaves were felt as we third graders in Miss (Kathryn 1918-2006) Daniels's class discussed and even argued whether Kennedy's election might mean that all of us would have to "swear allegiance to the Pope."

Then, as now, children generally reflected the side of any debate they had heard championed in their homes. Already acutely aware of how my family's peculiar Mormon faith was viewed by many of our neighbors, I was especially sensitive to the question and its outcome.

Two years later, in October of 1962, our fifth-grade class, like every other one in the country, rehearsed together, under the watchful eye of Miss Mary Whitehurst (1890-1971), how to seek shelter beneath our wooden desks if a nuclear attack resulted from what then was happening in Cuba. As if it were only yesterday, I can recall my teacher asking a visiting county official what he thought might happen as Russian ships approached the limits of the American Navy's blockade of the island nation. My heart sank to my stomach as I heard him suggest, though only in a whisper so that we children might not be alarmed, that he felt there was going to be a "war."

Though we were only ten years old, we were mature and sufficiently informed to sense that war in 1962 suggested something quite different than it had meant to earlier generations of school children. We had read enough "Weekly Readers" to know that in this war, not just soldiers at the battlefront would suffer from the "ultimate weapon." Seldom in the years that have followed have I felt the relief that I sensed later that week when our teacher joyfully proclaimed to the class, "the Russians have turned back!"

But events moved quickly then as now and there was little time for jubilation. Only one year later, on that memorable Indian summer afternoon, we were sitting together again as Miss Sudie announced to us that our President had been shot and killed in Dallas, Texas. In the coming days, she would try to explain many other things to us, such as why our flag was flying at half-mast. Unfortunately, there were some things she was never quite able to make clear. It took only a few hours for some and days or weeks for others, but

The Education of an Island Boy

eventually, we returned to the games and pleasures of childhood. Still, more than we realized at the time, at that early point in our lives, we had been shocked into reality; the reality that even in the fairy tale land of America, we were yet to overcome ignorance, bigotry, and violence.

Because of our special situation on an Island that really is an island, we were spared from having to witness first-hand the cataclysm that surrounded racial "integration" in so much of the South and the nation. But we had ears to hear and eyes to see the televisions to which, by then, most of us had access. Perhaps because of our isolation from the main battlegrounds of that struggle, I recall that many of my classmates and teachers had a deep sympathy for the plight of Blacks in the South. Names like James Meredith, Medgar Evers, and Dr. Martin Luther King Jr. were not anathema to us that they were to some other white schoolchildren throughout our region. On the contrary, some of them would become our heroes.

Finally, by the time I had entered the later years of grade school on the Island, some of my classmates were beginning to see brothers, uncles, cousins, and friends drafted and shipped off to fight in places whose names most of us had never heard of. But by the time we graduated from high school, nearly all of us could reel off names like Saigon, Hanoi, or DaNang as easily as if they were situated just across the Bridge.

Few of us questioned then, as some later would, the reasons for America's latest effort to "make the world safe for democracy." But when those same relatives began to come home wounded, scarred, and sometimes not at all, we realized that the toy soldiers of our childhood were all too rapidly giving way to the realities of a grownup world; harsh realities that could not be swept away merely by deciding it was time to go home for supper.

But those distractions were very much the exception to the normal routine of the life we knew and enjoyed on the Island of my youth. For most of us, most of the time, life played out in splendid slow motion — slow enough to be savored and enjoyed, and then to be remembered. As the years have passed those memories have loomed larger and larger. Rather than fading them into the distance, the prism of time has brightened their luster.

School's Out!

When I reflect on my childhood friends and the life we shared together growing up, the one quote that keeps coming back to me is attributed to Mark Twain and goes, "All the summer world was bright and fresh, and the sun rose upon a tranquil world, and beamed down like a benediction." There must have been some bad days and troubling moments, but most of them have been erased from my memory by time and by experience. A popular cliché of recent years has been that "It takes a village to raise a child." I'm not sure if our neighborhood would qualify as a village by itself, but I am comfortable that, for the most part, it managed the tasks that a village might be assigned.

The boys and girls I grew up around, especially the former, were familiar with not just the exterior but also the "inside" of all the homes in our neighborhood world. If we had not spent the night inside it or enjoyed a full meal at the table, we at least shared a light roll or biscuit, or maybe a mullet roe or boiled egg that had been prepared in the kitchen.

Our playgrounds were fenced-in yards, along with the spaces around and in between them. The entire shoreline was considered communal property and unless we were there or in the sound, we were always within hearing distance of some adults, as some of them seemed always to be with and around us. Most of the grown-ups, especially the women, accepted parental authority over making sure that we children "behaved." And even those whose assumptions didn't extend quite that far, still were willing to "tell our mothers" if they thought we had said or done something that we shouldn't. "Do you want me to tell you Mama?" was a frequent reminder that we were always — always — being watched.

Another refrain often heard whenever it seemed to an adult that we children were not getting along as we should, or were just a little too loud or aggressive, was to "play pretty!" We came to accept that "play pretty" meant that we had to change what we were doing, even if it was not immediately evident as to why or how.

The Education of an Island Boy

In summer months, we would spend the largest portion of the day at the Landing and in the sound. With no parental supervision, we took care of each other to the extent that the most serious injuries I can recall were feet cut on oyster shells or the remains of a broken bottle or jar. Besides being a respite from the summer heat and humidity, playing on the shore and in the sound was such strenuous exercise that we children all appeared to be "fit as a fiddle."

Men's tools and equipment often were "boy's" toys — from boats to net spreads to hammers and saws. It was a boy's world as it seemed to me that most of the children in my world were boys. In our neighborhood, the offshore dock of what had been called "Danky's fish house" was our gathering spot. By then, Danky had passed, and the operation was run by his son-in-law, David Yeomans (1921-2006). So, to us, it was "David's dock." From there we would fan out to the scores of boats that swung at their stakes and moorings nearby and served as our bases.

There was always a deep "steamer hole," dug by revving the engine of a boat while anchored, to remove sand from the bottom underneath and behind it. The hole was on the east side of the south end of the dock and was maintained at about six feet or more to allow boats to get in or out, even on low tide. Just inshore of that was a high and white sand shoal that had been created in the process of digging the steamer hole. It often was out and dry when the tide was at its lowest during a strong summer sou'westerly breeze. That was when we would get into a running start from atop the shoal to plunge headlong into the adjacent hole.

At other times we used the hoisting bone that swung out from the dock to propel out over the hole and then fall to the water below. But most often, we just dove from the dock, or one of the wooden pilings that held it in place, straight out towards the deep. By mid-morning, as many as a dozen youngsters, usually all boys, would have gathered in the area, and we would play games around the dock and on and around the surrounding boats for most of the day. Often, by the time we got back to our homes, our fingers and toes would be wrinkled and shriveled from our day spent underwater.

Mending nets at the Landing around 1960. L-R William Willis, Houston Salter, Manus Fulcher, Willie Guthrie, & Mart Lewis. David's Dock and Fish house is in the background, and Willie's net house is at the right.

Washin' Off with a Water Hose

Were I to mention to my grandchildren that they should wash off their swimsuits and bodies with an outdoor hose after returning from a day at the beach or in the sound, I'm sure some of them wouldn't even know or recognize what I was asking for. But for my generation of Island boys and girls, that was not just a request. It was an everyday requirement.

The sound-side water that surrounds the Island is salty, nearly as salty as the ocean itself. It has been that way since time immemorial, but it became even saltier after Barden's Inlet was opened by the "Storm of '33," permanently separating Shackleford Banks from Cape Lookout. That breach allowed another avenue for the free flow of ocean water into Back Sound from Onslow Bay and immediately changed the nature of the ecosystem forever. But those of us who spent a major part of summer days swimming at the Landing were hardly aware of those changes. We were even less concerned with the salinity of the water that we swam and played in. As far as we knew, all water, fresh or salt, felt the same.

The only distinction we noticed was how warm or cold it was to our half-naked bodies.

After long mornings and afternoons spent playing in or around the sound, it was not unusual for a chalky film to form on our shoulders and forehead, and even on our eyebrows and in our hair. Arriving home after hours in the salt and sand, the first thing we heard from our mothers was a reminder to "wash off" before we came into the house. They had to remind us not because we didn't know what was expected, but because we dreaded the ordeal of shivering under cold water pumped from deep below the ground when we had just the moment before dried off from water that was as warm as 80 degrees in mid-summer afternoons.

I must confess, there were times when I fudged on doing a complete rinse. And on a few occasions, I might hardly have rinsed at all. The cold water that spouted from the hose was that uncomfortable — at least until your body adapted to the change. Sometimes we resorted to filling a bucket with water and then lifting it up and pouring the whole contents over our heads at once to shorten our time of exposure to the shock of the seemingly ice-cold deluge.

There was, however, at least one way to comply with Mama's wishes and avoid the cold shock that resulted from the cooler fresh water. When the mostly plastic garden hoses were left out in the sun, as they often were, the hose itself, along with the water inside it, would heat up considerably. The trick was to get to the hose before my brother or my cousins and take full advantage of the warmer water before handing off the hose to the next in line. Although the initial burst from the hose could be so hot that it was hardly bearable, within a few seconds, the temperature would begin to drop, and for at least a while, it was as warm and comfortable as the showers we now enjoy in our indoor facilities.

Eventually, if you paid close enough attention, you learned to sense exactly how much of the "just right" water there would be, and how much time you had to complete the washdown. Pure joy was finishing just as the water turned to the "frigid" normal that was the penalty for everyone who lost the race up the path to the water hose. Pure horror was winning the race only to find that someone else had so recently used the hose and that there had not been enough time for the water to reheat. Usually, that was when I resorted to the "bucket over the head" approach.

Made-up Games

Even when the weather was not exactly right for swimming, there was always something to do. Try as I may, I cannot recall ever hearing or using the word "bored" to describe anything about life as a child on the Island. In fact, I may have been in high school before I came to understand that there was a homonym for the usual word that made that sound; "board," you know, the same one that I could use interchangeably with a wooden "plank."

The butt end of those planks often became toy boats that we pulled along the shore. Tin cans were filled with sand and dragged by a string along the roadway. Slits of rubber from worn-out tire tubing became "rubber bullets" that were shot from wooden pistols rigged with a clothespin trigger. Smaller pieces of that same rubber were fashioned into slingshots that propelled "chaney (china)-berry" seeds as if they were bullets and nearly as fast as the real thing. Strips, or slithers as we called them, of cloth torn from old clothing were hung as tails on kites that could stream wildly in the southwest breezes as they blew on summer afternoons. In short, nearly anything that was no longer of any practical use could be made into a toy of some sort for or by us children.

There were no curfews or schedules. The setting sun primarily signaled the end of our daily routines. Sometimes, that alone was insufficient to end our day. When the approaching darkness failed to end our games, sooner or later, a chorus of voices would begin calling us home for the evening. Then, early the next morning, soon after roosters began to crow and hens started to cackle, the daily routine of our summer would begin again, and not a minute too soon.

Those days, even school days, were packed with the fun and excitement of day-to-day life, especially for boys growing up on the Island.

The Education of an Island Boy

My Rooster that was a "Chicken"

"What ya looking for?"

That was not an unreasonable question to ask in the situation. Here I was, bent over on my hands and knees, with my head touching the ground, peeking under our neighbor's house. I was trying to find an angle where some of the morning sunlight was bright enough that I could maybe detect if anything moved. My older cousin, Sno'ball (Creston Gaskill), whose house it was, had stepped outside not expecting to see me, especially not there, so he was wondering just what was going on.

"I'm looking for my game rooster," I told him. "He's run away, and he's camped under your house and won't come out for nothing, not even some corn pellets.

"I think he's scared that I'll try to get him to fight again," I explained. "He's not much of a fighter, and he'd rather play hide-n-seek with me than risk having to 'rassle with another very angry rooster."

With my bantam rooster, Junior, standing by the steps in front of our house

I was only ten years old, but I had learned enough about chickens, at least this one, that all these years later I'm still convinced I was right. That rooster stayed under Sno'ball's house for another two weeks. He must have come out some at night, waiting for everyone to go inside, so he could eat the handful of feed that I used each day trying to lure him out in daylight. We could hear him under the house, and occasionally he would peek out around the block foundation that lined it. But he was determined not to get anywhere close enough to the outside that I, or anybody else, might reach to retrieve him.

Finally, acting on a tip from my cousin Paul who lived across the road, we pushed another fighting rooster into the same space my bird was using, and sure enough, my game rooster ran out a cacklin' to where my brother Teff was able to fall on and hold him. A few minutes after that, the chicken-rooster was back in the coop in the corner of our yard. Later that same day, we took the bird back to Mike Rose, who had sold it to us just a few weeks earlier and told him to keep the bird and the four dollars we had paid for a full-blooded "War Horse" fighting rooster.

Thus ended my days as a chicken-fighter. Don't get the wrong idea. The chicken fights that were orchestrated by a small group of Island boys were far removed from the "cock fighting" that remains an ugly part of some cultures. And though our version may not have been pretty, at least by today's standards, it was more an exercise in showmanship than in fighting.

We would stand in a circle consisting only of the boys who were watching and launch our birds into the middle. The roosters would then raise their wings, spread their feathers, and ready themselves either to attack or defend, depending on their temperament. After just a few seconds, one of the roosters would begin to lunge at the other, and the two birds would bounce off and start again. As they did, we would grab the ones that were ours, and that was it. The parade that preceded the contact was what we loved to see. Once the fighting had begun, for us at least, the show was over!

For one thing, genuine fighting roosters cost money, sometimes lots of money, unlike the laying hens that everyone had in abundance. Two dollars, five dollars, sometimes even ten dollars may not seem like a lot now, but it was a small fortune then, especially if it had been earned by picking up and selling bottles out of ditches or opening scallops on the dock. No one was about to see that investment go to waste in an exhibition that offered neither money nor rewards; only the excitement of watching two birds dance in circles.

The Education of an Island Boy

There were dozens of adolescent boys in our neighborhood, and several of them had taken to the sport of roosters. My cousin, Paul (Hancock 1944-2016), along with Rennie (Moore b.1948), Billy (Beaman 1945-1990), Jeffrey (Willis 1946-1992), and especially Dallas Daniel "Dack" (Guthrie 1942-2014), each had at least one prized bird that they loved to show off against the others. Watching them perform, I came to marvel at both the beauty and grace of the majestic roosters. Sensitive to my interest, my daddy found me a small bantam rooster that had the same traits, if not the size, as the larger roosters. But "Junior," that's what we called him, soon became so much a part of the family that I couldn't risk even a "show-dance" that involved the chance of his getting hurt.

My brother, Tommy Hancock

Thus, I eventually started hinting to my parents and siblings that I was anxious for one of the bigger and more storied fighting birds. Because of my young age and my family's finances, I remained an onlooker until my brother Tommy came home for a visit from his Coast Guard assignment in Louisville, Kentucky. (We used to say that he was stationed off the coast of Kentucky.) When he learned what was going on, he offered to buy me a "game rooster" if I could find the one I wanted, and it didn't cost "too much." Mike Rose was a few years older than me and lived two miles to the east'ard, but he was recognized as having the best birds that could be found anywhere on the Island. One Saturday afternoon, Tommy drove me to Mike's house, and a few minutes later, we headed home with my chosen rooster nestled under my jacket and arm, and for less than half of what we had expected to pay.

After just a couple of days, Tommy had arranged for Paul to bring over one of his bevy of fighters so we could see just how willing my new pet was to be part of the combat dance. It was then that we learned why Mike had been willing to part with this particular bird for such a low price.

He was pretty, and he was loud- you could hear him crow from anywhere in the neighborhood, but it was immediately evident

Livin', Learnin', and Playin'

that he was more a lover than a fighter. He refused even to make the stance of a fighter. He just turned his back and ran for any opening he could find to get away from the fighting circle. Not only did he leave the circle, he kept on running until he found a haven under Sno'ball's house. And that's exactly where he spent the next two weeks.

By the time we finally got hold of him again, Tommy was back in Louisville, and I was too ashamed even to watch another chicken fight. So, my "War Horse Game Rooster" ended up where he had started, and I moved on to some of the thousand other things that made being a boy on Harkers Island such a never-ending adventure.

Hollering For (Not At) Your Children!

"DELMAS Leeeeeee- aaah!"

It's hard to spell out just how it sounded. But it was a sound and a voice that everyone recognized and knew exactly what it meant. When you heard that sound ringing through the oaks and cedars, it meant that Rowena was ready for her son, Delmas Lee, to head on home.

Rowena's call was distinctive, and so were the sounds of all the mothers in our neighborhood. We came to recognize each of them as they stood on their porches and hollered at the top of their lungs, calling for their sons and letting them know that supper was ready, their father was home, or that it was time to call it a day.

To a generation that has grown up around whole-house heating and cooling, with windows pulled down and compressors roaring, it might be difficult to imagine just how quiet the outside could be, and how much could be heard by a listening ear. In fact, you had to be careful of what was said, even inside your own home, as anything spoken in a normal voice could generally be heard by anyone near an open window or door.

But usually, a little before the time for any meal, most children were signaled to head home by the sound of their mother "hollering" to let them know that dinner or supper was ready.

The Education of an Island Boy

Thinking back, it seems remarkable how far and clear a female voice could ring and echo in our neighborhood. Each mother had a distinctive sound and cadence. Like fledgling birds, we grew to recognize and respond to the pitch and tone of the sounding voice even more than to the words or instructions that were hollered.

Sunrise was announced by the crowing of roosters and the cackling of hens, and depending on the time of the year, by the sounds that came from the Landing. When fishermen and shrimpers tied up at their moorings or at the dock, seagulls would circle overhead, awaiting the scraps that were thrown in the water. The squawking of gulls and the level of that sound was a sure indicator of just how successful that morning's haul might have been. There were other mornings when the prevailing sound was not of birds, but of the crewmen of shad boats that were working a haul in the Island channel. Their chants and chatter resounded across the water so loudly that we could hear them through our bedroom windows as we awoke on calm summer mornings.

But in the later afternoons and evenings, even if the wind was blowing to squelch the echoes, you could still hear the sounds of mothers as they called in their children in for the day. My mother was not much of a screamer and seldom took part in the chorus of voices that rang through the neighborhood. But there were some that you could count on hearing every day.

Besides Rowena, there was Esther (Moore, 1928-2013) hollering for Cecil Arendell (Rennie), Vivian (Gaskill, 1929-1981) calling for Manley and "Brother," Elva (Irvine, 1927-2014) rounding up Kenny, Robert, and Kyle, and Ollie (Moore, 1919-2008) telling Dallas Daniel it was time to come home. And there was my Aunt Mary (Hancock, 1924-2004). Actually, she was married to my cousin Norman (Hancock, 1920-2008), but since they were a generation older, we grew up calling them Uncle Norman and Aunt Mary.

Mary had been raised at Chincoteague Island on Chesapeake Sound, and she maintained an accent, even when she hollered, that set her voice apart. When she called out for her son, Paul, the name rolled out in several syllables that sounded like "P-a-a-o-o-u-u-l-l."

Livin', Learnin', and Playin'

Her house was just across the road from ours, so we usually got the full force of her hollering as it bounced off our front porch.

Every neighborhood had its own set of boys and their mamas. And most had at least one so distinctive that everyone else, including those who lived far down the road, knew of it, even if they had not heard it themselves. None was more celebrated throughout the Island than that of the children of Luther (1893-1943) and Lettie (1902-1986) Guthrie. Although it was before my time, it was still so well known that most people could mimic the sound and the rhythm of Lettie's daily call to all five of her sons, letting them know that she wanted them home.

Standing on her porch, she would take a deep breath and then bellow out in one long and loud verse: " L u t h e r   M e r r i l l, M a r i o n   L e e, C h a r l e s   C u r t i s, C u r v i s   L e e!" And then, without taking a breath, she ended with a final flourish of "J a y P e r r y´ (with the final letter accented as if it were the French pronunciation)."

My Daddy's Very Personal "GPS" Monitor

"Where did you go?" he would usually begin.

"Just to Wade's Shore and across to the beach," I might respond.

"Did the engine run alright?" he would follow.

"Never missed a pop," I would assure him.

"Did you have a good time?" he would ask as he headed back up the path and towards our house, satisfied that nothing had gone wrong with me or with the boat.

"Yeah," I would tell him, maybe adding something along the lines of, "but the tide was so high that ...," or "There were so many yellow flies that ..."

A few minutes later, we were both back at the house. I was washing off under a water hose, and he was back at work on his net or on something he was building or repairing in our small backyard.

The Education of an Island Boy

Such were the conversations that followed an "unsupervised" day at the Banks in my father's boat when I was a boy. A half a century before I was born, and before hurricanes had left it largely uninhabitable for people, Shackleford Banks had been the home place of my ancestors for many generations. But for my era of young boys, it was a summer wonderland. Lying less than three miles across the sound, it was always visible on the southern horizon. It was bordered by both a gentle ocean and peaceful sound and it seemed to call to us to come and enjoy — a natural theme park that charged no admission.

Most Island families had a boat of some kind, and by the time we approached our teenage years, we were deemed responsible enough to use those boats without adult supervision. Usually, our chosen destination was the Banks. And once we got there, we could play and enjoy ourselves to our heart's content. Swimming in the ocean, diving, and skiing in the sound, chasing after herds of wild horses and sheep, blazing trails, or digging for clams — time seemed to fly on wings as the days raced by. But each day eventually came to an end, and we were obliged to return to our boats and head back across the sound to home.

It was at the end of that return trip that a mystery began to unfold in my life. Each afternoon or early evening, as our boat approached our family dock, I came to expect that my father would be standing at the shore and awaiting my return. As we secured the boat together, he would ask about my day of fun, even as he inspected the boat to make sure all was in good order. All along, I assumed that the latter was his primary concern.

As the youngest of seven boys, I had the good fortune of enjoying the freedom of the Banks even earlier than my brothers. And as the years passed and I grew older, and my brothers eventually had boats of their own, the time came that my father entrusted his boat to me alone. Now, with my friends and younger cousins, we would repeat the same routine that had become an irreplaceable part of summer life on our Island.

But even as I matured and the dynamic of using his boat became more routine, one thing about my father did not change. No matter what the occasion or how long or short the stay was, he was still there walking the path from our home to the shore at the very moment our boat came into view.

It seemed to me as if he had access to some internal GPS or tracking device that allowed him to know the very instant that I headed home. Try as I might by staying later than usual or heading home early, I could not elude him. Intuitively, or so it seemed, he could sense my direction and knew exactly when I would approach the shore. Even after I grew up and had a boat and a family of my own, whenever we would go out for a day on the water, my father was always there to welcome us back to the dock. "How does he know?" I used to ask myself. "How can he tell exactly each time that I am headed for home so as to be there to meet me?"

The passing of time, and more especially, having sons of my own who asked for permission to spread their wings by boating alone, eventually revealed my father's great secret. For by then I had a deeper understanding of the dangers that could lurk in the water. The very first summer afternoon that my two sons headed out into the sound and ocean, I came face to face with the very sensitivity that used to draw my father to the shoreline. Because, from the moment that my sons' departing boat slipped beyond my view, I would stare without respite toward the same horizon and wait for their return.

After a few hours, that invariably seemed much longer to me, as my sons made their way back to our mooring, I could see them in the distance long before they could ever take notice of me. Then, just as with my own father, I would be there at the shore to reassure myself that all was well, not so much with my boat as with my boys. Since then, every time I catch the first sight of my children as they break the horizon for home, even in boats of their own, my mind is drawn to a specific verse in the Biblical parable of the "Prodigal Son." "When he was yet a long way off, his father saw him ..."

My father lived for ninety-three years, and for most of that time, he continued looking in the direction of his children and grandchildren who had ventured into the Banks and the sound— be it ever so tranquil and serene. A lifetime of experience had taught him that the waters of the sound, and especially the ocean, can quickly change demeanor and that even the most placid marine setting can hide unseen dangers. As age and experience have made me more aware of those dangers, I have come to value much more the mental image I have of my father waiting on the shoreline. There was a time when my overriding impression was that his constant attention was because of how little he trusted me. The wisdom of the years has convinced me that it was, rather, because of how much he loved and cared for me!

My father, Charlie William Hancock, sitting on the gunwale of a skiff at our landing. My brother Mike's trawler, "The Seven Brothers," is moored at our dock.

Harkers Island Cowboys

Growing up in the heyday of television Westerns and "Cowboys & Indians," the herds of wild ponies that roamed Shackleford Banks sent a veritable siren's call to every young boy and man on Harkers Island. Each time we went to or by the Banks, we could see them, generally in a group of four or more, feeding on the marshes or moving along the sandy shoreline. In our minds, we could fantasize about reining one of them in, putting on a saddle and bridle, and heading off into the horizon just like Gene Autry or Roy Rogers.

A recurring fantasy, even a dream, among boys of my age on the Island was that we might have one of those much-touted

Shackleford Banks ponies for our very own. For most of us, fantasy was all it ever was, but for some of us, including two of my brothers, it became a "dream come true."

The annual horse-penning that occurred at the height of each summer, and that most everyone on the Island got to witness, couldn't help but arouse the interest of a generation that was fed a daily dose of television shows of heroes sitting atop their ponies. Several times each evening, we watched in our living rooms as both Cowboys and Indians rode their horses gallantly into town, into battle, and eventually into the sunset. Knowing that there were large herds of seemingly free and wild ponies for the taking just across Back Sound was constantly on our minds and in our conversations.

The wild ponies were "wild," but they were not really "free." Most of them were claimed by owners from the Island and the mainland, and one of the main reasons for the annual penning was to identify young foals so they could be claimed and branded. My father even owned a few, and when I was about five years old, he allowed my brother, Mike (child number seven and son number four), to bring a young, roan-colored mare over to the Island to spend a summer.

After just a few weeks, and before the horse was fully "broken" for riding, the pony sustained a serious cut on its hoof while grazing in a wooded area between our house and that of our neighbor, Cliff Guthrie.

Riding a Banks pony with my brother Telford in front on Christmas morning in 1960. My cousin, Manley Gaskill is standing behind us in front of his new teepee. The outfits were Christmas presents.

Seeing how grave the injury was becoming and knowing that veterinary help was out of the question, my father decided to transport the colt back to the Banks so it could heal itself in the salt marshes that until then had been his home. He wrapped the wounded heel with strips of a bed sheet and tied it up with string, and then turned it loose in Cab's Creek, a section of marshes that lie directly across the sound from our house.

Sure enough, a few weeks later, when Daddy and Mike returned to check on the horse's condition, they found it running hale and free within a small herd of other ponies. Content that he had spent his only chance to have a mount of his own, my brother bade it goodbye and turned his attention to getting a car and courting a new girlfriend he had met that spring while attending Smyrna High School — his future wife, Drexell.

My brother Bill (child number five and son number three), however, had a much more fulfilling experience as an Island cowboy. In the spring of 1953, when he was fifteen years old, he was rewarded with a gift of fifty dollars for the previous summer of helping my father in the water. They had agreed to use the money to buy a Banks pony from an Island neighbor, Joe Neal Davis (1925-2001). Joe Neal had a two-year-old stallion he was keeping at East'ard (Core) Banks that was both bigger and more lightly colored than most other feral horses. Needing some immediate cash, he sold the pony for approximately half of the going price that similar stock would bring had he waited until the auction that accompanied the summer roundup.

My brothers Bill, Ralph, and Tommy with two of Ralph's children- Jacque Sue and Ralph Cornel - 1953

Livin', Learnin', and Playin'

Daddy and Bill pulled a skiff behind the "Ralph," my father's boat, to the Banks where the horse was captured, and then hobbled so he could be carted in the skiff back to our landing. The pony proved so spirited that both the capture and the fettering were much more difficult and time-consuming than my father had anticipated. Memories of that experience would resonate with my brother and would be evidenced when the time finally came to move his pony back to the Banks for the winter.

Bill stabled his new pony, which he named "Samson" after the long-haired Biblical strong man, in the grassy yards that belonged to our father, our Uncle Louie, and our grandfather, Ole' Pa. He soon had Samson gentled enough to ride, but when Daddy realized that Bill had begun a pattern of mounting on the horse's right side, Indian style as it was called, he demanded that his son retrain both him and his ride to the more traditional "left-sided mount." That was fine with my brother, but the horse, now used to the original routine, began to bite at Bill's arm every time he approached from what Samson assumed to be the "wrong side." It took several weeks of coaxing to convince the horse that the "left side" was going to be the "right side" from then on.

My oldest brother, Ralph, was already married and living in Idaho when he heard about Bill's new venture. As an expression of both love and admiration for what was being done, Ralph purchased a used saddle from a military surplus store and had it shipped all the way to the Island so that his younger brother would not have to ride bareback. Bill kept and cherished that saddle long after the horse it had straddled was gone.

The Island in 1953 might not have been densely settled, but it was still thickly wooded, meaning that there were few open spaces for riding or for running a new pony. Bill made use of a north-south path that stretched from the Landing, ran beside our house across the main road, and then back to the "old road," roughly a quarter of a mile, as his riding circle. After a while, the rider and his horse extended their range all the way to the Sand Hole at the west'ard, more than a mile each way.

The horse loved to gallop in the soft white sand that interspersed the dunes and bushes, and they were often joined there by Bill's good friend, Jim Sparks (1937-2014), who also had a pony of his own. While riding there alone among the hills one day, Samson was "spooked" and threw off his rider. Startled by the event, the horse ran all the way home without Bill, while my brother, who had punctured his side on a tree limb, had to make his way back using only his own two feet.

By the end of that summer, the sight of Bill riding his horse was recognizable to everyone in the neighborhood. Samson had been fashioned into a dependable mount and was much loved by his rider. However, the financial realities of the era did not allow for anything other than grazing for sustenance. Purchasing hay was out of the question, so Bill knew he would be able to keep him only until the grass began to die in late autumn. After that, he would have to carry his horse back to the Banks so that he could forage the same shrubs and beach grasses that had sustained the herd for three centuries.

As the sun moved farther south in the evening sky, and the summer grass quit growing, Bill realized that the time had come to retrace the same journey that had brought Samson to the Island six months earlier. At least this time he would be able to deposit his horse on Shackleford, much closer and easier to get to than Core Banks could ever be.

Anticipating the problems that had been evident when his horse had first been captured and transported, Bill began to prepare his horse and friend for the journey that awaited them both. More than a generation later, my mother and sisters would still wax emotional as they described my brother training his horse to get into the skiff; not just to make Sampson more comfortable, but also to avoid the frustration that my father had shown a few months earlier when the routine had first played out.

Day after day, Bill would walk his horse to the Landing so he and Samson could practice getting in and out of the skiff. Finally, the day arrived for departure, and much to everyone's relief and satisfaction, Samson comfortably climbed across the gunwale and stood erect, where, being held close by my brother, he was towed across Back Sound to his winter home.

Livin', Learnin', and Playin'

Teenage boys grow up much faster than horses, and by the next summer, just like Mike a few years later, Bill had turned his attention to other more "normal" interests for a sixteen-year-old boy. But he did so having lived out a fantasy that only a very few boys, even Island boys, ever got to experience.

Horsepenning

Some strangers called it "pony penning," but we always called it "horsepenning" (one word). Every summer, on or close to Independence Day, Islanders would cross Back Sound in multitudes, in a mass exodus, headed into Banks Bay and the shore of what used to be Diamond City. There, on Shackleford Banks, they would gather by the hundreds in their boats, along the shoreline, and around a small pen, maybe twenty-five feet square.

Men from the Island, and a select few teenage and twenty-something boys, would have arrived there hours earlier to begin the celebration. When I was a child, the young boys and men would fan out all over the Banks under the direction of the chosen leader, Allen Moore (1909-1974). In groups of five or more, they would herd the scattered groups of horses from the various dunes and creeks, as well as scrub oaks, cedars, and yaupon bushes, of the island as they drove the ponies towards the pen at Diamond City. Running, often on their bare feet, they would poke at and otherwise spook the horses to get them moving, and then, in concert with their sidekicks, herd the ponies in the right direction. This was long before the days of motorized vehicles like the three and four-wheelers that later overran the whole expanse. The ground was much too jagged to allow for cars or trucks to negotiate the terrain. And, for whatever reason, no one can recall ever having seen someone riding a horse to help in the roundup.

It was the speed, stamina, and savvy of the Island boys, and those alone, that was responsible for finding and bringing in as many as two hundred horses from the far corners of the Banks. Keep in mind that the distance from the Mullet Pond at the west end of Shackleford to Diamond City in the other direction was as much as eight miles. But in a matter of only a few hours, the horses, colts, mares, and studs, would all be herded together in that small pen near the tide line of what was called Banks Bay.

The Education of an Island Boy

By the time the horses were corralled, the crowd would have grown to several hundred. As many as a hundred boats of all sizes would be anchored in the bay, and scores of small skiffs would be pulled up on the beach. Men, women, and lots of children were gathered in lines and in bunches to watch and await the arrival of the horses. Adding to the festivity were the many small fires that started near the tide line, using driftwood and dead marsh grass, to roast oysters, conchs, and hotdogs for the swelling crowd.

Because of the number of people involved, and the relatively small space in which we gathered, the event could sometimes verge on the chaotic. Now and then one of the studs would get startled and break free, causing a panic among the onlookers until it could be restrained. Slightly less threatening were the men who celebrated the morning of horsepenning by getting drunk. It was usually the same ones every year, and most people knew who they might be and that they were to be avoided, especially by children.

One other risk was that if someone got too near the backside of a horse while it was restrained, it might resort to "kicking." I was made aware of that when one of my father's horses, a beautiful, tan-colored stud, kicked me in the chest one Independence morning, and I was carried to Beaufort in a boat to be checked out by Dr. Fulcher. There were no lasting effects except for a large

Horsepenning on Shackleford Banks in the 1950's.
CSWM&HC Collection

Livin', Learnin', and Playin'

bruise on my sternum and a lifetime of respect for what can happen when you approach a horse from the rear.

Once the horses were secured, either in the pen, or tethered to a post or a holder, the primary work of the day ensued as their numbers were noted, new colts were identified, some were branded, and many were traded or sold on the spot. One of the heirlooms I have kept and have on display is my father's branding iron of a large "H." My uncle Calvin had a special skiff with a high freeboard that was specifically made for moving stock, including the horses, to and from the Banks. He might have been charged with carrying as many as four at a time back to the Island, where they would then be moved to their new homes.

After the counting and trading of horsepenning day had been completed, the gates of the corral were opened, and the herds scurried away just as quickly as they had arrived. At about the same time, the cavalcade of boats that came from the north headed back in the opposite direction. By suppertime, many of the same boats and their passengers would be at Academy Field on the Island to watch the boat races there that concluded the day's celebration. It was always fun to be a boy at Harkers Island. But it was never better than on those extraordinary days when it seemed everybody was together as part of one big family — including even the horses.

Harkers Island's Little League Baseball team in 1964. Front L-R David Ronald Guthrie, Joel Hancock, Anthony Nelson, Alton Best, and Manley Gaskill - Back Row L-R Willis Nelson, Larry Mason, Rex Lewis, and Curvis Guthrie

6

Playin' Ball and Workin' the Water

[Baseball] is a haunted game, where each player is measured by the ghosts of those who have gone before. Most of all, it is about time and timelessness, speed and grace, failure and loss, imperishable hope, and coming home.
                    Ken Burns & Geoffrey C. Ward, "The Love of a Game"

For many Islanders of my generation and earlier, there was hardly any distinction between playing and working, especially regarding locations. On the water or the land, playgrounds and job sites were often the same. The fishing holes and beaches used for hauling a net were later or earlier that day the setting for swimming and diving and races along the shore. Open fields used for hanging and spreading nets were used for playing ball or games of cowboys & Indians. Backyards that were the homes of chicken coops and clotheslines were also perfect for a basketball goal suspended from a cedar or pine tree that used trawl bunt as a net hung beneath the goal.

Even the same roads and paths used for hauling and loading were an ideal setting for running, racing, and playing football, especially for baseball. Baseball as a game was meant to be fun. As we matured and the level of play improved, reaching your peak level could be like work. Working in the water was meant to be work, but it could also be fun in the right setting and with the right people

The Education of an Island Boy

— sometimes just as much fun as baseball or the other games we played while growing up.

Clayton Guthrie
CSWM&HC Collection

Islanders did indeed love to play, and of all their games, they loved playing baseball most of all. Even those who didn't or couldn't play loved to watch it. Everyone loved to tell stories that kept alive the prowess and the foibles of previous generations of players and their fans. Even when men were well past their prime, and it was challenging for younger boys like me to imagine them ever having played a game that required speed, agility, and skill, they and their contemporaries continued to identify them by how they had once been heroes on the playing fields. And they always seemed to weigh younger players against their memories of what old timers had been like, usually with the former coming up as having been less than their equals.

"He's a good shortstop, but not as good as Clayton Junior (Guthrie 1920-2005) or David Yeomans (1921-2006)," or "He sure is quick, but not nearly as fast as Ottie Russell (1909-1989)." The one comparison my generation heard the most often was, "He can hit it a long ways', but nobody else has ever hit it as far as Thomas 'Tookie' Willis (1918-1980)." I once told my Uncle Linwood that the older he got, the better baseball player he and others used to be.

We Didn't Even Get a Chance to Bat!

David Yeomans
CSWM&HC Collection

I came of age as a baseball player playing with my friends along the path to the Landing that ran beside our house. As I grew older and the boundaries of that narrow pathway became too constrained, our games moved over to Rennie's field, a half-acre open spot that

Playin' Ball and Workin' the Water

was near the center of our neighborhood and surrounded by drainage ditches on both sides. Later still, as both we and our numbers grew larger, we moved our games to the much bigger grazing area we called Johnson's Cow Pasture, which was close to the Bay on the Island's north shore. At other times we played at Academy Field, at the Sand Hole, and especially in an open field behind our church that was a parking lot on Sundays but was free for us to use as a playground the rest of the week.

Eventually, for some of the more dedicated players in the generation before mine, the neighborhood sandlot games began to give way to real games played on real diamonds with chalked foul and baselines, actual bases and pitching mounds, and, best of all, real baseballs. What I mean by real baseballs is that for our pickup games, the balls usually were so old that they were covered with tape and so misshapen that some of them looked more like an onion than the real thing.

By the 1930s, there were unofficial clubs of players that represented the "East'ard," the "West'ard," and the "Middle." My older brothers would have belonged to the final grouping, but the boundary lines were never official, and no one made any effort to enforce them. Not long after that, an "Island" team was assembled that played against similar squads from mainland communities from Straits to Atlantic, and even against the "real" teams from Beaufort and Morehead City.

The growth of inter-community contests initially took a hiatus with the outbreak of World War II when so many young men left home for military service or jobs in supporting industries—some of them as far away as Norfolk, Virginia. Still, the games themselves did not completely stop, even though some aspects of the rivalries did evolve due to the loss and, eventually, the addition of some new players to their rosters.

With the onset of America's involvement in the fighting, life on Harkers Island began a series of transformations that proved to have lasting consequences. Among those changes was the influx of soldiers and sailors assigned to Cape Lookout, and responsible for protecting this part of the North Carolina coast from the German U-Boats that frequented the Outer Banks of North Carolina in the

The Education of an Island Boy

early years of the war. In due course, some of those military personnel found a permanent home on the Island as was evidenced by the new surnames that became a part of the Island demographic.

One of those sailors, whose name has now been lost, was noticed by local baseball fans as a very specialized talent. This young visitor was a pitcher. But more than that, he was ambidextrous and could pitch the ball equally well with either hand. What a discovery! What a find! What a pickup! Here was a young man who could, by himself, take unlimited advantage of an age-old baseball strategy. Specifically, he could pitch right-handed to right-handed hitters, and, when necessary, could switch arms and throw with his left hand to the left-handed hitters.

Eager to exploit their assumed good fortune, the Island team invited their rivals from nearby Marshallberg — just across the Straits Channel — to a challenge match with the intention of settling an old score. Marshallberg had been on a winning streak in recent years thanks to several young players who had shown a consistent talent for hitting the best pitchers the Island had to offer. So confident were the Islanders that they agreed to play the game at Smyrna, literally in Marshallberg's backyard. Perhaps not suspecting that they were being set up for a ringer, the challenge was immediately accepted, and the game was on.

The contest began with the Island team in the field, they being the "home team" for having offered the challenge in the first place. It thus worked out that the ambidextrous Island pitcher got to show his stuff at the very onset of the contest. Unfortunately for the Islanders and their many fans who had come to witness the game, it immediately became obvious that although their intended hero indeed could pitch with either hand, he could not pitch very well with either one! Batter after batter from Marshallberg stepped up to the plate and swatted the ball soundly into play as if they were taking batting practice. It was even said that several of the cattle, roaming a pasture that sat just beyond the right field fence, were spooked by long balls that disturbed their grazing.

By the time the third out had been made, and the Marshallbergers headed out to take the field, the Island boys had decided that discretion was the better part of valor. The first half of the inning had taken so long that the sun was already beginning to fall behind the tall pines that were to the west of the Smyrna School. Rather than take their turn at bat, they stole away to their cars and trucks that were waiting to take them home.

Seeing their foes run off rather than continue the contest, some of the Marshallberg players and fans chased behind their fleeing opponents and heckled them with repeated chants of "We beat you; we beat you!" Leaning out of the back window of one of the departing cars, a Harkers Island player responded with the best retort he could muster, "I wonder how you know that. We didn't even get a chance to bat!"

That Ball was High!

With the end of the War and the return of the soldiers, sailors, and workers, matchup games between the Down East communities heated up again with an increased fervor. From May to September, there usually were games every Saturday and Sunday afternoon. Young men who had served together in the armed forces and who often worked together when they got back home, became passionate rivals once they got on the field of play. The intensity of the contests served to generate and then increase the community enthusiasm for the games, and the further interest in turn, just added to the fervor of the rivalries on the field. As both fed on each other, the on-the-field antics grew more and more passionate as a whole community's honor could hang in the balance. The results of that ardor led to some memorable schemes — and to at least one implausible incident.

My cousin, Creston Gaskill (1926-2003), called "Sno'ball" by everyone but his immediate family, loved to tell of a memorable game played between Harkers Island and its sister community of Salter Path. I call Salter Path a "sister" to Harkers Island because, like the Island, it was settled mostly by families who migrated from Shackleford Banks after the Great Hurricane of 1899. Even as late as the mid-point of the last century, the two villages shared not just their history and family surnames, but also a taste for stewed loon, a knack for catching jumping mullets, and an absolute hysteria for the game of baseball.

The Education of an Island Boy

Given their mutual love for the sport, it was little wonder that ball games played between the two were always a family squabble, and sometimes, to borrow a phrase from Major League Baseball great Ty Cobb, "something like a war." This was never more so than on a late summer afternoon, sometime in the late 40's, when the two teams met on the sandy field of Salter Path. The game was tight until the very end and came down literally to the very last pitch, even if it wasn't a pitch.

As related by Sno'ball, who was catching for the Island team, the Islanders held a one-run lead going into the last half of the ninth inning. But even after giving up two outs, the home squad was able to load the bases and put the tying run within just ninety feet of home plate. The Salter Path batter then worked the count full so that everything, yes "everything," would come down to one last throw to the plate.

By then the sun had begun to set behind the sprawling oak trees that bordered the first base line of the ballpark, and the late summer shadows already had extended onto the field and beyond the pitcher's mound and home plate. Realizing that the game and the pride of both communities now hung in the balance, Moe Willis (Amos Eston Willis 1922-1999), the pitcher, called his catcher out to the mound for a conference.

Moe was young and strong and was one of the best pitchers ever to play for the Island team, but by that time, he was spent and realized his best stuff might not be enough to close the matter out in the way his teammates, family, and friends hoped and expected. No one is sure exactly how he came up with the idea, but when his catcher joined him to discuss what the last pitch might be, the pitcher suggested that they just "fake it" and go on home!

What do you mean?" Sno'ball inquired. "How can you just fake it?" "Easy," the tired but ingenious young pitcher responded. "It's getting so dark, and everyone is so excited, I'll just wind up and pretend to throw, while keeping the ball in my glove. You (the catcher) set up your target right in the middle of the strike zone, and just pop your mitt really hard. If we act it out 'good enough,' the umpire will never know the difference. Since he's the only one that matters, we'll just go on home and chalk this one up as a win!"

So, that's exactly what they did. After a long, long glare at the plate (to allow the sun to dip a little lower), Moe Willis curled into a full windup and let loose toward home with all his might — but without a baseball. In less than a second, Sno'ball banged his right fist into his closed mitt with a mighty thud, and the umpire (who was said to be from Morehead) jerked his right hand into the air and screamed, "Strike three!"

A group of boys from the Smyrna area assembled for a pickup game of baseball.
CSWM&HC Collection

Pandemonium immediately broke out on the field and especially in the bleachers and among the crowds who had lined up three deep all the way down both foul lines. It was all the Island team could do to get to their cars without being trampled, but in short order, they had made their escape and were headed east to Atlantic Beach. This was where they planned to gather and celebrate before heading home to tell their story to the pitiful few who had not been able to see the game in person. But as the gathering commenced, it soon became obvious that their group was one player short. Sno'ball, it was feared, had been caught up in the tumult at home plate and was unable to extricate himself in time to get with the rest of his team as they hurried to their departure.

At that time, the road leading down Bogue Banks to Salter Path was still unpaved and covered only with several layers of seashells and discarded roofing materials. So, it was more than half an hour later that the main Harkers Island group reached their rendezvous spot at Atlantic Beach. It was several anxious minutes later before their catcher, and a new hero, came straggling in, looking even more spent than when the game was being played.

Anxious to know what had ensued in the aftermath of the final out and their rapid escape, everyone gathered around him to ask, "What happened? Were they mad at you? What did they say?"

"You'll never believe it" was all he could get out before pausing again to catch his breath. "Except for the crowd that swarmed around home plate, making it really hard for me to get out, I was hardly noticed," he finally explained. "They were mad at the umpire and not me. Every one of 'em swore that the last pitch was high!"

A League of Our Own

It was the children of the generation of ballplayers who suited up for baseball after the war that were my playmates and later teammates as baseball became an ever-increasing focal point of my attention as we approached adolescence. As was the case throughout the country, those former soldiers and sailors were the coaches who introduced my baby boom generation of ballplayers to how the games were meant to be played and enjoyed — both on and off the field.

Even though baseball had been played by all ages on the Banks and later on the Island since shortly after the Civil War, and maybe even before that, when it came to organized teams and leagues; well, that was something reserved for grown-ups. There were a few teenage prodigies who were skilled enough, or at least big enough to play, with adults, and who could represent their community on the field of honor — or shame, depending on the outcome. But that real, even if artificial, age boundary all but disappeared in a flash in 1963 when I was still just ten years old.

The various communities east of the North River Bridge may have appeared to be quite similar to casual visitors, but they were fiercely independent in most matters. Until the county board of education mandated a consolidation of high schools after World War II, each of them had its own fish houses, churches, and even schools. I don't recall any combined activities before the school consolidation, and only a very few since.

What may have been the first real exception to that rule was the "Down East Little League," with four teams that were loosely representative of several Down East communities, or at least those that were south and west of Nelson Bay. Its geographical boundaries were roughly a triangle that reached from Harkers Island on the southeast corner, to Bettie in the northwest, and to Davis Shore in the northeast. Harkers Island and Otway had teams of their own, but Marshallberg and Bettie joined with other communities to field a team — and not always neighboring ones. Marshallberg was joined with Tusk and Gloucester, and Bettie also had boys from Davis, Williston, and Straits.

The league had its genesis amid the care and concern of a cadre of young fathers. Each of them had played baseball when they were younger. They also had served in the military and had sons for whom they wanted something more than the mere sandlot games that their fathers and uncles had enjoyed. Sometime in the spring of 1963, Dallas Arthur from Bettie; J. C. Dickinson from Otway; J.D. Lewis and his brother, "Wump," from Marshallberg; and especially my older cousin, Creston "Sno'ball" Gaskill from Harkers Island — the same one who had helped pull off the maneuver that had won the controversial game against Salter Path — pooled their energies and resources to organize and then oversee what became

Creston "Sno'ball" Gaskill

The Education of an Island Boy

for me and my age group "a league of our own."

I can still recall how excited I was when Sno'ball's son, and my next-door neighbor and closest friend, Manley (Gaskill 1952-1996), let me know there was "gonna be a little league and that we were gonna have our own team." As the school year ended, Sno'ball, assisted by his good friend, Lomus Jones (1932-1992), began practicing with our group of about fifteen boys, most of us either ten or eleven years old, in the makeshift ballfield that sat behind our church.

It was mostly vacant and primarily used for Sunday parking, but with a wire backstop at the northwest corner. Yet for us it was our Yankee Stadium, Wrigley Field, and Fenway Park rolled into one. After just a couple weeks of practice there, we became a real "team" ready to take on the best that the rest of the world could throw in our direction.

The league itself had no official rules or by-laws, no regulation fields, and no paid umpires. That first year we didn't even have any uniforms. But we did have what Sno'ball loved to call the three "B's"; balls, bats, and boys. Seven years later, the final piece of that puzzle, the boys, who had started out in this "disorganized" league, were together at East Carteret High School. Before we finished there, we had won the regular-season championship of the Northeastern High School 3-A Conference, a league that included the largest schools in the eastern part of the state.

During my senior year we were even coached by another "Harkers Island boy," Joe "Boy" Willis, who was just eight years older than me. At the closely cropped and fully lined ballparks of Greenville, Kinston, New Bern, and places in between, and in towns as far away as Roanoke Rapids and Elizabeth City, we were able to use the skills and talents that a small group of caring fathers had first helped us develop and hone amid the sand spurs, crabgrass, and yaupon bushes of the original "down-east."

More than half a century later, it is hard to express how exciting it was for me and the others to play baseball in a real league, even if it was not "real" by some standards. An incident that occurred just one year earlier exemplified how I and the others felt. One

Playin' Ball and Workin' the Water

afternoon, while leaving Beaufort after a Saturday shopping trip with my family, we stopped by Huntley's Hardware, a building supply store that was adjacent to the Little League stadium for the town of Beaufort. While waiting in my sister's car, I saw a ball player, just about my age, walking away from the park wearing an authentic baseball uniform, the whole thing, including a cap with a raised letter, a pin-striped shirt with a number on the back, matching peg-legged pants with colored socks and black spikes (that's what we called cleats in those days).

I couldn't have been more impressed if Willie Mays himself had paraded in front of me in all his glory. That was the first time I ever remember seeing in real-time an actual "baseball player" uniform. To this day, I still can recall and even feel some of the excitement that all but overwhelmed me that summer afternoon. The suggestion that I might someday be able to wear a similar type of garb was so foreign to me that it was more fantasy than hope. Then, from out of nowhere it seemed, came the opportunity to be part of a team just like the one the boy with the real uniform had represented. Even if I didn't have such a uniform (our second year we did), I had the "real baseball," and that was what most mattered.

As to the games we played, everything was based upon the "unofficial" baseball rule book, both written and not, that our coaches had grown up with. No effort at all was made to adhere to the modified rules used by the nationally organized youth groups. All games were played at the field used by and across from the Smyrna High School. It had the dimensions of a park for grown-up players, so to make it work, the coaches simply shortened the bases by thirty feet and placed a pitcher's rubber fifteen feet in from the regular mound.

Other than that, we played baseball the way, according to Sno'ball, it was meant to be played. Runners took leads before the ball was pitched, stole bases when the situation called for it, and broke up double plays with both feet and arms spread in every direction. There were no "free" substitutions that allowed for everyone to get a chance to play. We played hard and we played to win, just like our coaches said we should.

There was no such thing as a "mercy rule" to save the losing team from greater embarrassment. With a group of coaches who had come of age in boot camps preparing for wars in Europe and Asia, little attention was paid to sparing the feelings of players or even teams that did not measure up. In their minds, the best way to avoid embarrassment and humiliation was to play good enough baseball that those emotions were never aroused.

Umpires were drafted from both adults and adolescents who happened to show up before the game got started. Sometimes it was even the parents of the players who were calling bases as well as balls and strikes. Despite the apparent conflict of interest, there was hardly ever a contested call — at least not one serious enough to interrupt the flow of the game. Even the accepted age limits for players mandated by the national organizations were not strictly enforced. Several boys, who technically were old enough for the "Pony League," and thus too old for our teams, instead became the oversized heroes of their "Little League" squads.

Two, and only two, new baseballs were unwrapped for each game. When one of those was fouled into the thick woods that lined the field, play was stopped until it could be found and returned. Other than just a few fathers and older brothers or cousins, there were few people there to watch us play. But that didn't matter. It was what was happening on the field that really counted, and as long as Sno'ball and Lomus were satisfied, and our teammates were not disappointed, we couldn't have cared any less for who was or wasn't cheering from the sidelines.

Once the season had begun, and we started actually playing ball rather than just practicing and getting ready, it was all over, or so it seemed, almost before it started. We had just one game a week played on Saturday mornings. We matched up against the other three teams four times each, making it a long season by today's standards. But our Harkers Island team was so good that by the mid-point of the season, we were undefeated, and the only real contest was for which team might earn second place. We ended the first season with only one loss. In our second year, we were undefeated. In fact, the most exciting match-up of both seasons was when as part of the closing celebration, the "Harkers Island Sharks" matched up against "all-stars" chosen from the other three teams.

Even then, the excitement was only in making out the lineups since we defeated the all-stars as handily as we had the regular squads.

After just a few more seasons, the original league gave way to one sanctioned by a national organization. By then, each team had matching uniforms, certified umpires called the games, and legions of parents eventually sat on metal bleachers or on lawn chairs to cheer for their sons, grandsons, cousins, and friends. At the end of the regular schedule, the league chose an all-star team that went on to tournaments with the hope of competing at the state and national levels. But in our league, this league of our own in the strictest sense imaginable, when we won the regular season title, we were "world champions," at least of the small world which we knew and were a part of.

We had no misgivings about not being able to play against other teams from other places. For most of us, the world we knew was all east of the North River Bridge. At least when it came to baseball, that world was our oyster, and we were eating it the best way of all — salty and raw!

Yet Another Generation

The memory and the influence of those early days of playing organized ball with my friends while being coached by my older cousin have persisted until now. Especially when I had sons of my own playing in a real league for the very first time, those bygone days came back in a flood of sentiments and emotions. Those memories were especially vivid as I watched Manley Gaskill, the same one who had been my Little League teammate, interact with my boys as their first basketball coach. There was one special occasion that carried me back in both time and place to when his father, Sno'ball, was teaching us about playing at the same time as he tutored us on other and even more profound lessons about life in general.

The event was a "Pee-Wee" basketball game that Manley was coaching. He had ushered the little boys, including my son Mike, in and out of the game on a regular basis to give everyone an equal chance to play. Keeping track of the coming and going of a dozen or more six-year-old boys can be hectic at best, and sometimes

The Education of an Island Boy

very frustrating. Some of that frustration was evidenced in Manley's response to Mike, my youngest son, just moments after he had been ushered out, Mike was back at Manley's side and asking, "Do I go back in now?" His tone suggested that it was more of a plea than a question.

"Listen, Mike," Manley responded, "You've played a whole quarter already, and everybody wants a chance to play."

My son, Charlie Michael Hancock

Manley was like a second father to my son, he being the same age as Manley's son Brent, and living close beside us. The boys were together so often that both Manley and I were as comfortable and familiar with one as we were with the other. So, Mike took no exception to the direct response that his question brought. Still, it was obvious to his coach that Mike was unhappy with the answer, even if not the tone. He was right. Unwilling to give up on his hope to get back on the playing floor, Mike replied just as directly as he had been answered.

"I know they do, but they don't want to play as much as I do!"

Manley was technically my first cousin, just once removed. His father, Sno'ball, was my actual first cousin. But Sno'ball was older than my oldest brother and thus of a "whole 'nother generation" from Manley and me. Manley lived next door, with literally less than twenty feet between our bedroom windows, and was just five months younger, so he and I came of age together at the same time and at the same place.

And together, we measured the steps in that process mostly in terms of ball — football, basketball, and especially baseball. Sno'ball loved those same games as much as we did, and because of that we had a mentor who was with us all along the way; from rolling a rubber ball in the grass to suiting up for high school teams that represented our school and community.

As we matured Manley and I developed a routine of playing ball in the front yard every afternoon, especially as supper time grew closer. It was not unusual for us to play all day long. But we were sensitive to the hour when Manley's father would be getting home from work. We knew that he would never venture to walk past us without stopping for at least a while to engage in whatever the game of that day happened to be.

Then, every evening after supper, he would come out again to hit us grounders, throw us passes, rebound our jump shots, or catch our best fastballs. Through it all, he was telling us stories about the games he had played and the players he had watched or known. Those late afternoons were as much skull-sessions as practice. He made sure we knew how to think and talk about the games he loved as much as how to field a grounder or run a pass pattern.

Neighborhood boys playing in my front yard with Sno'ball Gaskill's house in the background. L-R: Manley Gaskill, his brother who was called "Brother" (Walter), Anthony Davis- my sister June's son, and me.

In addition to having been our coach on the first "little league" baseball team ever assembled on the Island, he would continue his mentoring as we moved up in age and in the levels of play. Often, after having watched our entire practice from the sideline, he would join us as we left the field or gym and headed back home. Then, it was not unusual to get there just to start playing again, and to keep playing ball with him nearby until darkness made us stop.

Even after Manley and I matured into high school sports, it seemed that Sno'ball was always there. He was careful not to interfere with our coaches while we were in their care, but coming and going to practices and games included extended conversations about what we had learned or still needed to know. He loved us, and he loved our games, and he was never tired of talking with one or about the other.

As Manley and I grew older, especially after we had boys of our own, we better appreciated the stories and even the lectures that had been part of Sno'ball's tutoring. That "feel" for the game, and especially for those who played it, came out a generation later as Manley contemplated how to respond to my son's asking that he be put back in the game as soon as possible, even when it was not "his turn."

And those experiences shaped Manley's response more than a quarter century later as my youngest son begged him to get back into a contest he had left just moments before. Having been a young boy who loved the game with that much intensity, or even more, and understanding that not every boy on the team had that same passion for playing, Manley decided that treating them all equally was not necessarily treating them all fairly. On the spur of the moment, rather than treating all his players the same, he instead chose to nurture and reward sincere desire. Seeing some of himself in the pleading of his second cousin to get back on the court as soon as possible, Manley proceeded to reply in the way he thought, even if unconsciously, his own father would have responded.

"You're right. You go on back in there and play your heart out. And when this is over, you can remind me to explain something to you about ..."

Learning to "Work the Water"

Some summer mornings were so quiet you could hear a pin-drop both inside and outside the house. The absence of air conditioning meant that not only were windows and doors usually open, but there was little more than the sounds of nature to break the twilight silence. Roosters crowed and seagulls cawed as the sun announced the morning, but generally, there was little else to be heard either inside or out. In that stillness, even the least commotion was noticeable as the new day was about to begin.

Throughout the longest days of summer, it was not uncommon to be awakened on a "slick cam" morning by a din of hollering coming from well beyond the shore at the Landing. Sometimes we would run down the path to look toward that distinctive yet familiar sound. Frequently, out towards the Island channel, were as many as half a dozen small dories, each carrying several crewmen, heading out from a much larger fishing vessel.

Brothers Neal, Calvin, and Weldon Willis in a skiff at the Landing. David's Dock and Fish house in the background.
(Used by permission)

The voices that had pierced the morning were the sound of those crewmen, mostly African Americans, working on a "shad boat" that had found a school of menhaden in the deeper water that was just a few hundred yards from the shoreline. Usually, after their catch had been surrounded by their net, the "chanteymen" would morph into a musical chorus of brilliant harmonies even while they tugged on the heavy nets they were charged with hauling aboard. Their ringing voices would echo across the calm water so clearly that it sounded as if they were as near as the foaming water line that marked the incoming tide.

"Shad boating" was done on an industrial scale in nearby Beaufort, down the southeast coast to the Florida Keys, and then back along the Gulf of Mexico all the way to Texas. But it required more organization and capital investment than the Islanders of my youth had to offer. Watching the large and coordinated crews of experienced seamen work from a distance was the closest that most of us growing up on the Island ever got to being part of that culture.

The men of Harkers Island were another kind of fishermen. For the most part, they worked hard — just as hard as those who tugged on the giant purse seines that were carried on the shad boats. But they worked at their own pace and at a rhythm set by their internal clocks rather than by the beat of a work song. They deliberately chose to be unshackled by the constraints of bosses, foremen, and time clocks.

Whatever their job, in or out of the water, being at home and in their own beds when the day's work was over was of primary importance. Within those parameters, they used their backs and their ingenuity together to support their families in the only ways most of them had ever known. They hoped that if they worked long and hard enough, their children would have a chance for an even better standard of living than they themselves ever had known.

For my father's generation, and even for my older brothers, working meant only one kind of work, and they called it "workin' the water." Building and repairing boats was an integral part of that occupation, especially since a Harkers Island waterman was obliged to be both a fisherman and a carpenter for either building or maintaining his various watercraft. Truthfully, it could be assumed that with very few exceptions, every full-time fisherman was a part-time boat builder, and that every full-time boat builder was a part-time fisherman. By mid-century, there were as many as half a dozen, sometimes more, boathouses on the Island. Each of them employed anywhere from two to ten carpenters who specialized in building and repairing boats of all sizes — from small skiffs to large trawlers and sport fishing head boats.

Even working on automobiles was directly related to being a waterman in a special way, as most boats were powered by an engine that once had been in a car or truck. How a motor might work in a boat when eventually it was moved from the dilapidated or rusted-out body of a clunker — which generally was the case with vehicles exposed to the corrosion consistent with continual exposure to salt air — was an important factor when deciding what kind of used "old car" to buy or salvage.

Understandably, working the water mostly involved being in and around the sound or ocean, and the "catching" of fish and shellfish.

Seasons, winds, and tides considered together largely determined their targets based on what they reasoned to be the most practical. Practicality was based upon what was least backbreaking and the most likely to offer the best potential for bringing a check from the fish dealers the next Friday evening. No matter how cold or hot, wet, or windy, there was something to be done.

Boats and fish houses along the south shore of the Island in the 1950's
CSWM&HC Collection

Most of the preparatory work had to do with nets: hanging the "cork and lead lines," or later spreading them on net spreads to dry, thus keeping the cotton mesh from rotting from the moisture. Preparations and clean-ups were important and could not be overlooked. But none of that would matter much unless at one time or another, fish, or shellfish of some kind and in suitable numbers could be found and brought to the docks and fish houses for sale.

For the dozens and even hundreds of watermen on the Island and up Core Sound, there were as many kinds, or at least patterns, of working the water as there were crews, or even single fishermen. Some would concentrate on shrimping in the summer and fall and do little of anything during the colder months. Others would wait until the fall for hauling and sink-netting for their money. Still others would depend on oystering, scalloping, crabbing, and clamming to make a living. Many if not most of them were involved in a combination of these endeavors at some time during the year. Without exception, fishermen used at least some of their catch to feed their own families. Seafood of every kind might be a part of any day's diet. But primarily, it was for earning cash and supporting their families that the men and boys of Harkers Island "worked the water."

From before I can remember, I was schooled, informally but repeatedly, in many of the nuances of how to do just that. I learned to tell the tide by looking at the moon or by observing the amount of foam that gathered at the water's edge, and to know that a low tide on a northeaster could be higher than a high tide on a southwester. I came to understand that it was much easier to navigate the many shoals and sandbars of the inland sound during a low tide than when it was high, because the low water made those obstacles easier to identify. I was taught that wind direction was all but conclusive in determining what, if anything, might be caught or harvested on any given day. I saw that the lifting power of the ocean waves could help to hoist a heavy sink net over the stern of a boat and that pulling too hard on the lead line of a set net could cause the loss of most of a catch by lifting the bunt from the bottom and allowing the fish to escape. These and dozens more lessons were taught not so much by dictation or explanation, but by hands-on observation.

How Much Would you Take Right Now For the Whole Mess?

Understandably, there were varying degrees of commitment among the various fishermen and crews who worked the waters off Harkers Island in my youth. Some, especially later generations, were inspired by a profitable day of fishing to return as early as possible, even the next morning, to try and add to their bounty. At the other end of the scale of devotion to their task were those who considered a good catch as a sign that they could, and even should, rest for the remainder of the week. According to this way of thinking, since money to pay for their next "grub bill" was now assured, there was no urgency to add to what was already secured.

Most of the Island crews were somewhere in between those two extremes.

My father, Charlie William, mending net at the Landing in 1979.
"Coastwatch" May 1979

My Uncle Louie was not. He most definitely sided with those who were comfortable with toiling with pulling ropes and clearing nets for as few hours and days as possible. He had been that way for most of his life, but as he grew older, he encouraged the rest of those whom he loved to follow his example. One late summer afternoon, he did his best to impose that approach on my brother Mike. Earlier that day, Mike had paired his boat with one belonging to his good friend, Frederick Willis (1934-2017). Together they set out to "long-haul" for yellow-fin spots in Back Sound between the Island and the Banks, at a special place called the "Pollywag." It was on the west end of the Island channel and extended to just off Ole' Pa's landing.

After several hours of using boats at each end to pull nets that were more than a thousand yards long, the two crews finally reached a point where they could draw the ends of the net together. As they did, they created an oval that became increasingly smaller until eventually, their entire catch was trapped inside a circle that was no more than thirty feet in diameter. The smaller the circle became, the more obvious it was that this time, they had hit a jackpot that would yield as much as several tons of fish for the market.

Harvesting and moving that many fish by hand could take all day and into the night and could make for many hours of long and hard lifting and pulling. As the crews began the work of clearing and culling their catch, and it was obvious that it was so large that it would take the remainder of the day to finish, my Uncle Louie oared his little skiff out to get a better look at what was going on. My father had done the same a few minutes earlier, and I was sitting beside him holding onto one of the lines of the bowl that the shrinking oval had formed. As he slipped in next to us, Uncle Louie also grabbed hold of the cork line of the net just beside us.

From our vantage point we had a direct view as the men were busy dipping their scoops in and out of where the bowl of the net was agitating with thousands of pounds of yellow-fin spots. The fish were packed together inside the seine so thickly that they were brimming the surface, and their yellow dorsal fins, from which they got their name, made the water itself assume a yellow glow. After watching the men hurry and strain for a few minutes, Uncle Louie called to Mike and asked him to come to where he could ask a question.

"How many fish do you reckon you got there?" he asked my brother as the two of them looked at the teeming mass just inside the cork lines.

"I don't know, Buddy," Mike responded as he tried to wager a guess to satisfy our uncle's curiosity. "There might be as many as two or three thousand pounds when we get 'em all loaded in."

After mulling some thoughts for just a moment, Uncle Louie came back with another question. "How much would you take right now for the whole mess — the fish, the nets, the lines, and everything?" he asked my brother, who by then was a little bewildered as to where the conversation might be headed.

"Again, Buddy, I don't know. It would be hard to say. Why do you need to know that?" He responded, trying to get to the bottom of what was being asked.

Without any further hesitation, my Uncle Louie, who had been part of hundreds of similar endeavors over the years, and who was recalling the toil and sweat that had to be expended before this day's work was over, explained what he had in mind.

"I want to buy the whole thing from you so I can cut it loose, and you and everybody else can go on home. I hate to see anybody punished as bad as you are gonna be by the time you leave here tonight."

Obviously, that deal was never closed, and after getting a bucket full of spots to take home and clean (prepare) for his own supper, Uncle Louie headed back to the shore and turned his back on that day's remaining labors. But his concern for what was left to be done was a fitting commentary on how older fishermen sometimes viewed the tasks that were so readily assumed by the succeeding generation.

Joining a Fishing Crew

Even beyond baseball and other competitive sports, the most significant benchmark for coming of age as a boy on the Island was when he became a part of a "fishing crew." For most of us, our first fishing crew experience was with our immediate family of father and brothers, and often uncles and cousins. But by the time I was ready to be a real and contributing part of one, rather than just the youngest son who watched more than helped, Daddy had left full-time fishing. When I was ten years old, he hired on as a carpenter and boat builder working for Julian Guthrie (1914-1998) at Hi-Tide Boat Works on the mainland at Williston. He still had his own fishing boat, but from that time forward, fishing, shrimping, and working in the water had become a supplemental income rather than his primary way of making a living.

Two years later, in the summer of 1964, when I turned twelve years old, I decided to make some money of my own, since by then, money had to be my own or not at all. Even though he then had what might be considered a regular job, my father's income as a boat builder left no money for anything that was not a necessity. That reservation applied especially to an adolescent son whom he assumed was now old enough to support himself, at least in part.

I had been able to make some money before, mostly by mowing lawns or by salvaging the glass bottles of soft drinks that littered the ditches and roadsides. Lawn mowing jobs were at the mercy of the season and the whims of the relatively few Islanders who cared to "cut the grass" for anything other than the walkway to the path or roadside. Gathering bottles, mostly in roadside ditches, and returning them for a penny apiece at any of the local stores could be done at your own discretion as the need arose. Even before the days of litter bags and "Keep America Beautiful," it took quite a while and a lot of effort to find and pick up the one hundred bottles needed for every dollar of earnings. In truth, the most you could expect to do with "bottle money" was to make enough to buy Dr Peppers and Moon Pies.

But I was entering a stage of life where my spending needs were getting beyond that, especially after Daddy built me a twelve-foot skiff from juniper scraps left over at the boathouse where he worked. Then, in what might have been the biggest financial investment he ever made for me, that was not food, shelter, or clothing, he paid $20 for a second-hand ten-horsepower Evinrude outboard motor. When placed on the back of my skiff, that "stern engine," and the handmade wooden oar that he made from a piece of oak timber, opened for me the much larger world of the Sound and the Banks, and eventually even the Beaufort Cut. Still, there was one large caveat. I had to have cash of my own to buy fuel to run the motor. Getting that money was entirely my responsibility.

So, early that summer, I decided to try what was at that moment the option of first resort for making quick money —opening scallops. Waking up before daybreak, I would grab my scallop knife and a pair of gloves made especially for shuckers, and head to the Landing and to David's dock. Once there, I would join a group of a dozen or more women and "youngerns," taking our places along the benches where a load of scallops brought to the dock that morning or the night before would be laid out on a long wooden shelf for "opening."

Playin' Ball and Workin' the Water

I never approached the proficiency of some of the more skilled shuckers, but I did reach a point that by dinner time each day, I could have earned as much as four dollars. Working more hours than that to make money to buy gas would have precluded the very venture that I was looking to finance. So, an all-day job would have defied all logic and the very reason I wanted a job in the first place. For that reason, and maybe a little laziness, I never spent more than a few hours of any one morning on the scallop house treadmill. In fact, I seldom, if ever, worked more than a couple of days in any given week. Two gallons, twice a week, could earn me eight dollars. That was sufficient to fill the five-gallon fuel tank that fed into my outboard motor. With money to spare, I could be in the boat every day and still have more left over for baseball cards and junk food at Dallas's, Norman's, or Edith's stores.

By mid-August and as the school year approached, my first taste of financial independence led me to look for something with the potential of a much bigger return. I convinced Daddy to ask Calvin Willis (1912-1978) if I could go with him when he started "mulleting" just a few weeks before school was set to begin immediately after Labor Day. Calvin and Daddy were cousins, but in many ways, they were more like brothers.

After the death of my grandmother when he was only four years old, Daddy spent much of his childhood in the next-door home of his maternal grandmother, Emeline. Calvin was her oldest grandson by her second marriage and lived in the same house with her and his parents, Rennie and Aunt Gracie. He was the same age as my father and the two of them had been inseparable friends. I can't imagine that Daddy could have asked Calvin for anything that would have been refused. This was in equal parts because neither would have asked anything of the other that he didn't really want or need, and because neither would have refused the other even if he did. So, when Daddy said he would ask, I knew I had earned the chance to be part of Calvin and Neal's fishing crew.

Neal (Willis 1926-1994) was Calvin's slightly younger brother and his sidekick in everything that either of them ever attempted. I really do mean everything, since neither of them ever married, and both seemed to spend every waking moment together. Calvin had a large fishing boat, over thirty feet long, named the "Barbara" after their youngest sister, and both owned nearly identical twenty-five-foot open boats that were known simply as Calvin's boat and Neal's boat. Most of their ventures were either together in just one of the boats, or when they were mulleting or long-hauling in the late summer and early fall and were obliged to use them both.

Because of how close they were, both in proximity and in relationship to Daddy, they were very much a part of my life. It was not unusual to wake up and find one of them sitting on our porch, or even in the den, waiting for Daddy to come down, or for Mama to start cooking breakfast. Neither of them ever had a regular job — meaning anything other than working in the water — so they seemed always to be nearby and around.

They were either hanging or mending nets, maintaining their equipment, or working to convert a junk engine that would someday end up in one of their boats. It was especially with the latter that they acquired a well-earned reputation for being able to "cuss" better than just about anybody on the Island. For them, "cussing" was not so much a profanity as a folk song through which they vented against whatever frustrations they had in trying to make a living in the sound.

Rest assured, neither of them was the kind to use curse words as part of a normal conversation. You could walk and work with them all day, or even all week, and never hear one of them use a single word of profanity. But when they were head-over-heels in preparing or repairing something for their boats, and especially when they worked on the dilapidated car engines that they routinely transformed into marine motors, things didn't always work as they wanted.

Sometimes the engine would not start, or if it did, it would miss on one or more cylinders, or a wrench would slip when trying to work off a bolt or nut, or a belt would break just when they thought they had a starter or generator ready to go. From out of nowhere, shot out a voice loud enough to be heard all over the neighborhood. Either or both would let loose with a litany of profanity and curses that would turn into a rhythmic verse of cussing that was both long and loud. Then, just as abruptly as it had begun, it would wane, and within a minute or two, they would be back on task and working away.

Since it was so routine and understood, most of us didn't even think of it as profanity, at least not in the same vein as if uttered by someone other than them. As I said earlier, it was more like a chant, or even an elegiac poem that expressed frustration and vexation more than a lack of reverence or wanton disrespect. Especially since they both were otherwise so meek and even gentle, most of us came to understand their cussing, and to excuse it as an aberration rather than as a character flaw.

It was this same kind and gentle Calvin that I will tell about later who loved and doted over his stray dog that I was looking to go fishing with, and not the one who sometimes cussed as if he were singing to sailors. And it was this Calvin that readily agreed that I could be part of his crew once mulleting started in mid-August, or at least until school started, and took me away from doing anything useful in the morning. For the next three weeks, I woke up before the sun broke over Eastard Banks and walked to the Landing where I would meet up with Calvin and Neal, and with a much older, Luther Willis (1894-1968), who rounded out our crew. Together we would oar a skiff out to the deeper water and to either Calvin or Neal's open boat, already outfitted with several hundred yards of mullet net, and head into the rising sun to start looking for mullets.

It was the "looking for" part that was the primary reason why the captains were not only willing but even anxious that I go with them as part of their crew. Despite my youth, or rather because of it, I had something that neither of them still did, the sharp eyes and clear vision that could see a solitary mullet as it jumped and cleared the water on a placid morning in Core Sound. Mullets are somewhat unique in that they gather in large schools, but usually only one, or at most two of them, will betray their location by jumping up and clearing the water as if ready to fly. Then they splash back down below the surface with a distinctive "swoosh" and a cascade of water.

Calvin used to say that if you saw one mullet jump, it meant there were a hundred more that you could not see. My job, or at least my assignment, was to stand on the forward "thought" — that was how Harkers Islanders pronounced "thwart," the bench seat that ran across the beam of an open boat — and keep a lookout for anything that broke the water. That in and of itself might seem like an easy and simple job, but it didn't always turn out to be that way — at least not for me.

The "looking" itself was not all that difficult, but maintaining concentration and staying awake could be a whole lot harder. Try and imagine what it would be like to be moving along very slowly and gently in an open boat, just after sunup and after having been aroused from sleep at least two hours before my normal wake up time. The salty air was heavy, and the boat engine was running so softly as to sound more like the purring of a kitten than the clanging of pistons. Add to that the fact that I was generally staring into the rising sun that was getting brighter and harder on my eyes with every passing minute. The result was that one of the things I remember most about my mulleting career is how hard it was to keep my eyes open. I must admit that there were a few times that my head fell forward, jerking my neck, and thereby reporting my condition to Calvin and the others. I remember that one time he asked me, with affection and with humor, if I wanted him to put me ashore so I could go to sleep.

My father, Charlie Hancock, doing finishing work on his last fishing boat, the "Miss Margarette"

Calvin and Neal were among the best and most respected fishermen ever to work the sounds and shores of the Banks and the Island. Fishing was their livelihood and a major portion of their lives. They wanted to catch as many fish as they could and then sell them for as much as possible. So, there was an urgency in their endeavors, even if there was no sense of rush or hurry in their efforts. They brought me with them so I could help them both to find the mullets, and then to catch them. I didn't want to let them down. At least, as far as I could tell, I don't think that I ever did. My recollection is that though we never caught enough that people would gather around the dock to watch us unload, we always seemed to catch enough to justify both the time and the expense of a long morning on the water.

Boats are always given names that are important to the family owning the boat. My mother was particularly happy when my father named his last big boat after his wife," Miss Margarette."

Next to my father and brothers, Calvin and Neal were the ones who taught me most about what it was like to be a progger and a fisherman. All these years later I still can envision an image of them standing together behind the steering stick of their vessel. They are silhouetted against a rising sun and headed towards Barden's Inlet at the east end of the Island. Once there, they will turn either for the bays off Shackleford, the Hook of the Cape, or even offshore into the ocean. No matter what their chosen destination, they will reverse their course sometime before sundown and head back towards our landing. When finally, they have moored their boat and made their way onto the shore, they will have logged yet another day of "workin' the water."

Aerial photo of the middle of the island taken in the late 1940's. The fish houses along the shore are those of Danky Willis and Cecil Nelson. Carl Lewis's store sits across from the Methodist Church at the bottom of photo.
(Used by permission of Gary Bacon)

7

Kith & Kin — Women & Men

Granpa said back before his time "kinfolks" meant any folks that you understood and had an understanding with, so it meant "loved folks."
                    Forrest Carter, "The Education of Little Tree"

I grew up surrounded by family and kinfolk; and not just figuratively, but literally as well. Because of the way they shaped both my character and personality, they were also among my most important teachers. Life lessons were written in daily conversations that were illustrated on a chalkboard of ongoing and day-to-day routines. They were heard in stories while sitting on a porch or under a tree, or while standing around a net spread, or on the gunnel of a fishing boat.

Through them, I came to know my deceased ancestors as intimately as if they were still walking along the shore or up the path to the Landing. And the binding ties were as much horizontal as vertical for they served to tie me to my living and contemporary kinfolk even more as I was made aware of our multi-generational bonds.

"That's the same as when ...," "He looks (or acts) just like ...," or "I'll never forget about ...," introduced so many sentences that the lines that followed those phrases eventually drew pictures in my mind. These have, in turn, left images that are as clear and alive today as when they were first uttered to me more than half a century ago.

The Education of an Island Boy

Still, it is the people themselves, even more than their lessons and stories that linger in my consciousness.

But it is only with the stories told by or about them that I can hope to convey something about why and how a small group of people

One of the "scallop house" crowds
CSWM&HC Collection

in a tiny neighborhood on a remote coastal island were able to leave such a lasting and happy impression upon a young boy's mind and heart.

What follows is a collection of stories and anecdotes — some of them sublime, others verging on ridiculous — about a few of the more memorable people of my neighborhood, all of whom were family. Later chapters will focus on other persons and tales about Islanders that I knew and who helped to form and give color to the world and lifestyle I inherited. These stories are intended to serve only as a glimpse of some of the interesting characters that were around me every day.

Also it is more a tapestry than a single or coherent narrative. Obviously, each of these anecdotes offers only an incomplete picture of the rich canvas that was their lives. But taken together, they provide a window that opens into the time, place, and extended family in which their stories unfold, and where I grew up.

Aunt Gracie's Scrambled Eggs

Everyone called her "Aunt Gracie." Maybe her children and grandchildren didn't, but nearly everyone else did. Perhaps it was because there were so many nieces and nephews, Hamiltons, Willises, and Hancocks — or more likely because she perfectly fit the mold of what an ideal aunt was supposed to be. She just seemed like she should be everybody's aunt.

She was born Gracie Hamilton in 1896 (d. 1976). She and her husband, Rennie Willis (1884-1940), had nine children of their own; eight of whom grew to be adults. Most of them lived within a short stone's throw of their mama's porch, and two of her boys, Calvin (1912-1978) and Neal (1926-1994), remained in the same house they were born in all their long lives. But it was the many offspring of her eight siblings that grew in numbers so large that it may have caused her to be identified as everyone's "aunt." Add to that her kind and gentle nature, the nurturing attention she offered to everyone who caught her eye, and the way she shared her home and food with anyone who passed her way, and you can better understand why she was considered as family by everyone who knew her.

"Aunt Gracie" with her granddaughter Veta Ann Willis.
(Used by permission)

Aunt Gracie's home sat on the Island's south shore, facing the Banks and directly to the west of Ole Pa's place. Her husband,

Rennie, had been born just a few feet further to the west in a house built by his parents, Cal Farr Willis (1856-1923) and Emeline (1853-1923). Emeline was my great-grandmother. There was a small stoop porch facing the Landing, and from her kitchen window she had a view of the dock that belonged to Rennie's brother, Danky, and the many boats, large and small, that dotted the shoreline. On the north side of her home was a long porch, with a swing and several rockers, that looked out on a small pasture, called "Rennie's Field," and in every direction she could see the huddled homes of legions of her immediate and extended families.

In front of her home there was a dirt path that ran directly parallel to the one beside our house and on the west side of Aunt Ezzer's and Uncle Louie's. At various points it was cobbled with clam, scallop, and oyster shells, and led directly from the porch to the Island's main road that was no more than two hundred feet to the no'thard. Beside the path was a drainage ditch that was sometimes maintained by the county using prison workers as laborers, but the trench itself usually was so full of brush and vegetation that it was more a lengthy mud pond than an outlet for run-off water.

There was a constant stream of traffic up and down that path of people headed to and from Aunt Gracie's porch. Some may have been on specific errands, but most were just part of the daily flow of friends and family who viewed her home as a gathering place.

Among those frequent visitors was a peddler from Marshallberg, Julian Brown (1871-1961). "Mr. Brown," as he was called, was known by everyone and revered by many, not just at his native Marshallberg, but anywhere from Beaufort east and north to Cedar Island. He was especially recognized at Harkers Island. In fact, Browns Island, the much smaller and uninhabited island that sits between the mainland and Harkers Island with only Eastmouth Bay in between, took its name from his family who had owned it for as long as anyone still living could remember.

Julian Brown was tall and heavy set, what his generation called "stout," with a full head of graying hair. He was as much an "entrepreneur" as a peddler, at least in the early 20th-century connotation of that title. He did some farming and fishing, raised livestock on his privately owned island, and marketed his crops, catch, and other assorted wares up and down Core Sound. He was renowned for several things, including his skills as a trader, his thriftiness, his generous heart, and most especially for his immense appetite. In short, his personality and his reputation were much larger, relatively speaking, than the small island he used to pasture his herds of sheep, goats, and cattle."

It was said that Julian Brown would open his home, and especially his kitchen, to anyone who needed it or him. In return, he expected and assumed that others should be similarly charitable to him should he ever need it. As he worked his way along the shores of Core Sound, when mealtime arrived, he was prone to drop in on whatever friend was nearest by, and then join them at their table. His impromptu visits were so commonplace that, eventually, they were expected and taken for granted.

Julian Brown
(Used by permission)

Early one summer morning, while peddling his wares at the Island, Julian Brown made his way up Gracie's path and to her kitchen as she was preparing breakfast for her children. Treating him just like she did her own, she continued to crack and fry egg after egg, as many as her skillet could hold, and kept dropping them onto the plate of whomever seemed ready for another serving. After a while, all the children had left the table, but Julian Brown remained in his seat and accepted every new portion his hostess placed in front of him.

Eventually, both he and Aunt Gracie noticed that, along with the biscuits, bacon, and potatoes, Julian had finished off the last of the eggs still available. Uncertain if anything else was wanted or expected, Aunt Gracie got his attention and asked if he was aware that, so far, he had eaten a full dozen eggs. Washing down his meal with a cup of coffee that had been refreshed several times, the grateful visitor took stock of the situation and then responded to his host with a compliment and a simple request.

"They were really good, Aunt Gracie," he offered, "but if you cook any more eggs, would you please scramble 'em?"

"Dack" and the Egg Man

Near the westward end of our family neighborhood was the office of the Rural Electrification Administration, known most simply as the REA. The acronym was for one of the many programs that dated back to Franklin Roosevelt's New Deal. Its stated purpose was to extend electrical power via local cooperatives to small and remote communities that were still without it more than three decades after electric lighting had become commonplace in more urban areas. Harkers Island was the very first community in the entire country to get electrical power using an underwater cable. The relative timing and the way it was delivered mattered little to most Islanders, but the facility that housed the REA's operations was a source of great pride to the entire community. Right beside that building was Dallas's store, and when it came to the daily routines of boys in our neighborhood, that store was just as vital.

Dallas (Guthrie 1915-1964) was a son of Cliff (1888-1967) and Carrie "Cottie" Guthrie (1894-1985), whose house and yard joined ours on the southeast corner. His wife, "Little" Ollie (Willis 1901-1979), was my Daddy's first cousin through her father Danny (Danky) Willis (1891-1952), and the brother of Gracie's husband Rennie. At Dallas's store neighborhood boys would gather in packs, especially when his son, Dallas Daniel (1942-2014), whom most of us called "Dack," was behind the counter. Dack was the same age as my brother Mike and, thus, ten years older than me. But for years he had kept a firm grip on his "extended adolescence" so that he was a virtual contemporary with boys who were as much as two decades his younger.

There was something else besides the store that caused boys and young men to gather in such numbers all around him. Behind the store and his parent's house was what could have been labeled as the "Harkers Island Zoo." It was disguised as a chicken coup nestled under a bevy of oaks and cedars, but mostly that was just a façade for what really was there. To be sure, there was an assortment of chickens — Bantams, White Leghorns, Dominics, Rhode Island Reds, and others — and there were just as many breeds of ducks and geese.

But at various times, there were also calves, goats, sheep, guinea pigs, marsh hens, rabbits, and any other animal or bird to which Dack might have taken a liking. During the summer months, there were usually one or more horses grazing in the backyard. And because of how he nurtured and tended his menagerie, especially when they were sick or injured, Dack often was referred to as the Island's own "veterinarian."

Early on, Dack had been a victim of one of the many polio epidemics of the era. Poliomyelitis was such a scourge that my mother told of keeping her children inside on the hottest days of summer, fearing that heat and humidity were a contributing factor in contracting the disease. In later years, she often spoke of her appreciation and admiration for Dr. Jonas Salk, the researcher most often credited with developing a vaccine that all but removed that disease from existence. Before he did, it had left one of Dack's legs much weaker and less developed than the other so that by the time I knew him he had a noticeable limp.

But beyond that, Dank was a strong and well-built young man who could "lift weights" as well as any, and better than most of the troupe of youngsters who always were around him. When he tended the counter at his daddy's store, he usually kept his thin and short-sleeved shirt at least partially unbuttoned so that his large chest and stomach muscles could have ample "room to breathe." In fact, during the hottest summer months, he was as often shirtless as not. On one memorable sweltering summer afternoon, as many as a dozen boys were wasting away the afternoon on the store's aging wooden benches and in front of the window fan that ran from sunup to sundown. That was when we saw Dack put on a show that none of us would ever forget.

One of the regular visitors at the store was the "Egg Man." He was called that because at least once every week he would deliver and drop off several dozen freshly laid eggs from his backyard coop to be resold at retail in nearby country stores, including Dallas's. On this day there was a new egg man, one that none of us recognized and who was subbing for the regular vendor who, for whatever reason, could not make that day's rounds. Recognizing his wares, if not his person, Dack decided to greet the newcomer in his own unique way. Knowing him as we did, I and the others who had wasted the better part of our morning doing nothing useful could tell that something was up.

At first, Dack proceeded to welcome the new delivery man as if everything were normal. Suddenly, and without any obvious warning, he began to say over and over, "I feel one coming on me!" but a little louder and with more urgency each time he repeated it. That phrase, "I feel one coming on me," was recognized by us as a verbal signal that something unusual was about to happen.

Then, in a flash and without any further warning, he rolled across the counter and landed lying on his back on the main floor of the store, where he commenced kicking, screaming, and hollering – seemingly uncontrollably. Seconds later, the egg man, leaving behind his cartons, had bolted from the store, jumped into his truck, and headed toward the west'ard. In just a moment, Dack was back on his feet and behind the counter, acting as if nothing at all out of character had happened.

At the very same time we who had been witness struggled to recover not from our fear but from our laughter. Just as remarkable as what had just happened was the understanding that what we had beheld was quite unremarkable – at least in this setting. So, that was the end of it. According to Dack when I asked him about it many years later, no one had heard from that same egg man ever again.

The Prettiest Sound in the Whole World

Depending on his mood, Dack could entertain us for hours telling stories of what he had heard from the parade of shoppers and loiterers who came in and out of his store during a given day. Aside from those tales, lingering at the store gave young boys like me an exposure to stories told by the older men who often dropped by on lazy summer and fall afternoons; many of them were told in a vein and about subjects that would have been avoided in the more polite and mixed company of older family and friends.

One day Dack shared with us an account of a conversation he had the evening before with two of his friends, one of them much older than he or the other. From the way he explained and told it, we sensed right away that this was one of those stories we had best not repeat to or around our parents.

He related that the subject had arisen as to what was "the prettiest sound a man would ever hear?" Dack himself had been the first to offer his opinion. An avid hunter who kept a large array of hounds in a nearby kennel, he maintained that the sweetest sound he had ever heard was "the special bark and howl of hunting dogs as they locked in on the smell of a deer in the woods." That sound alone would arouse the thrill of the chase and hunt that was soon to follow. "Nothing," he explained, "could ever sound better than that."

His cousin of about the same age, "Peter" (Weldon Edward Willis 1945-2010), who lived directly beside him, was the next to chime in with an opinion. "No," he interrupted; there was something even better than the sound of dogs on a chase. For Peter, a waterman through and through, the sweetest sound in the world was one that could be heard only on a calm summer evening when "setting a mullet net" around a shoal or rock in the marshes off Shackleford Banks. If everything went exactly right, in the stillness of a moonlit night, you would hear the chorus of "swashes" that meant a school of mullets had just hit your net. "That," he argued, "was the sweetest sound a man could ever want to hear."

Weldon Edward Willis "Peter"

Listening nearby was an older and more experienced friend (to remain nameless) who had built and earned quite a reputation as a philanderer. He had paid close attention as the younger boys gave their take on what sounds aroused the fondest emotions a man could imagine. "You're both wrong," he explained as he stood to his feet and prepared to head out of the store and back into the real world. "The prettiest sound in the world, and believe me, I know, is to be in the woods at night, waiting for a woman who has agreed to meet you — and hearing the leaves begin to rustle!"

Pickin' Mule Hairs

Another of my older cousins, Paul Hancock (1944-2008), lived directly across the road from our house. He was eight years older than me, but because we shared so many interests and he was always so nearby, he remains a fixture in many of my childhood memories. He and his close friend, "Sambo Pete" (Guthrie 1944-1997), who lived up the road to the west'ard at what was called "Red Hill," loved to play "strikeout," a two-man baseball game played with a rubber ball, in his side yard. They were happy to let me chase foul balls and wild pitches for them.

But most of all, and even more than baseball, Paul was enthusiastically into "rooster fighting;" at least the mostly benign kind that we practiced on the Island, where we were satisfied to let the birds prance and cackle for a while as they danced in circles without ever coming to blows. The roosters themselves were much too valuable and dear for us to have risked their being hurt in a real fight. Paul always had several "game roosters" in a chicken-wired pen behind his house, and I was often beside him when he fed and sometimes groomed them early in the morning.

Years later and long since I had outgrown my childhood interest in chickens, and after Paul had served a stint in the US Army, Paul regained his interest in the fighting birds, and eventually, his involvement extended to the "real fights" that by then were illegal almost everywhere. So, several times every summer he would borrow his father's car and be gone for a day or more pursuing his latest passion. Traveling to places as far away as western Virginia and central South Carolina, he would come back home each time with a set of stories about his adventures that would entertain his friends for weeks to come. How he was able to learn about where and when these covert events were scheduled in the days before modern mass communication remains a mystery.

One time, while driving to South Carolina late one evening, he had the misfortune of running his car headlong into a stray mule that had wandered onto the darkened highway somewhere just before he reached the state line. He was not badly hurt, but the mule paid the ultimate price, and his father's Plymouth was totally ruined. The car's front end was smashed like an accordion from the front bumper to the steering wheel, and the mule itself had been thrown so high that it crashed through the front windshield.

The next day, Paul was back at home, thankfully not seriously injured, but with a story much different from the ones he usually related. And this time, and long after the accident itself, my cousin was constantly spitting, seemingly for no reason. Eventually, when asked why, he laid the blame directly on the car wreck of the wasted weekend as he explained, "It seems like all I'm ever doing now is pickin' the mule hairs out of my teeth."

Donald Guthrie- We Ain't Gonna Get Nowhere if You Keep Stopping

One of the most colorful and best-loved characters in our neighborhood was a distant cousin, Donald Guthrie (1923-2004). Some folks called him by both his first and middle name, "Donald Eukirk," but even more referred to him as "Red-Headed Donald." By the time he reached middle age, his red hair had turned mostly white, but even then, he was known for the color of his youthful mane.

Donald's parents, Willie (1898-1966) and Carrie (Moore 1903-1985) Guthrie lived just a few houses up the path from us, but his paternal grandmother, Evoline, was our next-door neighbor. For whatever reason, Donald spent as many days and nights with her as at home, and thus he was very much a part of our family's everyday lives.

His was one of the few generations of Island boys who had the privilege of herding horses on the Banks, and it was said that no one was better at it than he. The wild ponies of Shackleford were rounded up at least once a year, sometimes more than that, and steered into a pen that had been built near the shore of where Diamond City once had been. Unlike elsewhere, where cowboys

The Education of an Island Boy

rode their own horses to herd mustangs, the ponies on the Banks were driven by mostly young men who ran behind and beside them as they were guided into a waiting corral.

Donald had a reputation for being able to run fast and for long distances without rest. In addition, he had acquired a keen sense of how to think like horses as they galloped freely along the shore or through dunes and thickets. As he chased behind them, he was often heard shouting out directions to others, and usually was able to herd the galloping ponies in exactly the direction he wanted.

His running came in handy for more than horses — he was equally adept at herding sheep. On one occasion he was put ashore from a sailskiff at Drum Inlet, twenty miles north along Core Banks from Cape Lookout. His job was, by himself, to run a small herd of sheep along the beach towards the Cape. The plan was for another runner to meet him off Davis Island, the midpoint of the journey, and there relieve him and pick up the chase. But Donald was so good at moving the sheep that he reached the juncture even before the boat and crew, and thus just kept on moving to the south'ard. When the rest of the group finally got to their destination near the Lighthouse, they found the sheep already safely in their pen. Donald was sitting alone on the railing, his feet swinging in the wind, and, according to one of those who were with him, nothing left of the shoes he had been wearing but the strings still dangling around his ankles.

Even more endearing to most of us than his speed afoot was his flair for saying some of the funniest things you could ever imagine, even when it was not intentional on his part.

An oft-told story is of the summer morning when he went to his father's small boat, "The Ram," that was moored close to the shore at the Landing. In those days, the late 1930s, battery-powered starters were not yet available for the gasoline engines that had all but replaced sails and oars. In lieu of electrical starters, the boaters used metal hand cranks to jerk the crankshaft of the engine and start the ignition. This morning, when Donald reached for his crank and prepared to head out on the water, the crank was nowhere to be found! He searched all over his boat to no avail, and the harder he searched, the more annoyed he became.

Finally, reasoning that further searching was useless, and assuming that someone had pilfered the crank, his frustration reached a boiling point. Tied to a stake in the southerly breeze, the aft of his boat pointed directly at the shoreline where it was typical for scores of people to be gathered as they worked away on the boats, nets, and net spreads. Hollering to get their attention, he climbed on the stern gunwale and screamed at the top of his voice, "Whoever stole that crank is a damned liar, ... and I can do it too!" Obviously, his boast had no real meaning other than to express his frustration. But those who had heard him clearly gathered as much and knew to stay out of Donald's way for the next little while.

When he was drafted into the Army shortly before the Normandy invasion in 1944, Donald's talent as a runner was soon made evident. And it was also clear that he carried with him his penchant for making others laugh. Donald loved to tell a story about when, early in his basic training, his company set out on a twenty-mile hike. At the midway point, the drill sergeant called his men to a halt to give them a rest. When Donald, who early on had assumed the lead and was setting the pace for the march, heard the order to "halt," he ran up to his commander. Then, while pumping his arms and legs to remain in motion, he exclaimed, "I'll tell you, sergeant, we ain't gonna get nowhere if you keep stopping every ten miles!"

Donald Guthrie
CSWM&HC Collection

Because of his experience as a waterman, after basic training, Donald was deployed on the coast of France and assigned to a unit that ferried soldiers back and forth from their ships to the staging area. An important part of that job was keeping the boats running by servicing and repairing the engines and other mechanical equipment. His sergeant there was not nearly so experienced in working on watercraft or around the water, and Donald grew increasingly frustrated at having to be instructed about things he already knew. Eventually, he went over the head of his sergeant to the commanding officer and demanded, "Can I be transferred to the infantry?"

Amazed and even dumbfounded, the officer was speechless for a moment. "Why in the world," a startled lieutenant eventually Donald, "would anyone want to leave the safety of a motor pool and ask to be sent to the front lines of battle?"

"Because" Donald replied, "I can't stand to stay in a job where I know more 'bout it than the one who's giving me orders!"

His request was considered but denied, and soon after the end of fighting in Europe, he was back home running horses and sheep and entertaining everyone in the neighborhood with his wartime stories.

Blind Lilly

My Daddy's aunt, Lilly Larson (1870-1942), was blind and had been since birth. Like many others with her condition, she learned to compensate for the loss of one sense by the sharpening of another. For her, it was her touch. Her fingers became her "eyes" of a sort. With them, she not only negotiated around the home and neighborhood, but more especially, she learned to recognize faces by their feel. She would make her way around a room, feeling as she moved to learn and then recognize the chins, noses, ears, and even the eyelids of the people she knew and loved.

"Blind Lilly"

She was the older daughter of my great-grandparents, Louie and Emeline Larson. Left fatherless at only two years old, she became part of her mother's new family after Emeline married Calvin Farr Willis and moved her two small children, including my grandmother Agnes, to the spot adjacent to what later would become Hancock Landing. She would live there with her mother and other relatives from that point on. She was soon surrounded by a mushrooming group of relatives, including her sister and her two half-brothers, and seemingly countless cousins, nephews, and nieces. Because of her disability, she never married or lived on her own and remained dependent on her family for sustenance throughout her entire life.

Even as others most certainly could see and sense her disability, she remained happily oblivious to any distinction and was content in knowing that she was a special part of her extended family. She moved freely about the pack of houses that made up her small world as her friends and family served as both her eyes and her guardians.

As Lilly grew older, the physical deformities associated with her blindness became increasingly pronounced and apparent, but by then she was so familiar that it was more a distinction than a difference. Rather than intimidating the children she met, her soft hands, accompanied by her gentle voice, evolved into a welcoming ritual that was comforting and not at all frightening. It was familiarity as much as sensation that allowed young children to feel so comfortable in her presence.

Lilly had passed on before I was born, but she was very much a part of the day-to-day lives of my older brothers and sisters. Once, looking at a picture of her as an aged woman, and noticing the obvious deformity in her eyes, I asked my older brother, Tommy, if he was uneasy or scared by her in any way. "Scared?" he responded, "Why would you fear somebody you loved so much?"

An aged woman, carrying all the baggage of a lifetime without sight, was comfortably at home around an entire neighborhood of children of all ages. She, like dozens of her contemporaries, was not confined to an institution, or even to a secluded corner. She remained very much a part of the world she had known from her own childhood. For Tommy and the others in his age group, intimacy and affection had allowed love and compassion to overcome the innate tendency of children and adolescents to shy away from anyone they considered unfamiliar or unusual. A lack of the same familiarity, especially with older people, could be why so many of today's youngsters seem so uneasy in the company of some adults, even if their only deformity is being older and a stranger.

Except for a few formative years with Ol' Pa, my paternal grandfather, and his enduring influence and aura, I never knew my grandparents. But that does not mean that my childhood was devoid of time with and around older, even aged people. On the contrary, old people; aunts, uncles, older cousins, and scores more whose exact relationship I didn't really know at the time, were a constant part of my daily childhood experience. Indeed, they were both the source and subject of most of the tales that have formed the fabric of these stories.

In a time before rest homes and assisted living, there was no place for aging, even infirm seniors to be other than with their younger family members, either nuclear or extended. As I learned to love and respect that older generation, I also gained an appreciation and confidence in interacting with them individually and as a group. Having to listen more attentively and speak a little more clearly and slower was a small price to pay for the lessons they told and taught.

They Were Keeping Me Awake at Night

In early spring each year, the brownness of the Harkers Island winter gives way to abundant greenery that marks the height of the blooming and growing season. On the map, it may look like just another sandbar of the lower Outer Banks, a large shoal at the junction of Core and Back Sounds. But the Island has surprisingly rich soil as evidenced by the lush vegetation that covers both the virgin and developed plots for at least nine to ten months of every year. I don't know that there was ever anything here that was large enough to have been considered a farm, but there were lots of gardens — a whole lot of them —and they were all over the Island, from Red Hill and Oak Hammock to Academy Field and Shell Point.

Summer gardens had a little corn, and maybe a few beans, but they were mostly for tomatoes and cucumbers. A few sweet potatoes were planted in the early fall, and some "Arse" (Irish) potatoes in the early spring. Winter gardens were generally a domain for collards, and after the first frost, you could smell them being cooked with fatback everywhere you went.

"Will Odie" (Willie O. Guthrie 1893-1986) had one of the biggest gardens. It was beside his house, nested at the foot of Red Hill, and it seemed as if something was growing there year-round, as he could be seen in his garden as often as every day. Aaron Moore (1898-1970), just up the path from our house, also had a large garden, and he nurtured it as if it were a baby. He spent many hours either bent over pulling weeds or chopping with a hoe to cultivate the soil. His efforts were well-rewarded, for him and the whole neighborhood, when his potatoes and corn were ready for digging or picking.

The same shad and pinfish that were used to bait crab pots, or thrown to the gulls, were often used for fertilizer. I recall seeing Aaron with a shovel, opening a crease in the soil next to his plants, and then dropping a small shad into the hole just close enough to the root so as not to "burn it" with nitrogen when it decayed. He must have known what he was doing, because his garden was always green and grew so tall that we children sometimes could hide inside the corn rows.

While it was true that many families had a garden, nearly every home had a chicken coop or pen. The sound of hens cackling and roosters crowing in the morning was even more familiar than the squawking of gulls and shore birds. As a child, I was often sent to the coop early in the morning to gather eggs. Several times each year, Mama would allow the hens to "set," and soon there would be a bevy of "biddies" following close behind their own mama as she scratched around our yard.

It was while observing this phenomenon that I came to appreciate a saying that I would hear and use all my life. Once you have been around one, you will know exactly what is meant when someone is said to be "as mad as a wet-setting hen." Even after having experienced that firsthand, I came to enjoy being around chickens so much that I eventually had both a "Bantam" and a "Warhorse Game" rooster of my very own.

But chickens were kept for more than their eggs. I can't say that I ever got used to the ordeal of watching my father trap and capture a hen, and then "wring its neck" so that Mama could clean and cook it for supper. In fact, I tried hard not to watch and usually would run to the Landing or hide behind my Daddy's "little house" (shed) so that I wouldn't have to see it. My reservations must have been limited because I was usually there to watch as my mother plucked or else "singed" away the feathers, and then cut the torso, legs, and wings into enough parts that all of us had at least one piece of fried chicken that night for supper.

My Uncle Louie had both a large garden and a small chicken coop. That was especially so after he married his second wife, Verna, who had been raised on a farm at Core Creek, several miles inland from the Sounds and a prime farming area. Once they were together, he and she had something to eat out of that garden for every meal. The chicken coop was filled with a dozen or more "Rhode Island Reds" that would lay a fresh supply of eggs every day. They cackled so loud you could hear them even when the windows were shut. His garden plot was just to the westward of his house, and the chicken coop was to the southward of the garden. In early summer, the garden and chickens, along with several large fig trees, a grapevine, a silver maple, a persimmon tree, and an old hand pump on the edge of his porch, turned the southwest part of his yard into a bucolic dreamscape.

Eventually, after both he and Verna grew too old to "mess" with the chickens any longer, he got rid of the coop and extended his garden to where the chickens had been for several decades. In that small plot, maybe six by ten feet, but no larger, he planted some peppers and tomatoes. Anyone who has ever struggled to grow either of them can imagine what those tomato plants looked like as they took root in soil that had been organically fertilized for such a long time. It was so much a phenomenon that my Daddy and others would go by every evening to see just how much taller they had grown that day.

Ultimately, on one of his visits, he found the tomato plants lying on their side and piled together for the trash heap. My uncle had cut them down. When asked why, he quickly explained that "the tomatoes had become more of a bother than they were worth. They grew so fast that the noise they were making was keeping me awake at night!"

A Goat in Bed with Me!

That same Uncle Louie had been born seventeen years before my father and was like a father to his younger brother. Daddy had even lived with Big Buddy for a while after my father, as a young boy, had "run away" from their father's new home in Beaufort. As they grew older together, Daddy was careful never to do anything to offend or worry his older sibling, and as Big Buddy grew frail late in his life, Daddy took it upon himself to be a caretaker as well as a brother.

For as long as I can remember, a day never passed that the two of them did not spend at least some time together. And since our yards were adjoining, and our homes less than a hundred feet apart, it was as if the two families were one.

Uncle Louie, "Big Buddy" in his yard at the Landing mending net.

After the passing of his first wife, France (Rebecca Francis Guthrie b. 1895) in 1941, Big Buddy had been left alone at home with his youngest son, Louie Hallas (1930-2007). His three older boys, Linwood (1914-2007), Guyon (1917-2007), and Norman (1920-2008) by then all were married and on their own.

My older brothers, Tommy and Bill, were close in age to Louie Hallas, and the three of them did practically everything together. Once, the group decided that they wanted a "billy goat" for a pet, and so their fathers conceded to buy a pair of them from a farmer in North River, at a place called "Thomas's Turn," near what is now East Carteret High School. Early one spring morning, Daddy and Uncle Louie, along with Louie Hallas, Tommy, and Bill, who nestled together on the rumble seat in the rear, set out in Uncle Louie's automobile to make the purchase. By dinner time, they were all home, including two young goats that the boys held in their arms all the way back to the Island.

For a while, the whole neighborhood was excited, and the goats were the focus of everyone's attention. But after that brief period, as so often happens, the boys gradually lost their interest. The much-desired pets simply became another part of the neighborhood menagerie that also included pigs, chickens, dogs, cats, and sometimes even a horse.

Because Uncle Louie always maintained a garden, the goats spent most of their time there and amid a grove of fig and persimmon trees. They usually spent nights on his back porch, next to a hand pump and a tin can full of water used to prime the pump when it was empty. Near the middle of that porch was a window to the sitting room of the house through which southwesterly winds would flow on sultry summer nights. That made it an ideal place for slumbering away in the morning for an older man who hours earlier had left his regular bed after he had been awakened by the persistent alarm clock of old age.

The goats were resting on that porch one summer morning when a pre-dawn thunderstorm culminated with a strike of lightning and a loud clap of thunder. In less than a second, one of the goats bolted away from the light and noise, and directly through the screen that filled the open window beside the daybed where Big Buddy was sleeping. The whole neighborhood was startled by the clamor, including my father, who jumped from where he had been sleeping and hurried to see what had happened.

He found Uncle Louie still in his underwear and standing on his back porch while trying to clean up debris from the broken screen and window frame. Before Daddy could ask what had transpired, his older brother blurted out to tell him.

"I don't really know what it was other than that I woke up and found a goat in bed with me!" By the next weekend, both goats were gone.

The Closest I Ever Come to Having a Job.

Late in the summer of 1976, I returned home to Harkers Island. With me were my wife and our little girl, Emily, who was less than a year old. Coming home meant more than finding a place to stay. Even more urgent at the moment was that it meant finding a way to support my family. We were welcome to live with Mama and Daddy until we could arrange to get our mobile home moved from Greenville to the then vacant lot we had purchased from my Uncle Earl here on Lewis Street, and on which we have remained ever since. But finding a job was not quite so simple.

Every morning, I would head into town and check out leads I had read or heard about. Days turned into weeks, and I was getting a little discouraged as the pittance I was making mowing lawns and clamming (both Susan and I) was not enough to meet our needs. It was in that mood that I returned home one afternoon to find my father and Uncle Louie working together in our backyard. The two were hanging a "shot" of mullet net they planned to use a few weeks later when "big roe mullet" season began. As usual, I reported to Daddy about how the day had gone. Listening to our conversation, Uncle Louie interrupted to say, "Let me tell you about the time I went to Ocracoke to work on the dock."

My uncle was already eighty years old, and, as noted earlier, a whole generation older than Daddy. At this stage in their lives, Daddy deferred to him as if he were his father. In keeping with that, our relaxed conversation immediately gave way to his story. It went as follows:

"During World War II, we got word that the Army was building a dock at Ocracoke and that they were paying a dollar an hour to anybody who would work on it. So, I got in my boat one Sunday morning and headed up Core Sound and into Pamlico Sound to get there before the sun went down."

As mentioned earlier, this was the same dock and work project that my father had pursued while awaiting the birth of my brother Mike. The distance was more than fifty nautical miles, and his boat was powered by a five-horsepower air-cooled engine. It would have been a one-way trip of at least eight hours. This was quite a

The Education of an Island Boy

journey for someone who might never have ventured that far from home in his entire life.

He continued, "When I got there, they had already started building the dock, so I tied up to it and tried to climb off the gunwale of my boat onto one of the piers that was already finished. Well, as I was doing that, my leg hit a nail that was left sticking out the side of one of the pilings, and it started to bleed really bad. Seeing that, I decided that the best thing I could do was get back in my boat and head back home. That's just what I did, and I got back at the Landing about 4:00 the next morning."

With that, he had finished his tale and went back to his needle and twine and attaching corks to the line on my father's mullet net. A little confused as to the intent of what I had just heard, I asked him, "Big Buddy, that was interesting, but ... what was the point of that story?"

"Oh," he said, shaking his head as he realized that he may have lost his train of thought as he told his tale. "I just wanted you to know something. That was the closest I ever come to having a job."

He wasn't just joking. He was telling the truth and making a point for me to keep in mind during my current job search! He had lived his whole life and supported a family of five children without ever having worked a single day for someone other than himself. His was the life of a "Back Sound Progger" who went after fish, shellfish, or shrimp, depending on the season, in his own little boat or as part of his own father's crew. Indeed, he was never wealthy in financial terms, but neither did he appear impoverished in any way.

In fact, he could always pull out a few "bills" of different denominations from the crumpled wallet he carried in his back-hip pocket. And, when showing those "bills," he always held his wallet up to just below his nose, to hide the rest of the contents from anyone who might be looking too closely.

Thus, my Uncle Louie taught me a lesson that I have never forgotten on a fall afternoon when I was looking for employment but found something that has served me even longer: an understanding that a job is not a life — it's just one of many ways to make a living.

The "Booze Yacht," A Journey, and the Sweetest Fumes I Ever Smelled

Two weeks before Christmas in 1923, an incident occurred near the Cape Lookout Lighthouse that has been spoken of ever since. Nearly everyone who has grown up or lived in Carteret County has heard the story of the "Booze Yacht," and just as many have heard the song by the same name. The late Grayden Paul (1899-1994) of nearby Beaufort helped to preserve and popularize them both. The misfortune of "The Adventure;" the actual name of the ocean-going vessel that came to be known for its cargo of illegal whiskey, gave birth to the song that has been sung and to stories that have been told ever since.

Ralph Saunders (1876-1956), the headmaster of the fledgling Harkers Island school at the time, composed the lyrics that were sung to the tune of the then-popular "Sidewalks of New York." It also spawned such a host of stories that it has assumed the status of legend. For that very reason, some blithely assume the whole account to be anecdotal, dismissing the fact that just a generation before, there were real men and women who still remembered the actual incident — and especially its aftermath.

According to the stories of some who witnessed the events and others who had heard them told, this is what happened. The Eighteenth Amendment to the US Constitution had been enacted four years earlier, in 1919. That Amendment and enabling legislation had made illegal the sale and distribution of alcoholic beverages anywhere in the United States. To circumvent those laws, there arose a whole network of smugglers who found ways to supply what became a booming market for illegal booze, especially in the larger cities of the American Northeast. One of the primary methods of evading federal authorities was to buy and ship supplies of whiskey and other banned beverages from the Caribbean islands while avoiding the watchful eye of federal officials who were on a constant lookout for them.

"The Adventure," eventually nicknamed the "Booze Yacht," was one of those vessels, often referred to as a "rumrunner." As it maneuvered up the Atlantic coastline from a distillery somewhere south of Florida to a supplier for "speakeasies" in and around New York City, the crew of "The Adventure" made a fateful error of judgment. Passing close by Lookout Bight, a natural harbor at the foot of the Cape Lookout Lighthouse, they noticed the lights carried by surfmen of the U.S. Lifesaving Service as they patrolled around Cape Point in the darkness.

They assumed them to be the searchlights of Revenue Cutters working for the U.S. Treasury Department. Expecting to be boarded, the crewmen dumped their entire payload overboard in large, netted sacks with the intention of retrieving them the following day. To the chagrin of the boat's captain and crew, early the next morning, fishermen working that area discovered and pulled in the whole stash. Within hours the news of what they had found began to spread like wildfire along the Banks and at Harkers Island.

My father was fourteen at the time, and vividly recalled the real thing. As he remembered it, he had been too young to go with the others to the scene, but until his final days, he told of watching as older men dropped overboard sacks full of illegal whiskey attached to buoys for hiding and safekeeping. He described how he stood on his father's shoulders to reach overhead and stash bottles between the attic floor and the bedroom ceiling. He recounted how Uncle Louie, whom he called "Big Buddy," dug holes in the ground of his chicken coup, deposited his bottles, and then allowed the chickens to scratch over the fill to hide all traces. He could even recount the names of those unlucky ones who were caught with the illegal contraband, a few of whom ended up serving time for having violated the laws of prohibition.

Uncle Louie, who died in 1985 at the age of ninety-five, not only recalled the event, but he was one of those who had "enjoyed" the full Booze Yacht experience. One of the stories he loved most to relate was of how he, then in his early thirties, gathered his own cache from the booty left by the rumrunners. Like many of the other Islanders, Big Buddy had scurried to get to the Cape as soon as he heard from his neighborhood friend, Clayton Guthrie Sr.

(1898-1949), that some lucky fishermen had hauled in a net full of whiskey. Along with Clayton, and his uncle Danky, they dropped everything they were doing and made for the Banks. In his little boat, the "Best Bug," they hurried across Back Sound and into Banks Bay and onto the shores of what had been Diamond City. He knew the area like the back of his hand, for Ole' Pa still had a fishing camp there, near where the family's homestead had been before the storm and exodus of a generation earlier.

Uncle Louie - "Big Buddy"

The spot was as practical as it was convenient. Once they landed, it was a mere half mile walk across to the Cape shore, where burlap sacks full of liquor now lay awash in the surf under the late fall sun. This was about the best that the scavengers could hope for since this was a full decade before there was an inlet between Shackleford and Core Banks. A boat trip all the way down the Banks toward Fort Macon channel and back east to the Hook, as Lookout Bight was called, would have taken so long as to be impractical. Still further, the cargo of "The Adventure" was illegal and that's why it had been dumped overboard in the first place. Loading and hauling that stuff back through Beaufort Inlet and under the nose of local, state, and federal officers, would have been foolhardy, even for the rugged and carefree watermen of that era.

But the most compelling reason for the straight-shot route that necessitated walking across the Banks was that neither Big Buddy nor most of the other pillagers had sufficient fuel to make only the shortest of excursions. In fact, it was customary, when time was of no concern, for the fishermen and sailors of the Island who were lucky enough to have a gas engine to power their rig, to turn off

The Education of an Island Boy

their motors and hoist a sail whenever possible, just to save their precious fuel. So, substituting a fifteen-minute walk for a two-hour boat trip was no great concession for this pair of eager young voyagers.

Arriving at the shoreline of Diamond City, the group found the bay at the "Hook of the Cape," as Lookout Bight is often called, already crowded with the boats of many others who had come to the Banks with the same intention. In fact, Big Buddy would often remark, the trip across was like a parade, as an ever-increasing flotilla headed in the general direction of the Cape, either to claim their share of the booty or just to watch others do the same.

The "Best Bug" was left anchored far enough offshore to assure that it would not be stranded by the ebbing tide, and the eager young threesome ran swiftly off and across the banks and through the sand dunes. As they made it to the Cape shore, they found a veritable circus as the throng rummaged through the strewed bags and sacks to find just the exact cache they were looking for. Louie and his companions picked up the first two unopened cases they could find and headed swiftly back northward toward their boat.

About halfway across on their return, Danky decided to open the sacks to inspect and maybe even sample what they had collected. To their disappointment, they saw that they had picked up containers of "quarts," rather than "pints" as they had supposed. They much preferred the smaller bottles, so they immediately decided to leave their bags right where they were and return to the shore to get what they had wanted in the first place. So large had been the stash that even by the time they returned, there still was plenty to choose from. This time they made sure they had the right size bottles and once again headed for their boat.

Within less than an hour, they were back aboard the "Best Bug." But to their disgust, they learned that their boat had been relieved of its fuel supply, most likely by one of their fellow travelers who had come along without checking that he had enough for the round-trip. If necessity is the mother of invention, it can also be the midwife of improvisation. Having sampled the whisky in the quart bottles just minutes earlier, Big Buddy had noted that it was some of the strongest he had ever tasted. "If alcohol can be used to light a flame," he thought, "why can't it be used to run an engine?"

Thus began his experiment with the combustive powers of distilled liquor. With Danky at the helm, Big Buddy held his thumb over the open mouth of a bottle of Caribbean Rum and allowed it to seep into the down-draft carburetor of his six-horsepower Bridgeport engine. Sure enough, the engine fired up, perhaps from the residue of gas left in the fuel line. But as the trio made their way back across the Sound towards the Island, the motor held its fire and never cut off — not once! As Uncle Louie stood at the back of the engine box holding the bottle, he could feel and smell the exhaust as it fumed from the straight iron pipe that extended from the manifold. He said that he positioned himself so that the exhaust vapor would blow directly into his face. He did so, he insisted, because it was "... the sweetest fumes he'd ever smelt in his entire life!"

So, they made it back with their booty, except for the two bottles they had been obliged to use as fuel for their engine. Big Buddy never found out who had stolen his gas tank that day, and really didn't much care to investigate it. But he never forgot how he had improvised to make it home, nor the smell that lifted from the pistons of that internal combustion motor as it "put-put-putted" across Back Sound. The "Booze Yacht" was much more than a legend to him and to those of us who heard him tell his stories. It was just another part of what life had been like in the early days of Harkers Island.

The Education of an Island Boy

The "Booze Yacht"
Words by Ralph Sanders

Down around the Beehive, Harkers Island retreat
Every night and morning, the fishermen would meet
One day there came a rounder, a rushing by the door
Said "Boys let's go to Cape Lookout,
there's a booze yacht run ashore."

That's when lots of rounders, for miles and miles around
Kept their gas boats busy, cruising through Core Sound
Some of them were happy, and some of them were sore
But King Lock stoppers stood ace high
when the booze yacht run ashore.

(Chorus)

This way, that way, to the Cape they run
The coming of the Adventure, put fishing on the bum
Some folks lost religion, and back-slid by the score
King Lock stoppers stood ace high when the booze yacht run ashore.

Things have changed since those times, some are up in their G's
While others they are down and out, but most feel just like me
Some would part with all they got, and some a little bit more
To see another time like that, when the booze yacht run ashore.

Ivey Scott put the words for "The Booze Yacht" to music to the tune of "The Sidewalks of New York".
From Harkers Island Music Legend CD
And CSWM&HC Collection

The year after returning to the Island, my wife Susan and I welcomed our second daughter, Joella, to join Emily in our growing family.

The Education of an Island Boy

Telford Willis, my Grandmother Bertha's brother

8

The Wisdom and Wit of Ordinary Days

They were rememberers, carrying in their living thoughts all the history that such places ... ever have. I listened to them with all my ears, and have tried to remember what they said, though from remembering what I remember I know that much is lost. Things went to the grave with them that will never be known again.

Wendell Berry, "Jayber Crow"

... I could go out in the street for an afternoon, and I would see so much that, when I came in the house, I'd be talking and talking for what seemed like hours. Dad would say, 'Boy, why don't you stop that lyin'? You know you didn't see all that.' But I knew I had.

Claud Brown, "Manchild in the Promised Land"

Mark Twain claimed that his experiences growing up in Hannibal were an "inexhaustible source" of inspiration for him. "... When the tank runs dry," he wrote in his autobiography, "you've only to leave it alone and it will fill up again in time, while you are asleep ..." So it was with my everyday encounters with the men, women, boys, and girls I knew while growing up.

The people who lived around and with me, mostly older, but some barely so, were my teachers as I came of age on the Island. Their lessons were not so much about what it took to survive, since for me and most others, that was so simple as to be mundane — and not all that hard. They taught me how to make the most out of that simple life and enjoy it to the fullest. Instead of chalkboards and reading assignments, they used stories, yarns, and everyday experiences to explain and make sense of what happened around us and prepare me and others for what was to come.

Many of those experiences involved making a living in and from the nearby sounds and ocean. "Working the water" involved lots of talking and listening, as very few people worked the water alone. There were some things a "progger" could do by himself, like clamming or oystering or dragging a small shrimp trawl. But making enough money to support a family usually involved a crew of men and two or more working boats to make it happen. The teamwork needed for success necessitated mostly verbal coordination. "Let her out here," "There he jumped," or "Cut her into the wind," were among dozens of routine expressions that were part of gillnetting, pound-netting, or trawling, and anything else that involved two or more men working together to find and harvest the bounty of the sounds and ocean.

Still further, preparing for each day's venture sometimes required as much time and effort as the work itself. After the catching was done there was still the culling of a drag, the clearing and cleaning of a net, or the shoveling into boxes that was a normal capstone to a day in the water. All of this usually required more than one pair of hands, so oral communication was at the heart of every day's routine.

The intricacies of the routines could have become tedious had there not developed a unique set of terms and expressions that youngsters learned as part of growing up next to the water. This vernacular led not only to more efficiency on the job but also came to involve a set of stories and characterizations. These yarns, as my mother often called them, were a large part of the cultural backdrop against which life on Harkers Island played out for nearly a century. Unlike the far-fetched tales told by raconteurs like "Lying Willie," these narratives were based entirely on real people

The Wisdom and Wit of Ordinary Days

and actual events and offered a window into what daily living on the Island was really like.

Beyond the jargon of the everyday waterman were the myriads of stories about life itself, about families and friendships, and about dealing with the ups and downs of day-to-day living. They explained to me and my "classmates" how the wisdom — and the foibles — of our recent ancestors had already solved many of life's mysteries. I needed only to be patient enough to listen and to remember. That is the reason that from my earliest years I became fascinated with the seemingly endless tales that were a part of daily conversations or discussions.

When my mother, along with some others, heard the more outlandish ones repeated, they sometimes would throw up their hands and exclaim: "That just don't bear telling!" Unlike my father and most of the other men who were swapping the yarns, they didn't seem to sense that the relevance of a story was not entirely dependent on its veracity. I recall that once, after Mama questioned what she was hearing, my Uncle Terrell patted her on the shoulder and consoled her, "I know, Margarette, it might not be true. But it oughta be."

My father's sister Lurena and husband, Terrell Scott.

In the days before television came to dominate the soundscape of most mornings and every evening, long and unhurried discussions that involved mostly brief but sometimes intricate stories were the fabric of every day's routine. In our neighborhood, after supper, the men would gather, often on my family's front porch. Later, the women and children, including me, would filter onto the scene and somehow find a place to sit and, occasionally, take part. As I remember, the younger children often ended up on someone's lap and usually remained there until they fell asleep. The men did most of the talking, and the women were called upon to add details or to affirm what their husbands had just told.

Some stories and some lessons had been told so often or were so well learned, that they needed only to be mentioned or cited to make a point, or to prepare the setting for yet another tale that was about to follow. When someone wished to express unbridled affection and exclaimed that "She loves her dog more than Mart loved TomTom," it was assumed that everyone already was familiar with the story of how much Mart had loved his son, TomTom, and could appreciate and accept the allusion. That was how I, as had several generations of youngsters on Harkers Island, came to know and understand a set of anecdotes that became the parables by which we lived and learned, and communicated our feelings to those with whom we shared a special place and time.

Each one of the stories I have included has a name attached to it. Some of these names, however, will live only in my mind due to a sensitivity for how their families or friends, hearing or reading them for the first time in an open setting, might perceive them. In fact, in a few places I have altered the circumstances just a little to err on the side of caution and make more certain that no offense might ever be taken. Despite that, let there be no misunderstanding. I am comfortable in knowing that the characters themselves would have no problem at all with my stories, especially since many of them were the men and sometimes women who told them in the first place — to me and to others.

All of them, even those whose names are withheld, were and are dear to me, and are included because of the special place they still have in my heart and mind. Indeed, this entire project is meant as much as a tribute to them as a narrative about me. Other than this small caveat, these stories are told just as I heard or saw them unfold and any mistelling is an error of my memory rather than a license with the truth.

These stories are independent of each other and can stand alone for retelling. A later chapter will focus on other persons and tales about Islanders that I knew and who helped to form and give color to the world and lifestyle I inherited. On their own they may tend to suggest an incoherent message or less than that — just another farcical description of when someone acted capriciously or unwisely, or simply misunderstood what really was going on.

The Wisdom and Wit of Ordinary Days

It is when offered up together and in the context of life as it happened in real-time, that they were like shoulder pads or a helmet that allowed those who listened to stumble and even fall, but then get back up and move on — usually with a smile on their face. Trying to weave them into a coherent narrative with a beginning and ending recalls the maxim with which Mark Twain introduced Huckleberry Finn to the world: *"Persons attempting to find a motive in this narrative will be prosecuted; persons attempting to find a moral in it will be banished; persons attempting to find a plot in it will be shot."*

As noted, I first heard many of these stories while sitting on our porch. Others were learned while I was leaning on a bench or a wooden drink [soda] crate that was turned upright to be used as a seat against the wall of a neighborhood store. Sometimes I listened in as old men swapped yarns while working on their wares around net spreads at the Landing, or on the dock of a fish house, or waited in line for their place in a barber's chair. Still more were repeated to me by my older siblings when we were just passing time and were sharing things they already had learned, and felt I needed to know them too.

My brother Tommy was seventeen years older than me. In addition to having had the added experience of those years, he was my next-door neighbor for the better part of fifty years until his passing in 2021 and thus a part of nearly every day in my life. He remembered and told even more stories than I could ever imagine. Each of my older siblings had a knack for relating events in a memorable way, but it was Tommy's memory and humor that is the most evident in the stories I have included throughout this account.

What follows is my attempt to catalog and retell some of those stories, and to give them a relevance that might extend even to those who are far removed from the tiny Island that spawned and nurtured the characters involved.

I might add one additional note before a select few of those stories unfold. I must have been at least in high school before ever being introduced to the word "hyperbole." But when it was finally explained to me, I knew exactly what it meant—because hyperbole was an integral part of how people on the Island told their stories and made their points.

Telford Willis & Brady Lewis – You Can't Have it Both Ways!

My Mama's Uncle Telford (Willis 1898-1949), Grandma Bertha's younger brother, had passed four years before I was born. But because he continued to be mentioned, described, and quoted so often in daily conversations, it was like he never really left. What follows are two of those stories and another about his wife, Gertie (Guthrie 1899-1979), still told by his descendants and others even seventy-plus years after his passing.

"Teff," as most people called and knew him, had dark hair with a round face that was always either sun or wind-burned from his days out in the water. He would have been deemed a little short by today's standards, but at around 5' 8", his height was average for his day. He was stockily built with a waistline that often remained partially hidden under his somewhat oversized belly. It was said that he laughed with his whole body, and he was eager to shower his affections on not just his wife and children but on his extended family and anyone else he deemed to be a friend. He wore his emotions upon his sleeves, and when he spoke, he gathered the attention of everyone within his earshot.

Gertie was not native to the Island, but she shared her husband's Diamond City heritage. She was from Salter Path, a community on Bogue Banks and across the Beaufort Inlet. The people there, like most Islanders, traced their ancestry to Diamond City and Shackleford Banks. She was as slender and fair as Telford was stout and tough. Teff and Gertie had scrimped and saved together for most of their adult lives to have enough money for the workboat of his dreams. He had been a part of fishing crews since he was hardly old enough

Telford and Gertie with one of their seven children

to lift a lead line. He already had owned several small boats of his own, including a sailskiff. But now he was ready to build the vessel he had dreamed of and planned for during all those years of working for and with others.

Not only that, his new boat, to be christened "The Frances" after his oldest daughter, was being built by Brady Lewis (1904-1992), the boat builder from the east'ard who even then was a legend both on and off the Island. Teff had come the two miles from his house to Brady's boatyard to visit his builder early one morning, and to tell him of yet another idea he had conjured up about tweaking "The Frances" even as she was being built. Perhaps it was something he had noticed on another boat, or maybe something he figured out on his own while heading back and forth to the Banks or the Cape.

Brady Lewis was by then in the prime of his life as a marine craftsman and designer. His workshop was merely in his own backyard that sat between his small frame house and the shoreline less than a hundred feet to the south'ard. At any given time, there might have been half a dozen or more vessels pulled up onto his yard or anchored at his landing. They could range from small skiffs that needed planks or timbers replaced to the full-size open or cabin boats that were the staple of every Island fisherman.

There were piles of rough-cut juniper lumber everywhere waiting to be planed and later cut into the small strips used for planking the intricate shapes of his trademark style of boat building. The smells of sawdust and shavings from that lumber were as fragrant as rose petals to most Islanders as they recognized it as the smell of new boats about to come to life.

Vessels he built already lined the shoreline from Red Hill to Shell Point. And his reputation extended well beyond the Island up and down the Outer Banks. He had built enough boats that he had seen or heard, and even invented, about everything that could be imagined when it came to what was already being called the Harkers Island "flare bow" boat in other places, but simply a "Brady Lewis boat" in eastern Carteret County. Assuming that everyone else was aware of his skills, the master carpenter and boat builder had grown a little frustrated at having to make changes, even small ones, in the design of something he felt he already had perfected. Eventually, Brady dropped the block plane that he was using to shape one of the juniper planks and looked my Uncle Teff squarely in the eye to make sure he had his attention.

"What's it gonna be?" he asked with a plaintive voice that suggested he had about reached the end of his patience, "Do you want me to build her for fishing, or do you want me to build her to go fast? You can't have it both ways!"

The old boat builder posed a question that by then was at the heart of a quandary besetting a new generation of Island fishermen — a group that earlier had been obliged to work strictly for subsistence but now had some margin for leisure and fun. They still needed to make a living in their boats. It was all they had for supporting their families, but by the late 1930's some of them were earning much more than what was needed merely for subsistence.

Eventually, there had developed among them a love for "going fast." And the crafts they looked to for that, and even for racing, were the same boats used primarily for hauling nets, trawls, and the day's catch. Uncle Teff was one of those who had fallen in love with the fast-boat craze, and he was determined that his new one would never be left in the wake of other boats when hurrying along the shore.

By that time, engine-powered boats had totally replaced the sailing vessels that had been piloted on Core Sound for two centuries. Making use of the advantages that the new motors offered, some fishermen built large "trawlers" with masts, booms, and cabins that included bunks. Even more of the locals opted for smaller open boats that were less than twenty-five feet long. With a skeg in front and a rudder behind it, that propeller, or "wheel" as most of them called it, could propel the smaller boats to upwards of forty miles per hour.

They usually had an engine salvaged from an older car or truck. It was placed somewhere to the aft of the boat's center and fitted with a straight metal shaft, without a transmission, which fed through a water-tight alley to an underwater propeller. In general, the farther back, the faster it could go. But that arrangement left a smaller and less practical area for working with nets and catches. Thus, the dilemma of utility vs. speed.

Some devoted speed boaters would spend hours disk or hand sanding the sides and bottoms of their boats hoping to make them smoother, and thus faster, by reducing the drag caused by a rough surface. One particularly resolute craftsman claimed to have given his boat such a smooth finish that it was impossible for it to sit still in the water — continually rocking back and forth, seeking balance. He added that when he pulled it up on the shore to work on the motor, he was obliged to anchor it to keep it from sliding back into the Sound.

More speed was not without its advantages for a fisherman. It could be important when chasing schools of fish, when hurrying to the dock with perishable cargo, or when getting to or through a channel before the tide went out completely. But it soon came to be valued most of all in "racing" against other boats. Whole groups of boaters were apt to spring into competition whenever and wherever they were headed in the same direction.

Every summer day, or any other time when the weather allowed, boats could be seen and heard zipping up and down the Island channel. Especially on Saturdays, the same boats would race across the strait that led to Beaufort for the weekend shopping in town. Even when no trips were planned, Saturday mornings were race days at the Landing. The sounds of growling motors could be heard all along the shore and swells from the speeding boats would create a constant flow of waves washing up along the sandy beach.

Every summer, on the 4th of July, late that afternoon and after everyone had returned from the horse penning at Diamond City of that morning, a substantial portion of the Island's population would gather at the shore of Academy Field for races that lasted until dark. The day's winner was awarded a small cup as a memento, but the greatest prize was the reputation earned as "having the fastest boat on the Island."

All of this, in some form or another, was churning in the mind of Uncle Teff as he pondered his response to Brady Lewis's ultimatum about how he wanted "The Frances" to be fashioned by the greatest boat craftsman the Island would ever know. But it was with only a moment's hesitation that he made his decision and blurted out his emphatic response: "You make her go fast, and I'll fish her the best I can!"

Telford Willis - You'll Freeze to Death This Winter

Like so many others on the Island, Uncle Teff was an avid loon hunter. How that scavenger waterfowl became a delicacy on the Banks and later at the Island and Salter Path has never been fully explained. But fancied, and thus hunted, it was — and remained as much well into the last century. It was even said that young men from the Island who were away in the military or other services would sometimes write home with their arrival plans, and a request that at least two stewed loons be waiting for them to enjoy — one for themselves and the other for whomever was there to greet them.

The fact that loons eventually became a protected species only seemed to enhance the excitement of bagging one of these migratory birds. In the early spring of each year, hunters lined the south shore of Harkers Island to prepare a one-sided gauntlet that stretched at least two miles long. Each hunter would, in turn, take his chances at shooting the birds as they flew just beyond the tideline each morning looking for the small fish and minnows that schooled there in late winter and early spring.

On one spring morning, a gallant and solitary loon made its way along the shore in the direction of the rising sun as hunter after hunter fired shells in its direction. The fusillade eventually sounded more like a cannon barrage as each fired shot echoed as subsequent rounds were discharged. But because the tideline had formed a bit farther out than usual, most of the shooters either missed the bird entirely, or else their shots broke through only the bird's outer feathers and failed to pierce the skin. After that, with fragments of their plumage trailing behind, the loon continued its path eastward toward Shell Point.

As the sounds of gunfire grew closer and closer, the fleeting bird eventually came into view and abreast of my uncle. Having anxiously awaited his turn, Teff arose from his perch and fired two shells he was confident would hit their mark.

Just as with the other marksmen, a few feathers drifted out and around. Yet the bird kept flying as if nothing had touched it, making its way to and past the next awaiting hunter. Greatly frustrated by his failure to bring down the loon, Teff quickly stood erect and raised his fist in the direction of his prey as he shouted, "Fly damn ye, you may live now, but you'll freeze to death this winter!"

The Handsomest Man in the World

In the decades of the 1920s, '30s, and '40s, Mormon missionaries walked the paths and shoreline of Harkers Island daily, passing their time at the homes of the several dozen Latter-day Saint families that by that time had established a growing community on the Island. By then, a second generation of members was reaching its adolescence, including several dozen young "Mormon girls" who couldn't help but notice the handsome young visitors from the West. Not only did they speak with a "peculiar accent," but those young "elders," as they were called, always were dressed in "store-bought" suits and ties, and had clean-shaven faces and well-trimmed hair.

Their outfits were markedly different from the threadbare jeans and wrinkled shirts that were worn by most local boys of the same age. Further, those Island boys often had disheveled hair, were barefooted or wearing knee-high boots, and sometimes smelled of the fish and shrimp they had harvested earlier that day.

Teff and Gertie lived at the foot of Red Hill, near the southwesternmost point of the Island. It was a large- at least by Island standards at the time, and even a stately two-story dwelling. It had a large front porch shaded by two

Telford and Gertie Willis's home was across the road from the south shore.

large oaks that were positioned midway between the house and the Island's main road. Friends and family often gathered there to enjoy the cooling southwest summer breezes and interact with the steady stream of passersby who daily followed that path in both directions.

The family's five daughters; Margaret (1922-1938), Frances (1929-2016), Phyllis (1933-2013), Joyce (1935-2003), and Carol (1941-2007), loved to sit on the swing and rocking chairs while bantering back and forth about whatever was that day's topic of discussion. One afternoon, while Teff had gone fishing or was just working at the Landing, Gertie listened through the open front windows while her daughters and some of their friends talked about the two elders who then were serving and living on the Island. Gertie, decided to chime in on the conversation as she had noticed that each of the young girls had chosen a recent visiting missionary to label as the "most handsome man she had ever seen!" After each of her daughters had described in detail their choice, and why he was chosen, Gertie decided to end the conversation with her own definitive answer to the question at hand.

Moving gently through the screen door that opened onto the porch she waited for the girls to acknowledge her presence. Then with a voice that could never be confused for just levity, she announced to her daughters and their friends, "Every afternoon, at just before supper, I look towards the Landing, and eventually I see a tired, often wet and sandy fisherman walking this way — usually with his worn-out pants rolled up to below the knee and smelling like fish. But even from a distance, and especially when he grabs me by the shoulders and kisses my forehead, your daddy, Telford Willis, is the most handsome man who ever lived!"

Are You Now or Have You Ever Been ...?

Online Dictionary: **common** - *an adjective (commoner, commonest) showing a lack of taste and refinement supposedly typical of the lower classes; coarse; vulgar ...*

For my generation that came of age as the war in Vietnam was erupting, turning eighteen implied something more than just filling out a card at the post office. It meant having to go to the selective service office at the county seat in Beaufort and registering in person for "the draft." The most important part of that process was an interview with Miss Ruby Holland of nearby Smyrna. She had been secretary for the local draft board for half a century — a tenure that spanned World War II, Korea, and Vietnam. After registering, if your number "came up," the letter you got inviting you to take a requisite physical exam and, if you passed the physical, to join the armed services, had her prominent and handwritten signature at the bottom.

Miss Holland's office was in an old Georgian-style building on Courthouse Square in Beaufort, the county seat, that dated back to long before the turn of the previous century. She had no secretary or other staff to assist her as she considered herself uniquely qualified to manage her office all by herself. There was a local draft board made up of several county dignitaries — all of whom were male — but it was assumed that the board was there merely to "rubber stamp" whatever choices and decisions she came up with. Just the mention of her name could provoke anxiety in anyone approaching the age of military draft eligibility.

By the time I turned nineteen, the selection method had been changed from a purely "selective service" to a "lottery system" based on your date of birth. Cards representing every date on the yearly calendar were placed in a bin and were drawn out one at a time. The order in which they were drawn was used by every draft board in the entire USA to determine in what order that year's list of eligible young men would be called upon to serve.

My birthday was number one-hundred-twenty-seven in that year's lottery — a number high enough up the list that mine was never reached. Several friends were not so lucky, including my then-college roommate from Beaufort, whose birthday was chosen as number three. That left him little option other than to enlist. However, prior to 1970, every young man of the given age was eligible to be chosen to serve and was evaluated based on several specific criteria. It was up to the local draft board, under Miss Holland's direction, to decide both "if and when" he might be "selected."

The Education of an Island Boy

So it was that one of my older friends from the Island went to register a few years before my age group and was interviewed by "Miss Holland" to determine his eligibility. She had a list of questions, most of which were straightforward and required a simple "yes" or "no" response. All proceeded normally until the Secretary came to a question that had been a required part of the interview as a result of the so-called "Red Scare" of the previous decades.

"Are you now or have you ever been a Communist?" she asked the young man as he sat attentively across from her desk. Pausing to ponder the question for a few moments, the boy finally summoned up what he thought would be the most appropriate answer. "Now, I'm 'common,' I'll grant ya. But I'm not the 'commonest' person I know. I think that would have to be [name withheld]. He's a whole lot commoner than me. Just about anybody on the Island would tell ya that."

It was then that the local draft board Secretary took her own extended pause. Finally, without so much as a single follow-up question, she thanked the young man for his time and allowed him to be on his way. Just a few weeks later, he got his notice of induction.

Dallas Rose- In Two Hours, We'll Be Headed Out Again

Not all Island fishermen were created equal. Some were more successful than others, and some were more diligent than others. Dallas Rose (1913-1988) may not have been noticeably more successful, but no one could fail to notice that he worked harder than just about anyone.

If most other fishermen left home just as the sun was rising, Dallas was by then already beyond the Inlet and waiting on a set (a placement of a fish net in a lengthy line or circle.) If other boats headed home in time to reach the dock by sundown, Dallas's boat was still offshore when the sky grew dark. And even as he worked longer, he also worked with more vigor and intensity. While others would put out only a few hundred feet of net to "try a sign," which meant testing to see if a school of fish might be present, Dallas would put out a full thousand yards or more.

Understandably, it sometimes was a challenge for Dallas to keep a regular crew to work with and beside him. Not that he was unsuccessful, for Dallas's crew shared out more than most. But there were very few others who were willing to go at it as persistently as he did. Usually, he depended on his family — his brothers, cousins, and nephews. Later, he had sons and a son-in-law of his own. It was one of these family helpers who told a story that, better than any other, illustrated what it was like to fish with Dallas Rose.

One fall evening, as his boat, "The Wasted Wood," approached the dock, he asked one of his crew members to reach for and pull in the "mooring stick" that was tethered to the anchor that would secure the boat for the evening. As the young man reached into the night air for the stake, Dallas noticed that his eyes were watering, but not due to the wind or the evening mist. He was crying and shedding real tears as he struggled to hold onto the rope and secure the boat. "Why are you crying?" Dallas asked as he gazed into the face of his exhausted helper. "We're almost home, and soon you can rest."
"I know," his young but worn-out crewman responded. "That just means that in two more hours we'll be heading out again."

Cletus Rose- Why Don't You Fly Somewhere?

Dallas's younger brother, Cletus Rose (1916-1984), was a "renaissance man." It seemed He could do anything, and most of those things he did exceptionally well. He was a carpenter, painter, plumber, electrician, roofer, cabinet maker, architect, engineer, and boat builder. He designed and built houses and shops from the ground up, and his cabinet work was as much artistry as carpentry. He worked side by side with Brady Lewis in building some of the Island's most distinctive vessels. He was a boat craftsman in his own right, building everything from small skiffs to large trawlers.

Cletus Rose

The Education of an Island Boy

He was a musician and singer, and with a chorus of his daughters, could entertain and inspire an audience or a congregation. He was a devoted family man, close to his parents and siblings, and idolized by his wife and girls. But what was most memorable to many about "Brother Cletus," as he loved to be called, was his essential kindness and goodness. He was a leader in his community and church. In those positions, like his father, George, before him, he often took it upon his own shoulders to help an individual or a family that had fallen into hard times.

Everyone who ever knew him has their own stories that are a window to the heart of his unbounded compassion. Clem Willis Jr. (1938-2019), his nephew known as "Bud," once explained that while working with his uncle on a job site in the western part of the county, he chose "not" to commute with him back and forth to work. This wasn't because Bud had his own car, and not because of any scheduling conflict. Bud eventually determined that he could get back and forth quicker on his own, even if he had to hitch a ride. His Uncle Cletus, he learned, would pick up every hitchhiker he saw, and then take him wherever the "bummer" was going, even if it was far off the path to their job. "I would be back and eating supper," Bud remembers, "long before Uncle Cletus would ever make it home."

In the heyday of his time as a carpenter and boat builder, Cletus acquired a collection of specialized tools that was the envy of other less successful journeymen. Knowing of Cletus' good nature, his friends often prevailed upon him to borrow one or more of those tools to work on some special or temporary project. But many times, "temporary" turned out to be permanent and the borrowed items were never returned. Eventually, feeling shame or guilt about their failures, some of the borrowers avoided being with or even greeting Brother Cletus when they approached him on the road or at the store. Even though they knew full well that he would never mention it, they preferred not having to come face to face with a reminder of their own failure to keep their end of what had been a very one-sided bargain.

Just sensing their hesitation even to greet him was more than Cletus could bear. To remedy the situation, he offered a preemptive gesture of forgiveness that, he hoped, would remove any

The Wisdom and Wit of Ordinary Days

misgivings among his friends who had "borrowed without returning." He posted a sign in a local store, telling everyone who still might be holding on to any of his tools, that the items were henceforth theirs to keep, with no hard feelings, but with one simple condition. He asked that they be his friends again when and wherever they saw him. He couldn't bear the anxiety of feeling that anyone would hesitate to greet him over something that, to Cletus, was as inconsequential as an electric drill or hand saw.

My own favorite story of Brother Cletus' personality, and one that combines his talents, his attention to detail, and especially his gentle nature, is of the time he tried his hand at duck hunting. Having heard his friends extol the joys of stalking and bagging waterfowl in the marshes off the Banks, he determined one summer to be ready that fall to become a hunter with the best of them. He built himself a stand on the edge of a marsh that, as recalled by those who saw it, was more like a home than a "duck blind."

He acquired different shotguns that could be used for the various types of shooting that he planned. He carved and painted several bags of working decoys of many different species of birds to make sure he had the right ones when the time approached. He acquired the necessary licenses and permits and outfitted a skiff so that he could transport his equipment to and from the Banks.

Eventually, all that was left was for the season to open and the hunting to begin. On the very first day, as the morning sun rose over Core Banks, Brother Cletus was sitting alertly in his decked-out duck-blind, shotgun on his shoulder, decoys on the water, and with his skiff hidden in the marshes. As soon as there was enough light to make out an image, he caught sight of a "bufflehead," one of the smallest of the duck species, as it landed at the very foot of his blind and began to swim among his decoys.

Very gently Cletus steadied his gun on his shoulder and looked down the barrel at what was going to be the first prize of his career as a hunter. But, at the critical moment, and before he could bring himself to squeeze the trigger, the small bird turned and looked him squarely in the eye, and then tilted his head ever so slightly to the side. As the hunter gazed into the miniature eyes that were staring into his own, his trigger finger went limp. He lowered the gun from his shoulder and stood up and stared back at the bird for a few seconds. Finally, his inner self having overcome his desire for the sport, Cletus waved his arms and shouted, "Why don't you fly somewhere before somebody shoots you?"

Within a couple of hours, he had gathered his decoys and dismantled the blind. Along with his guns and equipment, all of what remained was loaded on his skiff as he headed back to the shore at the Landing not far from his home. He never again ventured to hunt for birds. More importantly, Brother Cletus never lost the caring compassion that made him a failure as a hunter, but a "Prince of a Man."

My Mama's Aunt Mary- Just Look at You Crowd

Anyone who lived on the Island before the days of thermostatically controlled heat and air conditioning can recall the sounds of seagulls in the morning. When windows were left open, the cascading cries of the gulls announced that fishing and shrimping boats were back at the Landing. Large flocks would gather on warm summer mornings as fishermen cleared and culled their nets, waiting impatiently for the refuse — pinfish, shad, or tonguefish — that were shoveled "o'er board" as watermen sorted through their catch.

As the process concluded, and the fishermen used a big flat-head shovel to pile up his scraps, the gulls could sense that their booty was ready. Especially then, they circled and squawked, anxious to pounce on what would soon be thrown over the boat's stern or side gunnel. The noise was so loud that it could be heard far away, up on the shore and even through the paths that dissected the vines, yaupons, cedars, silver maples, and oaks that still were abundant just above the tide line.

All of us recognized the sound, and even if we had no need to hurry and help in lifting baskets or shoving skiffs, we had been there enough that in our mind's eye we could see it as clearly as if we were standing on the shore. Seagulls, in both sight and sound, were as much a part of our environment as sand and saltwater. Indeed, we were so accustomed to them that we could describe people or things by ascribing to them the traits we saw most often in these scavenger birds. "Soaring like a gull," "hungry as a gull," "mouth open as wide as a gull," and lots of other similes were parts of our lexicon.

For that reason, no clarification was needed when my mother's Aunt Mary (Willis 1890-1939) one day made just such an allusion to express her exasperation. Mary was what might be tactfully described as "simple," and as she grew older, according to my father, was "just as wide as she was long." She also could be very loud and opinionated and was often heard protesting what she thought were the injustices of her lot in life. The combination of her simplicity, her appearance, and especially her frequent and outlandish protestations served to make her somewhat of a comical figure to those who knew her best and were around her most.

She never married and had spent her entire life in the care of her parents. During the lean years of the Great Depression and the beginnings of the social services that most of us now take for granted, Mary learned that the local "welfare office" was offering handouts for those who were in dire need. Along with many others, she stood in line at the county courthouse in Beaufort for the chance to explain her predicament and, hopefully, get some of the food or other supplies to be handed out. Unfortunately for Aunt Mary, because she had no dependents and lived in the home of her parents, when her time came to make her case, she was deemed unqualified to receive any kind of assistance.

Obviously disappointed, and just as much frustrated, she rose from the desk where she had been interviewed. Turning around and making her way to the exit, she was obliged to stand face-to-face with the long line of others who were awaiting their own chance to explain why they needed help. Having already told the interviewer in graphic terms how she felt about his decision, she now placed her hand on her hip, leaned a little to the side, and then hollered at all those who were still standing between her and the doorway. "Just look at you crowd. You look just like a bunch of damn gulls!"

The Education of an Island Boy

Ed Russell- What About that Oak Tree Over There

After the devastating Hurricane of 1933, known to Islanders and throughout Down East as the "Jimmy Hamilton Storm," federal disaster workers visited the Island to offer help to those who had lost or were forced to abandon their homes. Among those was Ed Russell (1872-1943), whose home amid the tall oak trees of the West'ard showed gaping holes in the outer walls and in the roofing. Ed had never been known as being mild-mannered or patient, even under the best of circumstances. Now in his sixties, his innate mannerisms had hardened all the more, and he never missed an opportunity to let others — and especially anyone who crossed him — know exactly how he felt about things.

At the beginning of what he knew was destined to be a long and grueling day, the inspector was, no doubt, predisposed to make each inspection as brief and straightforward as possible. So, after making some abbreviated notes and an introductory conversation, the inspector looked at and pondered over what was left of Ed Russell's house. Judging from those parts that were still standing, he concluded that although there was some obvious damage from the storm, it also was evident that it had been in an advanced state of disrepair for quite a while.

Taking a few more notes and then reviewing what appeared to have been a set of guidelines and tables, the inspector announced his determination as to what, if any, financial help to make repairs that he could offer. "Mr. Russell," he began, "your house seems to have been in pretty bad shape even before the storm!" He then began to point out the obvious problems that, he felt, precluded the rendering of anything other than the most basic of assistance.

As he appeared to listen, Ed remained focused on the inspector's original observation of his home's condition before the storm had arrived. He held his tongue for as long as he could, and then, while looking around him, he pointed out with increasing emphasis the devastation that was visible in every direction. In close proximity to his small home, and in every direction, there could be seen a dozen or more oaks and cedars — some more than a century old but now uprooted lying on the ground.

Finally, struggling to keep his emotions under control, the sixty-one-year-old Russell responded to the visitor with a pointed question of his own. "What about that oak tree over there lying on its side? Was that in bad shape before the storm?"

Fishing with Calvin Rose- All I Wanted Was a Chance

Calvin Rose (1932-2008) had a big trawler called the "EsCal." The name was an abbreviated combination of the name of his wife, Esther, and his own. It was equipped with lots of nets and the finest equipment that could be procured for commercial fishing in that era. In late fall and winter, the "EsCal" was used for sink netting off Cape Lookout. Calvin was good at what he did, and he made a good living in those few months when croakers, spots, and sea mullet schooled on the back side of the breakwater at Cape Lookout. For that reason and because he was so easy to work with and for, there were always plenty of men and boys eager to join his crew and earn a part of the money that he shared out just about every Saturday.

Calvin Rose
CSWM&HC Collection

The system used by Island fishing captains to pay their crewmen was one of the most egalitarian that could ever be imagined. Each one, no matter his age, strength, or skill level, was paid the same. Even the captain and boat owner himself was entitled to only one equal share. His only advantage over the others was that his boat was also awarded the same share as the other crew members — meaning that a greater number of helpers ultimately meant a proportionally smaller share for the boat — and thus for the captain. Thus, most boat owners understandably tried to work with as few extra hands as was practical.

Early one fall, when large schools of fish started showing up at the Cape, one recently married young man who had no boat of his own and only his hands and the strength of his back to offer to an employer, determined to seek out Calvin Rose and plead for an opportunity to join his crew. Early one evening, he spied Calvin leaving one of the Island's stores. The jobseeker made just the briefest of greetings before beginning to make his case to the man he hoped would be his employer. He explained that times were hard for him and his new wife and that he really wanted and needed a job on Calvin's boat — and the sooner the better.

But the older captain was wise to the younger man's history and habits. The younger man had never held any job for more than a few weeks, and often only for days. When he did work, he was prone to come in late and leave early. And what was most worrisome at all was his reputation as a scrounger and of asking for his wages in advance — and then never showing back up.

Still, Calvin was friends with the man's family and had known him since he was a small boy. Largely for that reason, the captain was unwilling to offend either him or them. He knew he couldn't just turn him down right there on the spot. Instead, he quickly came up with a scheme that would allow the jobseeker to retain some dignity, and the boat to have only the crew the captain wanted.

"Here's what you do," he told the would-be crewman. "Tomorrow morning at 6:00 sharp, you come down to the dock where we keep our boat. If the boat is still there, it means 'we' are not going. If the boat is not there, it means 'you' are not going!"

"Thanks," the man said as he headed toward home. "I'll be there. All I wanted was a chance!"

An Unexpected Holiday Visitor

The man at the door was wearing a suit and tie, a really nice one, and his shirt was so heavily starched that it was glossy. It was obvious that he was a stranger not just by his looks or his accent, but by how he acted, as if he knew he was on unfamiliar ground, and maybe even a little lost. It was just after sundown on December 23rd, more than forty years ago, and it was highly unusual to see anybody, even a traveling salesman, working on that day and especially at that hour. Even more ominously, the stranger had pulled out and opened his wallet, and from it he drew an identification card and badge to show who and what he was.

The Wisdom and Wit of Ordinary Days

As my cousin opened the door of his small rented mobile home, what we then called a trailer, the visitor stretched out his hand with the picture showing and announced, "Good evening. I am a special agent of the I.R.S. (Internal Revenue Service)."

Within no more than a minute he would explain who he was looking for and why he was there. But in those seconds, and before he could utter those words, my cousin's whole life history passed swiftly through his mind.

He was reminded that he had dropped out of school even before finishing the eighth grade — and thus avoided having to leave the Island for high school. He recollected that he had never held a job other than working in the water, and that unlike most of his family, he had never owned a boat of his own. He had instead worked as a crew member for any of ten or more friends or family who took him along for a share of the catch. Like everyone else he had been paid strictly with cash, in a barter economy that kept no records and reported no earnings.

He contemplated that he didn't even get a social security card until he was in his thirties, and then only because he had been told that this was the only way he or his wife would ever be able to draw any pensions or even claim welfare assistance. And most of all, he thought about how he had never once filed his taxes — neither federal nor state, since as far as he was concerned, he had never earned a real income. In only a second or two all of this came back to him, and not just that. He was certain that the man standing in front of him was an emblem of his past that finally had caught up to him!

As my cousin struggled for what he might say or do, at first pretending that he did not hear or understand what he was being told, the stranger at the door tried to continue his introduction. He wanted to explain that he was there only to ask for directions. You see, in the days before 911 identification, homes and even streets on the Island were not marked, except for an occasional mailbox with a "Star Route" number that had absolutely no order or sequence. The agent was looking for a recent newcomer to the Island, one who appeared to be a successful businessman searching for a quiet place to retire. But he obviously had some unresolved tax issues or else a government agent would not have been seeking him out in person less than two days before the most important holiday of the year.

Before the Special Agent could continue his introduction, my cousin gave way to both the fear and the resignation that had overwhelmed him. Having watched at least one too many detective dramas on television, he stretched forth his arms with his hands held close together so that he could easily be shackled or cuffed. As he did so, he looked the stranger in the eye and asked, "How come you waited until this close to Christmas to come get me?"

Disappointed at Her Proofs

Sometime near the middle of the 1960s, the local power cooperative sponsored a "family portrait fundraiser" and contracted with a photo company to use their building as their studio. Families were invited, even encouraged, to sit for portraits that would be offered at a discounted price, and the co-op would share in the proceeds. Appointments were made, and a schedule was posted. Early one Saturday morning, a line of families, young and old, small and large, all began to make their way to pose in front of a professional photographer to make a family keepsake they hoped would last forever.

All that day, as well as through the next afternoon, the parade continued. Each family wanted to do their part to support the small co-op that was the pride of their community and, at the same time, to show off and preserve an image of what their nuclear family had been like. A short but steady line formed outside the front door of the REA (Rural Electrification Administration) office, as the co-op building usually was called. Folks from all over the Island, dressed in their Sunday best, waited patiently for their turn in front of a pale-blue painted screen that would be the backdrop for a cherished reminder to them and their descendants.

The excitement of the moment was only slightly diminished by the realization that they would have to wait several weeks to see the results of their effort. The company planned and slated a return visit, with a schedule similar to the original sittings, for each family's representative to review their "proofs." After that, the final product, usually a package that would include at least one 8 x 10s, two or more 5 x 7s, and several sheets of "wallet size" prints, would not be available for even a few more weeks.

Eventually, the waiting was over, and yet again, a line began to form in front of the glass door that opened into the Island's only full-fledged business office. It was while those proofs were being sorted and chosen that there ensued a conversation that has become a part of the consciousness of Islanders ever since. The final response of the frustrated "picture man" has been repeated so often that most of us use it anytime we are confronted with a similar scenario, especially when we are implored to "make a silk purse out of a sow's ear."

Late in the evening, after a long and arduous day of sorting through hundreds of packages for people who "talked funny" and shared many of the same names, the company representative sat down with an older lady who was unhappy with what the camera had recorded of her and her family. The photo expert mentioned several alternatives to resolve her concerns: a touch-up, an airbrush, more or less lighting, and anything else the technology of the day would allow that might offer the woman something she might find acceptable.

But as the conversation ran on and on, and he sensed that other customers were growing restless from waiting long past the time of their appointment, the exasperated salesman finally reached his breaking point. When the matriarch insisted that she would not buy any of the photos until and unless she and her family were made to look "purty," he concluded the conversation by shouting loud enough that those waiting in the hallway could hear.

"Listen, lady!" he exclaimed as she made her way toward the doorway, her face showing her disappointment. "I can't undo what God Almighty already has caused to be done!"

Do You Wanna Cut the Grass, or ...

When I eventually had a family of my own, an oft-repeated question heard around our home was directed by me to our children and went something like this, "Do you want to (do the dishes, wash the car, mow the lawn, etc.), or do you want me to ...?" Each of my children knew how the query ended and the desired response, so we never had to complete the sentence — or at least, hardly ever. The statement had its genesis in a long-ago story of an Island father and his relationship with his teenage son.

When he grew up, he and his family, which included his wife as well as a son, lived in a home he had inherited from his parents near the edge of our neighborhood. He was at least ten years older than me but was a part of the gang of neighborhood boys that often gathered for games. Eventually he found a permanent job as an engineer for one of the many tugboat companies that worked along the Southeastern and Gulf coasts. Even then, whenever he returned home, he remained a part of the cadre of boys, teenagers and younger, who gathered and played together all day long — frequently until sundown, even when school was in session.

But as he advanced in his career, the work schedule for his new profession involved extended periods of being away from home, interrupted every month or so by coming back home for several weeks at a time. At least at first, when he did make it home, he fell back into his old routine of being just one of the neighborhood boys. Inevitably, once he was married and had a family, he put that part of his life behind him for good.

Many of this man's friends and neighbors had observed how the son was always hard at work around the home, keeping busy helping his parents with routine chores or even working on specialized tasks like painting a porch or trimming the hedges. While sitting around at a store one evening, his father was asked what special parenting skills he had used that caused an adolescent son to be so helpful and industrious, especially at an age when many youngsters shy away from even the most menial of household jobs.

"Well," the father affirmed, "I don't feel like you oughta make children do things against their will. I like to reason with 'em and help 'em understand the why — as well as the possible consequences, now and still to come if the job ain't done. Then I let my son decide for himself if he wants to help his mother and me or, if he's just gonna be lazy and take advantage of us.

"For example, I might say to him, '(calling him by name) do you wanna cut the grass, or do you want me to beat the hell out of you?"

"Then he decides for himself, cuts the grass, and I sit back and drink a cup of coffee."

Point made. Point taken.

Wouldn't That Be an Unsafe Movement?

Most of the Down East communities had something the people there were known for or by. Harkers Islanders were called "looneaters," folks from Marshallberg were called "hard crabs," and the people of Williston were called "beantowners." And for Otway it was accepted by everyone that they drove their vehicles harder and faster than anyone else! Hardly a weekend went by that there was not a wreck, many of them serious, in or around Otway. In the days before safety inspections required effective mufflers on all vehicles, whenever someone heard a howling or roaring engine streaking down the road, the most common speculation was that "... it must be somebody from Otway trying out their car."

It was against that backdrop that an older man from Harkers Island went to the state motor vehicles office in Morehead City to get a driver's license for the first time. He had driven cars and trucks all his life but had never ventured to get an official card to verify that he was legal. He had kept putting off any suggestion that he avoid the risk of driving illegally until finally he admitted the reason. He could neither read nor write! He, therefore, assumed he would never be able to answer the questions on the written portion of a driving test.

Eventually, the county sheriff, who was aware of the situation, worked out an arrangement with a friendly examiner at the DMV to allow for the test to be administered orally. The female officer was accustomed to working with much younger and more anxious applicants and was happy for the chance to help someone closer to her own age and temperament. So, after forty years of driving without a license, the older Islander sat across from a kind lady who read aloud to him each of the required questions. Everything proceeded routinely, even smoothly, in terms of his responses until there arose a question on the subject of "unsafe movement."

Sensing that the man was puzzled, the examiner sought to explain further her question to make sure that he grasped what was being asked. When he still seemed confused, the lady zeroed in by directly asking if he understood the term, and eventually she requested, "Can you give me an example of what you think is meant by the term 'unsafe movement?'"

He thought hard about it and settled on a response. "How's about this?" he finally replied, "A pulpwood truck being driven by a drunk Otwayer and passing somebody on a curve? Wouldn't that be an unsafe movement?"

The examiner must have agreed because a few hours later, the Islander was back home and showing off an official driver's license for the first time in his life.

Dead Man's Curve

At the southwest corner of the Island, and at the very top of Red Hill, the road curves sharply —almost at 90°. Since there were no reflectors or warning signs, driving onto the Island for the first time or for anyone unfamiliar with the lay of the land, it could be challenging to manage the turn, especially after the sun had set for the evening.

There were so many accidents there, at least a couple of them fatal, that the spot eventually became known as "Dead Man's Curve," a name referring to a hit single of the 1960s sung by Jan Berry and Carl Dean (Jan & Dean). The narrow black-top road is bordered on both sides by the largest oaks found anywhere on the Island, and the yaupon bushes that grew underneath them provided little cushion for cars that failed to negotiate the turn successfully. The oak trees themselves remained firm, and whatever hit them, man or machine, stopped immediately on impact.

Weekend nights in the 50s and 60s, when servicemen serving on the mainland at a station in Fort Macon or at Cherry Point would frequent the Island's movie theater and stores, were when most of the accidents occurred. It was approaching midnight on a midsummer Saturday evening when one of those happened. What ensued in the aftermath was told to me by a teenage witness who lived close enough to the scene that he heard both the screeching of tires and the impact that followed. He and his father were there even before a lone NC Highway patrol officer arrived to investigate and make his report. He later related what he had observed.

After an ambulance had removed the severely injured driver from the crash and sped away with lights flashing towards the closest hospital in Morehead City, the trooper retired to his squad car to prepare his preliminary report. In the warm summer air, he was quietly discussing with some of the onlookers what they first had heard and later observed as they arrived on the scene. It was while engaged in that conversation that someone noticed that asleep in the back seat of the officer's car was an older man wearing handcuffs, and apparently inebriated, who had been picked up by the patrolman just before he was called to respond to the accident at Red Hill.

As the back-seat passenger awoke, he grew increasingly restless and uncomfortable, not fully aware of where he was or why he was locked up in the back of a patrol car.

"What is it? Where am I? What's going on?" was all he could say as he looked toward the officer and saw the flashing lights from atop the car reflecting off the surroundings.

Still focused on the incident at hand, the officer paid him scant attention but eventually turned in his direction to say simply, "It was a bad accident."

Still more confused and curious, the detainee immediately followed up by asking, "Who was it?"

The officer paid even less attention than before and responded simply, "It was some drunk."

Now, totally alarmed and extremely agitated, the prisoner shouted out, "Oh me! Was I hurt?"

I Didn't Have a Dime in my Pocket, So ...

There were several auto mechanics on the Island, some of them very good ones: Johnny "Boo" (Willis), "Blacky" (Louie Caffrey Willis), and Thomas Lee (Willis) to name just a few. But there was just one garage and full-service station, and that was the one we called RJ's.

R. J. Chadwick's (1918-1993) little shop and store, just a stone's throw to the west of the intersection of the main roadway and Ferry Dock Road, was the one place that had service bays, a hydraulic lift, a tire machine, and basic repair parts on hand. It was right smack dab in the middle of the Island, and it was where owners who could afford it, or didn't trust themselves to do a particular job, took their cars to get serviced, repaired, or just "worked on."

The number of vehicles on the Island mushroomed in the boom years that followed the end of World War II. There were so-called "filling stations" at several points from Tommie Lewis's store at the east'ard to Claude's store at the west'ard. But gas, and a quart of oil or a gallon of antifreeze, was about all they had to offer in terms of service. R. J. and his parade of mechanics or helpers could do anything from overhauling an engine to changing a set of spark plugs. It was while doing the latter that something occurred that has remained a part of the folklore of the Island ever since.

R. J. reserved most of the challenging jobs for himself, but he usually relegated the more routine tasks to one of the several helpers that he employed over the years. One of those was a veteran from "up north" who had met and married a local girl and then made the Island his home — quite possibly because that had been part of the "pre-nuptial agreement" regarding where they would live that seemingly all Island natives make with their future spouses.

The helper mechanic had worked in an army motor pool while on active duty, and he appeared to have had ample experience at all the standard service jobs. Such was the case when a local driver brought in his late-model sedan for a tune-up. The car was driven around back to the primary service bay, and in short order, the oil was changed, brakes were adjusted, and a new set of spark plugs was installed. But when the car's owner started it up to drive away, the engine was "missing" so severely that he was unable, or at least unwilling, to take his car out on the road.

R. J. himself decided to check out the situation to find out what was causing the problem. After more than an hour of troubleshooting everything from the carburetor to the vacuum pumps, he finally pinpointed the issue as coming from the new set of spark plugs that had just been installed. Pulling them out one at a time, he found that each of them had an improper gauge — the minuscule distance between the tip and the base of the plug. When he asked his mechanic how such a mistake had happened, the young worker seemed a little dumbfounded himself. He had followed the standard procedure for setting the plugs; specifically, he had used a dime, a standard 10¢ piece, as the template for measuring the proper spacing.

It was only after extensive questioning that the new mechanic volunteered that he had not adhered precisely to what was the accepted norm for measuring the gauge. "I knew you were supposed to use a dime to set the thing," he admitted, "but I didn't have a dime in my pocket, so I used two nickels."

R. J. Chadwick's store, later owned by E. B. Gillikin
CSWM&HC Collection

The Education of an Island Boy

Some Lines That Ought to Never Be Forgotten

The following are some short, almost "one-liner" sayings that were known to nearly everyone on the Island. In each case, the story is less compelling than the response it elicited.

~   A newlywed Island husband walked out of his wedding at the Harkers Island Methodist Church with his new wife and crossed the road to Carl's store, at that time the largest and busiest enterprise on the Island. The new couple sat down at the counter near the front of the store and the groom excitedly ordered himself a bottle of Coca Cola. The groom noticed that Carl seemed to glance toward the bride and motion as if to remind him that he had not mentioned ordering anything for her. The man then sheepishly looked his bride in the eye and asked, "You didn't want nothing, did ya?"

~   It is told of an Island boy who once reported to his friends that he had wrecked his car. When asked what had happened, he explained that he had "backed her headfirst into a ditch."

~   Another Harkers Island boy who had grown homesick while working on a scallop boat off the coast of Florida decided to hitchhike home. Arriving at the Island a few days later, he was asked which was the biggest city he passed through while on his way. Without hesitation, he responded, "Baltimore!"

~   Two Island fishermen were working their nets along the shore one morning when they began a discussion of the news that they had gleaned from the radio and newspapers about World War II in Europe. One of them began by stating, "I heard that a lot of people got killed last week in a place called Normandy. I heard it was almost two thousand." His friend responded, "I heard it was more than that. I heard it was eighteen hundred."

~   After a church group traveled together to New Bern to donate blood as a charitable project, they were rewarded with a meal at one of the finer restaurants in town. One of the Island boys ordered a plate of baked ham, and reviewing the menu, asked for a side order of "yams." When the meal was delivered, he looked it over and then complained to his server, "Mam, I ordered yams, but I hate to tell ye, — that ain't nothing but sweet potatoes."

~   The Carteret County Sheriff once drove to Raleigh to pick up an Islander who had been released from prison after serving a sentence for domestic issues. Because the Sheriff was good friends with the man and his family, he volunteered to take his charge out for lunch before beginning the long trip back to the Island. Accustomed to fine eating while in the state's capital, the sheriff carried the parolee to the Velvet Cloak Inn, one of Raleigh's finer restaurants. After taking the officer's order for a plate of prime rib, the waitress turned to his companion and asked what he wished to order.

Anxious for something familiar after eating prison food for several months, he proclaimed that he wanted "two hot dogs." The server was more than a bit startled by the request, and condescendingly informed the Islander that, "This restaurant does not serve hot dogs." Looking up with his own expression of surprise he responded, "You mean to tell me that a café this big don't have no hotdogs?"

Such were the stories, the yarns, allusions, and lines that were a part of daily life and conversation on the Harkers Island of my youth. There were and are lots of others.

The Education of an Island Boy

Harkers Island as photographed by Lillie Miller. The 1970 bridge, replaced in 2023, can be seen on the middle left.

9

Special People and Their Stories — Life Lessons Lived Large

There isn't a person you wouldn't love if you could read their story.

Marjorie P. Hinckley

Being around older people so often was one of my youth's great blessings. These included many beyond my family and neighborhood, and they were there on such a routine basis that they were a genuine part of my life and learning. Even as a child, I could sense that I was often in the company of both men and women who were unique and who stood out amid the daily routines of life on Harkers Island. Some were exceptionally talented; others were just eccentric, and still more were remarkable in how their lives unfolded. There were others I knew only through stories repeated so often it was as if they were still alive and of our crowd.

Some have been mentioned earlier as part of the essence of Island life, places, and routines. Their stories, taken together, illustrate how seemingly unremarkable individuals, families, and neighborhoods stood apart even as they were meshed in the fabric of day-to-day living. The following pieces, mainly of the generation before mine, added a unique color and flavor to the routine of life that would have been more mundane but for their part in it. Though they may seemingly be unrelated on the surface, beyond their time and place, the underlying theme of each is that among the people of Harkers Island, these were exceptional individuals. Each one had a talent, character, experience, personality, or even a foible that exemplified the charm and variety of the small world of which we together were parts.

Has there been a blow or something? Tom C. and The Storm of '33

I spent most of my professional life in the insurance industry. For that reason, I have been especially sensitive to the barrage of hurricanes that have battered this area since the last era of storms began with Hurricane Bertha in 1994. Because of the time and effort involved in reporting and responding to the resulting claims, each has a particular niche carved into my memory.

My father, who lived to be just two months short of ninety-three years old, experienced several similar periods of intense hurricane activity. He knew what those storms meant to a waterman who supported his family with a boat hitched to a makeshift mooring at the Landing. Although he had specific memories of each of them, one storm stood out far beyond the rest. It occurred when he was still a young man, but married with three small children, and living in a small white-frame house less than two hundred feet from the shores of Back Sound.

It occurred before hurricanes had official names. He sometimes called it "The Storm of '33," but more often, he referred to it by the name of a fisherman from nearby Sea Level, Jimmy Hamilton (1878-1933), who lost his life after ignoring warnings and the pleas of his family. Two of Jimmy's aunts lived on the island, and many local fishermen were his friends. It was said that just hours before the winds arrived, despite indications that a severe storm was on its way, Jimmy Hamilton headed out into Core Sound with three of his four sons, looking for mullets.

When cautioned that a major storm, possibly even a hurricane, might be at their doorstep, he hesitated only long enough to explain to his family, "You can't eat hurricanes." Neither he, his sons, nor his boat were ever seen again. After that, every blow, nor'easter, tropical storm, and hurricane was measured against the

"Jimmy Hamilton Storm," and always, in my father's mind, paled in comparison.

He would relate vivid stories of the howling winds that caused the walls of his house to shimmer and the rising tides that surrounded his father's and his brother's homes. He would explain that the sea waters eventually reached his own backyard. Later, he would tell of the rapid ebbing of the water, which he would learn resulted from an inlet breaking through near the Cape Lookout Lighthouse. That inlet, today known as Barden's Inlet, would eventually be dredged and maintained as a permanent thruway to the ocean, running between Core and Shackleford Banks.

But for some reason, at least to me, none of those stories resonated as much as the account of what he saw and heard when the winds finally died down, and the people of his neighborhood ventured out to see what had been wrought, and especially what had been left by the monster storm. The humor, the irony, and the serenity evidenced in that tale capture in one simple story much of what made life for the people of our Island so unique and, at least for me, so memorable.

As told by my father, the heavy gale-force winds began around sundown. They grew increasingly stronger until shortly after midnight when they abated enough that he took Mama and the children, Ralph, Ella Dee, and June, across the dirt and shell path to the east of our house and to the home of Cliff (1888-1967) and Cottie (Carrie 1894-1985) Guthrie. He would later learn that what he had experienced was the eye of the storm passing directly over his home. Even though Cliff's house was closer to the shoreline than ours, it was bigger and higher off the ground.

Once he got there, Daddy found that several other families had the same idea, and that a group of over twenty had gathered on the chairs, around the table, and on the floors of Cliff and Cottie's living room. Soon after that, the howling gusts returned, and for another three hours, the storm-weary group looked, listened, and worried.

Finally, just before the break of morning, the winds died out, and as they did, it left an eerie calm as the sun rose over East'ard (Core) Banks. The new day shed light on the damage left by what would prove to have been the most destructive storm for more than half a century. What they saw when they stepped out on the south-facing back porch of Cliff's house was as follows: Trees, including mighty oaks, had been uprooted; boats had been torn from their moorings and were lodged in the brush and thickets near the shore; livestock from the Banks including horses, cows, and sheep had drowned as they were washed across the channel so that their carcasses dotted the shoreline; and porch posts and planks, along with shingles and siding that been blown or washed off homes, all were strewn in piles on every sound-front yard.

Hinckley and Polly with their granddaughter, Alicia Ann
(Used by permission)

Yet amid all of this, what my father and the others recalled the best, and talked about most often, was what they observed standing on the back-door stoop of the home of Hinckley (1905-1973) and Polly (1912-1989) Guthrie. Their house was at the Landing, between the shore and Cliff's porch, where the storm-weary group had gathered. Indeed, Hinckley and Polly were among those who had assembled next door with Daddy's family and the others. But left behind in their home had been "Tom C." (Thomas C. Lewis 1883-1935), Polly's aged stepfather, who had gone to bed as usual the night before, and from whom no one had heard anything since.

As he stepped out on his porch that early "morning after" after the most severe and damaging storm most of them would ever experience, the old man paused for a moment to observe the desolation that surrounded him, including a silver maple tree that had fallen at the very foot of his porch steps.

With his thin white hair gathered in the middle from a long night on a pillow, and wearing nothing but the faded burgundy union suit (long johns) that had been his night clothes, Tom C. rubbed his eyes to wipe away the sleep and to make sure that he really was seeing what had at first appeared to him. Then, looking to the north and at the family and friends staring in his direction from across his backyard, he asked, "Has there been a blow or something?"

Danny Boy Lewis- I Know Twice as Much as My Father!

Danny Boy Lewis was the son of Brady Lewis (1904-1992). The latter was and remains the icon of boatbuilding on the Island. Even today, his name is spoken of with awe and reverence when designing and building the wooden boats that once lined the south shore of Harkers Island from Red Hill to Shell Point. Sometimes, Harkers Island flare-bowed boats are referred to simply as "Brady Lewis" boats.

Brady and Elizabeth Lewis
CSWM&HC Collection

"The Ralph" docked at the Coast Guard Station, Cape Lookout, NC

Brady's son, Danny Boy (James Daniel Lewis 1922-1995), carried on his father's tradition of boat building and was true in every way to the example his father had set. Like his father, he not only built boats, always using his father's basic design, but often added a "tunnel" that allowed the boat to maneuver in more shallow water. And, again, like his father, he was fascinated with speed on the water and worked on making every boat he owned the "fastest boat on the Island." Neither Brady nor his son ever let functionality get in the way of making a boat

The Education of an Island Boy

"pretty and fast." Their lead convinced many other Island fishermen to follow their examples.

Brady was of my father's generation and built for him "The Ralph," the thirty-five-foot trawler that was my father's most prized possession for forty years. Danny Boy was much older than me, but I got to know him when I worked at Hi-Tide Boat Works at nearby Williston in the summers of 1968 and 1970. There was a small country store adjacent to the shop we worked in. On a daily basis, he would nod to me or one of the other two teenage boys who were working there, Eddie (Guthrie) and Curvis (Guthrie), to say, "Young Man, (the name he used for anyone younger than himself), go to the store and get me a BC powder." There was hardly ever a day that went by without him swallowing at least one of those renowned headache remedies — sometimes without water.

He was too involved with his labors to get to know any of us younger boys working beside and around him. In fact, after two whole summers of spending at least eight hours of every weekday somewhere near him, and after he had beckoned me yet again with his usual "Young Man," I got up the nerve to ask if he even knew my name. Looking at me, more amused than annoyed, he responded that he did, in fact, know it. When I asked him what it was, without any hesitation, he said, "You're that boy of Charlie Hancock's."

Along with his skills as a carpenter, Danny Boy was also known for how well and long he could wield a disk sander. Standing beside or even laying underneath a juniper-planked boat, he would lift the twenty-plus-pound grinder into the air and work unceasingly for hours at a time, stopping only every ten minutes or so to rub his hand over the wood to ensure that it was smooth enough to paint. Sometimes, the dust would cover his face so completely that it appeared as if only his eyeballs remained uncoated.

Though he was always Brady's son, Danny Boy was not content to be known for that alone. He took pride in his skills and felt that he was every bit the innovator his father had been. In fact, when someone once sought to compliment him by comparing him with his famous father, Danny Boy replied by boasting that not only was he just as good as his father, but that he "knew more than him when it comes to building boats!" Somewhat taken aback by that, the listener asked him how that could be. "Simple," he explained, "I know everything he knows, and I know everything that I know. So, I know twice as much!"

Loke and Lemmis- "Stewed Loons" and "Tied-up Chickens"

A little to the east of Hancock Landing, just past the Guthries, was a large flock of Willises. As usual, some other family names were also represented — Guthrie, Moore, and Lewis — but it was made up mainly of Willises, who were distantly related to the Willises of our neighborhood. One of the Willises from down the shore, "Lemmis" (George Lemus Willis 1860-1928), was gone long before I came of age, but he was mentioned so often I knew him. A little farther to the east'ard, on Ferry Dock Road, were several families of Roses. Brothers Tom, Danny, and Joseph all had families in the same neighborhood. But it was their brother "Loke" (John William Rose 1879-1943), whose life and "loves" became the stuff of legend.

Early on, I learned that other folks Down East, and especially people from "town," referred to us on the Island as "loon eaters." This came as no great surprise as I was already aware that Harkers Islanders were unique in their appetite for that migratory and scavenger bird. I also knew that shooting loons was illegal and had been for quite a while, but that some Islanders persisted in hunting them, nonetheless.

Among those hunters sometimes was my father. Because of the pungent smell, Mama usually cooked loon outside in a large pot over an open fire. She preferred the younger birds, which she called "Eel Trickers," a name they were given because of their skill at grabbing swimming eels as they broached the surface of the water. She maintained that their meat was milder and more tender than when they had matured. But Daddy made no such distinction. All he cared about was that there also be dumplings and gravy in the pot.

The Education of an Island Boy

Bertie Clyde Willis

Not everyone shared a fancy for this bird, especially my sisters, who always grimaced when asked to explain what eating it was like. But many folks considered it a delicacy, and some even demanded that it be served to celebrate special occasions. One of those was Mama's cousin, Bertie Clyde Willis (1918-1987), whom we all called "Uncle Bert." He was the oldest child and son Telford and Gertie. He had a lengthy career in the Army that kept him away for more than two decades. After he retired, he settled his family in Kinston, one hundred miles west of the Island on Hwy 70. But every time he returned from Kinston for a visit, his sisters made sure he had at least a portion of "stewed loon" to make him feel welcome. Once, while watching him savor a bowl of loon prepared in his honor, I mentioned to him that he "... loved loon more than anyone I'd ever heard of."

"I love it," he responded, "Oh, I do love it so, but not as much as Loke did!" He went on to tell a story about this same old-timer that I had heard my father mention so often, who, it turned out, really did love Loon even more than Uncle Bert. "How," I asked, "could anyone love it more than you?"

"Well," he explained, "Loke was partially blind and depended on his touch and other senses, even his taste buds, to compensate for what his eyes couldn't tell him. Loke wouldn't just eat the loon and dumplings. He needed something more to satisfy his cravings. When the pot full of loon was empty of meat, potatoes, and onions, he would lift the pot to his mouth and drink the gravy. But even that wasn't enough," Uncle Bert added. "Once he had drunk all the gravy, he would wipe his hands inside the pot and moisten them with what was left. Then he would run his hands and fingers through his hair."

Hearing that, I agreed that "Loke loved Loon more than anybody I've ever heard of," including my Uncle Bert.

Loke's fishing partner, Lemmis Willis, worked the water with his extended family and the other men of the neighborhood. He, too, was one of those who was called a "progger." He didn't have his own boat, but instead worked in the crew of others who did. Between the fishing seasons, and even during them, he and others like him would, on their own, rake and sign for clams, bend over for oysters, scoop for scallops, pot for hard crabs, or shed for soft crabs. They "progged" the sound to make a living. Like so many others, his everyday life was tied closely to the season, the tide, and especially the wind. Those three things, taken together, told a progger what he would or could do on any given day.

For Lemmis and others like him, life was simple and, fortunately, did not require much money. Food and shelter weren't just the beginning of their concerns. To a large extent, they were the end as well. After visiting and coming to know people on the Island at the turn of the 20th century, a Mormon missionary characterized this group of Islanders as "... good, humble, but very poor people. All they lived on was a few fish they would catch, then sell them, and not worry anymore until all the money was gone."

Despite anyone's relative poverty, real hunger was seldom a concern because fish and shellfish and an abundance of domestic birds and waterfowl surrounded their home, and because they lived amid a large extended family. Yet, shelter sometimes was. This was true even though most Island people and families were and are sedentary in a way that remains surprising to most visitors. Still, there were a few individuals and families that, although they always stayed within the confines of the Island, never really had a place of their own.

Even the poorest families, including that of Lemmis Willis, maintained a small flock of laying hens. On those occasions when a family was obliged to pull up stakes, the accepted way to transport the chickens was to tie their legs with a soft string, lay them on their backs, and place them in a wooden fish box until they could be "cut loose" and released at the new home. After a while, Lemmis had moved his stuff so many times that even his hens grew sensitive to how often it occurred. So sensitive it was said that when his chickens saw him coming, "they rolled over on their backs and crossed their legs!"

To this day, when we hear of someone who has frequently changed locations, it is common for others to ask if it has reached the point that "his chickens have crossed their legs?"

The "Tiny World" of Cecil Nelson

"I would prefer not to," said he. I looked at him steadfastly. His face was leanly composed, his gray eyes dimly calm. Not a wrinkle of agitation rippled him, ... not the least uneasiness, anger, impatience, or impertinence in his manner ...
Herman Melville, "Bartleby the Scrivener"

When I first ran across the above in a high school reading assignment, my thoughts immediately went back to an old man who lived just a few hundred yards from our house and whose dock was the next one to the west'ard from the one at our landing. In my mind's eye, I could see his faded but still yellow clapboard-sided house sitting between several very formidable "Island oaks." Most of all, I replayed in my memory the story told to me so vividly by my sister, Lillian, about her encounter with him, and how he became my very own version of Melville's "Bartleby the Scrivener." Here is how it went.

One summer morning, my father was working on his boat, "The Ralph," at the Landing when he hollered out for my youngest sister, Lillian. He didn't call her by name because, like everyone else before and since, he just called her "Sister." He gave her a dollar bill and sent her along the shore to the west'ard on an errand. She was to go to a store less than half a mile away and get a quart of "copper paint" that Daddy would then mix with kerosene to make sure he had enough to cover the bottom of his vessel.

"It should be less than a dollar, and you can keep the change," he promised her, knowing that the prospect of even a few pennies as a reward would cause her to hurry along her way. Within a few minutes, Sister, who was yet to reach her teens, was standing in front of the counter of a small wooden frame store and doing just what Daddy had asked. A middle-aged man listened to her request and reached to the shelf behind him, where he found the item my father had wanted. He explained to Sister that the cost was 95¢ and that he would have to get full payment before giving her the paint. She immediately laid out the dollar she had been carrying and waited anxiously for the change.

"I don't have any change in my pocket right now," the store clerk stated, "but I'll drop it by your house the next time I'm in your neighborhood."

"No, you won't," Sister quickly responded, "because you never leave your yard, much less come all the way to our house."

Taken aback by the unexpected response, the man hesitated and said, "You're a smart little girl, ain't ya?" as he reached under the counter and found a nickel. He handed the coin to my sister, who, as soon as she held it in her hand, grabbed the small can of paint she had been sent to secure and ran all the way back to our Landing.

The man behind the counter at the paint store was the store's owner, Cecil Nelson (1905-1966). For him, that store, and the dock that ran from it into the Sound, and the frame house that lay a few feet farther inshore toward the road, were his whole world — not just figuratively, but literally. Cecil suffered from what is often called "agoraphobia," a common symptom of which is an unwillingness to leave home — and sometimes even a room.

By the time I came to know him, most people could not recall ever having seen Cecil

Cecil Nelson, R- with his father, Samuel Nelson
CSWM&HC collection

anywhere other than on the small spot of land that held the home he shared with his wife, Myrtle (Lewis 1904-1985). My father, just four years his younger, could recall seeing him at the Banks when they were boys. He often mentioned that Cecil had been so pampered as a child that his father, Sam Nelson (1883-1962), would carry him on his back as they walked across to the beach side of Shackleford so that young Cecil would not have to strain or struggle while walking in the soft sea sand. The fact that he was married suggests that earlier, he must have had at least some social life outside his home and family. But those days were now long gone, and mostly forgotten.

His little store sold only paint ("Wolsey" was the preferred brand of the day) and nails, two staples for anyone who worked with boats. Suppliers and shoppers were obliged to come to him if they wanted to do business. He was not one to make a sale or buying call. The counter of the store was stacked with the magazines and newspapers he got by mail, which he read from cover to cover while passing what must have been long and frequent intervals between customers.

Some people still talk of how "smart" he was about news and affairs, and how he was often the first to know about many of the important things happening in the world. They also mention his beautiful penmanship, and how he wrote out receipts and signed his name as if he were preparing documents to be displayed behind glass or on a wall. But more than anything, they recall how he absolutely refused ever to leave his yard. They lament that near the end of his life, he grew increasingly more reclusive and, it was said, would not even step off his front porch.

In addition to the store, he supported the family with a small clam house at the offshore end of a short dock that jutted out from his shop. A high white sandy shoal on both sides of the pier was used as a bed for smaller seed clams until they were big enough to sell. Jimmy Fulford (1911-1989), Roosevelt Davis (1903-1983), and Ernest "Cooter" Davis (1906-1975) were his usual suppliers. They would dump their smaller clams on the shoal beside the dock and wait several months for them to grow. Then, after the clams were large enough to sell, they used forked rakes on a wooden handle to dig them back up. Cecil would buy their harvest and resell them to a dealer on the mainland in Otway.

For a while, he even had a truck he used to carry the harvested clams to the market. He would be seen sitting behind the wheel, steering it in a circle around his house, especially near his front fence, but not once venturing as far as the paved road less than fifty feet from his doorstep. Instead, he had someone on hire drive the truck for him and then return with empty baskets to restart the cycle.

One story, as poignant as it is revealing, was told to me by one of his younger neighbors, Bobby Russell (Robert Vernon Russell 1932-2019). Bobby was in his late teens and had just purchased his first automobile, and he was eager to show it to "Old Cecil," as he was called by then. He drove his car directly into the yard and in front of the porch and honked down hard on the horn. Within a few seconds, both Cecil and Myrtle stood in front of him, smiling broadly at the new automobile they were being shown. Cecil came down and stared into the window at the shiny leather, and even sat behind the wheel and tugged it in both directions, pretending to steer it as if it were moving.

At length, he arose from his seat to look more at the bright finish and the chrome bumpers. As he did, his young friend asked him pleadingly, "Why don't you jump in and let me drive you to Shell Point? It won't take five minutes. I want you to feel how she does when she goes into passing gear."

Without the slightest hesitation, Old Cecil just smiled, shook his head, and stepped back up on the porch as if he were retreating to safety. "I don't think so," he said, apologizing only for his friend's obvious disappointment and not for his decision. The scene would have mirrored what had played out in Herman Melville's fertile mind when he penned, "I would prefer not to," said he. I looked at him steadfastly. His face was leanly composed, his gray eyes dimly calm. Not a wrinkle of agitation rippled him, ...not the least uneasiness, anger, impatience or impertinence in his manner ..." Herman Melville, "Bartleby the Scrivener"

Cecil Nelson was comfortable in his own little world, but only in that world. He didn't invite or even want you to join him in it, only to respect its boundaries.

The Sad Story of Abram Lewis

Anytime we saw his red pushcart coming down the road, we ran as if to hide. He had never done anything to anybody that we knew of, but there was something scary and strange about the way he looked and moved, and our reflex action, whenever we caught sight of him coming, was to get far away, or at least out of his path.

His name was Abram Lewis (1922-1994), and when I reflect on my reactions to him, I am both embarrassed and ashamed. And the older I get, the more uncomfortable I am. Abram suffered from a severe form of cerebral palsy that left him nearly totally disabled. He could speak only to grunt and moan, and his limbs were so constricted that he couldn't stand or walk upright. He moved around on a worn and weather-beaten old Western Flyer wagon.

Abram Lewis
CSWM&HC
Collection

He steered with one outstretched hand while he pushed his cart along with a leg that extended over one side. The shoeless foot he used for pushing was usually covered with a sock worn through so badly that the bare skin of his toes was always visible.

He wore old clothes that fit poorly and were often tattered and torn. They always appeared soiled or, at best, unkempt. His face had a bearded stubble accenting a dark complexion, and his deep brown eyes evidenced simultaneously a smile and a profound sadness that still haunts me when I remember those eyes staring into mine.

Abram was one of several children born to a poor family, but hardly more so than most others on the Island. It was not poverty alone that made him sometimes an object of ridicule. Instead, Abram's decrepit appearance was caused by a lack of sensitivity, and even of compassion. In retrospect, there was at least some of both. It could be said that his life was less a life than a mere existence. The latter lacked the human dignity that might have been expected and should have been demanded.

In my memory, because of his handicaps and illness, Abram was seen and treated not with mercy but with begrudging pity and frequently with overt derision. Even some of his family seemed to feel he was primarily a burden to be endured. Some teenagers would mock and jeer him, and even those who were not the perpetrators were guilty of allowing the others to mock him, and even laugh at his humiliation. Most grownups simply ignored him; a response that was hardly more laudable than the pranks of their children. Smaller children like me just ran away, more because of what we had been told than because of anything we might actually have witnessed.

It would be comforting to think that Abram Lewis was the only person I knew who was victimized by his time and condition, but there were others whose situation differed only in the degree of their disability. Very few of them had the benefit of the special treatment they needed to make their lives more comfortable and bearable. I can't accept that this neglect was entirely because of a lack of love or concern or even of resources. It was, I presume, much more attributable to an unfeeling disregard by some for the plight of handicapped people in general.

Abram's story had a happy ending of sorts. When he was forty years old, he was placed in a state-maintained training school, in Kinston. There, he finally got the attention, therapy, and even the compassion he had been denied during those first long and formative years. Gladly for him, we eventually learned that Abram's disability did not extend to his mental capacities. In fact, he had been fully aware of the life he had been compelled to live.

For those of us who had either mistreated or ignored him came to understand that the victim of our neglect had not been so oblivious to our behavior as we might have assumed. Knowing that he had been aware of the indignity of his condition, as well as our apparent lack of caring compassion, has been a lasting shame for me and many others — if only because of how we passively witnessed it.

Abram lived for another thirty years at the facility that had saved him from the humiliation he had known as a child and man in the place where he was born. Friends and family who visited him there brought back stories of someone who would have been unrecognizable to most of those who once had belittled him. Thankfully, one of the ways that the Island and the world of today is far better than the one I knew as a boy is in how we treat and interact with people like Abram Lewis.

Archie Fulford- You Look Enough Alike

Archie Fulford (1915-1980) was loved by everybody. I mean exactly that! He was loved by everyone who knew him. Although in another place or at another time, he might have been known as the "town drunk," he was appreciated way too much to ever have been called that here. Besides, when Archie "got to drinking," he became even more lovable and was never a problem for anyone — that is, anyone other than himself. He was a die-hard fan of the New York Yankees, but that was the only bad thing you might ever say about him. (This, in jest, is the observation of a lifelong fan of the Boston Red Sox.)

The youngest son of one of the Island's longest-standing families, one that had been here for more than a century before the arrival of the newcomers from the Banks, he never had children of his own. But he was a kind and caring uncle figure for the kids of his many friends with whom he lived, worked, and played every day. By the time I came to know him, he was an older man, hardly more than five feet tall, with a face that evidenced the life he had lived, with heavy wrinkles and a ruddy complexion. But that same face always had a smile, and when he passed his time telling boys like me his farcical stories, his grin was often also a hardy laugh.

Near the end of his life, he was all but adopted by George "Billy" Best (1932-1998), who ran the biggest grocery store on the Island. By then, he had given up the bottle, and Billy used him as a combination stock boy and night watchman. He even spent most nights sleeping on a small cot, what we called a "day bed," in an office enclosure hidden in the very back of the store.

It was around the store, as he discussed the latest news and sports, and shared his yarns with other old-timers that I came to know him. Billy's son, Alton (1952-2022), was one of my best friends, and his father's store was just across the road from the ball field behind our church. So, a vital part of each day was meeting Alton and others at the store to organize a game, and then returning to the same place to get a soft drink and nabs when the game was over. Archie grew so used to seeing us together that he grabbed us both by our arms and said, "You boys look enough alike that you could be neighbors!" It was years later before I realized the whole irony of how we had interpreted his observation.

Archie Fulford
CSWM&HC Collection

Archie had a particularly deep affection for Alton, always playing with or picking on him in one way or another. He seemed especially to enjoy commenting on Alton's hair after it was tousled by swimming in the sound or playing in the woods. "Your hair is just like fine marsh grass," he once observed as my friend removed his cap after playing ball on a sweltering summer day.

But the remark I remember most is one day when we were a little older and dressed to go out in Al's car on a Friday evening. As Alton walked into the store, probably to get gas money from his father, Archie commented on his good looks and then feigned an added compliment, saying that Alton had really "kind hair." When my friend smiled in response, the old man added, "The kind that grows on a dog's tail." (Actually, he was even more explicit than that.)

The Education of an Island Boy

Ever since, using the adjective "kind" to describe a person or object has had a different connotation for me.

Harkers Island "Professionals" — Charlie Nelson, Raymond Guthrie, and Maxwell Willis

Despite having a growing population of well over a thousand and the opening of the Harkers Island bridge two decades earlier, in the mid-1900s, the Island remained separated from the mainland with its legal and business institutions. The relative simplicity of Island life allowed that there was little need for full-time professionals who hung a shingle to announce their special occupation. Instead, in many ways, the Island that I knew as a boy was a web of shared skills and talents that more than substituted for the lack of trained clericals or tradesmen.

In a very real sense, because of people like Charlie Nelson, Raymond Guthrie, and Maxwell Willis, Harkers Island was a "barter economy" when it came to some specialized services. Some among us could fill that void on any occasion that might call for an aptitude, ability, or skill beyond those needed in the routines of daily living. Many other men and women had unique talents; artistic, mechanical, or musical, that were known and utilized by their families, their neighborhood, and the whole Island.

The business offices of Beaufort and Morehead were much farther away than the actual distance that could be shown on a map. Most Islanders could not have afforded their services even if they had been closer. But because we had each other, that distance and price didn't matter as much as it otherwise might have.

One of the "specialists" who frequently was called upon was Charlie Nelson (1896-1971), a self-taught land surveyor. Early on, he assumed as his life's work a responsibility to legitimize the

Charlie Nelson and his wife, Letha
CSWM&HC Collection

Island's land parcels and boundaries, many of which, before him, were based only on oral agreements and handshakes making mention of physical landmarks such as trees, stumps, or fence posts. His drawings on the maps he created were the works of a master, and his artful lettering and numbers had the look of calligraphy.

He was often seen walking up and down the Island, carrying a bundle of equipment, including a tripod, compass, notebooks, and a surveyor's chain. His was not an easy task, and not just because of simmering disagreements over where one lot ended, and another began. Instead, his main challenge stemmed from the Island's shoreline running a few degrees off from what was assumed to be due east and west. The landlines were drawn perpendicular to that same shoreline so that when charted on a grid, they were hardly ever at the right angles that had been assumed.

Even today, many local deed plots appear as trapezoids and parallelograms rather than the shapes of planned rectangles or squares. Most of them still reference an initial survey that displays the name Charlie Nelson, Esq. Despite the challenges of the layout and topography, the old maps stamped with his seal remain artistic achievements as much as legal documents.

The same handwriting and descriptive skills that served him as a surveyor also led family and friends to call on him to prepare wills, deeds, and other personal legal documents, and to serve as the Island's "Notary Public." It was standard practice for any business agreement on the Island to conclude with the statement, "Let's go see Charlie Nelson and make it legal!"

Another of the men whom people on the Island looked to was Raymond Guthrie (1916-1987). I knew him well because he lived directly across the road from our house. For years, he ran a little store

Raymond Guthrie
Almeta Gaskill Collection

known simply as "Raymond's Store," even after passing it on to others. But he was best known, especially in our neighborhood, as our community "lawyer," although he had never studied for even a day in a school of law. So, he obviously was not an attorney in a technical sense. But even without so much as a high school diploma, he was the one to whom people looked when they needed to make their case in the form of a letter.

When did people go to Raymond for help? When a catalog order from Sears-Roebuck didn't show up or arrived already broken; when an outstanding bill came from a lender who threatened collection; when an appeal was needed to a congressman for a son or husband who served in the military and wanted a transfer closer to home; or when someone needed to complete an application to work at the military base in Cherry Point or on the ferry that left from Cedar Island. For these and a hundred other scenarios, Raymond Guthrie could prepare a letter to explain or plead your case — usually for a fee of five dollars or less.

Charlie Callis Guthrie
CSWM&HC Collection

Raymond never married. He shared a home with his parents and a brother, Charlie Callis (Guthrie 1914-1991). After the passing of their parents, the brothers grew increasingly eccentric and became the subject of gossip. They seldom ventured far from our neighborhood, leaving only in their fishing boat to go sink-netting at and around Cape Lookout.

But they, especially Raymond, had a cosmopolitan interest evidenced by the piles of magazines and newspapers that crowded his living room floor and tables. He would tell stories of calling telephone information, a toll-free call then, to distant parts of the world just so he could say, "I spoke to someone last night in New Zealand, Portugal, or Kenya!" Charlie Callis, who had served in the U. S. Army in Europe during World War II, would sometimes disappear for weeks, only to return home and announce that he had been back to Scotland visiting war-time friends.

Special People and Their Stories — Life Lessons Lived Large

As time passed, their home, once immaculately kept, became a haven for feral cats and other animals. He even had a pig that grew so large that it could no longer stand on its own. Eventually, in a case that drew "nationwide attention," as it was mentioned in national newspapers, the two were blackmailed for the return of one of their favorite cats — the one they called "Cry Baby." A ransom message demanded more than a thousand dollars for the animal's return. Happily, for Raymond, and for the cat, their pet was returned without any injury, and the perpetrator was arrested.

But now, three decades after both brothers have passed and their house sold and renovated, Raymond is remembered chiefly as an advocate and attorney who could write and say things on paper in a plain and straightforward way that his friends could appreciate, and that others would understand.

Another distinctive presence on the Island — and a man of many talents was Maxwell Willis (1912-1984). He had the mind of an accountant, the skills of an electrician, the mathematical acumen of a technician, and the vision of a civil engineer. With little formal education, but a lifetime of knowledge taken from hundreds of books he had read and studied, he played a central part in many of the changes that allowed the Island to emerge from traditional ways as it adopted the advances of the twentieth century.

Maxwell Wills
CSWM&HC Collection

He started as a clerk with a local electrical cooperative, the Harkers Island REA, when it brought electricity to the Island in 1939. But he quickly advanced to the position of director. He managed finances, including funding from several government sources, billing, payroll, and facility maintenance costs. But more importantly, he oversaw construction, repairs, and planning for an enterprise that eventually was valued in the millions of dollars.

Long before the age of electronic "gadgets," Maxwell was the ultimate gadgeteer. He was the first on the Island to have the latest phonograph, radio, and television equipment. His extensive library of books and manuals influenced what he knew and how he wrote and communicated that knowledge to others. He was equally adept and comfortable discussing electrical engineering with government scientists as when explaining construction or maintenance basics to a newly hired lineman.

Like other "Renaissance Men," he was eclectic in his interests. He loved art, music, and movies. His affection for animals and birds all but defined him to his closest friends. His place atop Red Hill was something of a menagerie, including even a monkey, "Choco," that delighted and fascinated Island children as it swung from the vines and limbs of the chinaberry trees.

Beyond his professional responsibilities, because of his engineering and architectural skills, he was a resource for anyone who needed to know how to make or fix something. Part architect, part electrician, and several more parts engineer, Maxwell could make plans and then see them become a reality. Carpenters, plumbers, and masons all sought him out when tackling a new or challenging project. His approval was a sure sign that a plan was ready to be implemented.

Earl Davis- Hardened Oak and Iron Nails

There were boards everywhere along the shore at the Landing — pieces of wood of different sizes, shapes, and kinds. It was obvious that they had accumulated rather than been placed there. They were usually at least six feet long enough to be used as a footing for sliding boats onto the shore. Placed side by side and end to end, they could make a runway atop the soft sea sand that enabled several strong arms, legs, and backs to pull a boat from the water and onto the dry land.

It was supposed that all of it was scrap lumber that either had washed up as driftwood on the beach side of Shackleford Banks or been salvaged from some abandoned building or porch before it was scattered or burned. In every direction, from Shell Point to Red

Special People and Their Stories — Life Lessons Lived Large

Hill, it was always there as community property to be used until it had either rotted or floated away.

One summer morning, my friend Alton and I were playing along the shore by the home of my aunt "Big Sister" and her husband, Earl Davis (1902-1988). Uncle Earl was home that morning, working at the Landing and trying to organize or dispose of the debris accumulated there after a long summer of sou'westers blowing off the Banks.

As often was the case, he soon engaged us in helping to gather and move the cans, bottles, tattered nets, and lines that marred his otherwise pristine shoreline. Unlike so many others, he was always generous in handing out nickels, dimes, and even quarters after we had "lent him a hand," so we were happy and anxious to help him that morning.

Earl was an extraordinary man in many ways. Sharing his pocket change with neighborhood boys was among the least important of his unique traits. He was both a college-educated and self-made man whose interests extended far beyond the boundaries of the little Island he was born and raised on. He loved his home and its people for what it was, but

Lillian and Earl Davis

unlike many others, he dreamed about what the Island might someday be. Beginning when he was a small boy and continuing to the end of his life, he was engaged with both head and heart, and often his hands, in one project or another to make his Island home a better place for him and others.

He was one of those special souls whose mind and imagination never rested. From the Island's first phone lines to an electric cooperative to a movie theater, and later a community water system, Earl Davis's handprints are even more indelible than are his signatures. And the latter can be found on every important document in the Island's modern history. Perhaps most importantly, he subdivided and then offered his family's inherited property for sale so that even the Island's poorest and humblest families could buy a "piece of land" to call their own. Several generations of Islanders now live in homes with deeds that include the phrase "Earl Davis Subdivision" somewhere in the legal description.

But all that was far from our minds that summer morning as Alton and I worked beside him arm-in-arm, moving, hauling, and piling the clutter that had amassed along his shoreline. When we finally finished, just as expected, he reached into his pocket and pulled out a quarter for each of us, enough to make us among the wealthiest boys on the Island for the next few days.

But, before we left, he pointed to a pile of boards we had stacked on the far eastern corner of his land, off the shore and up on his grassy yard that stretched over a hundred feet to his sprawling screened-in porch. This pile was markedly different from the others that lined the Landing shore, and not just because the boards were neatly stacked.

Most of them looked enough alike to suggest that they had come from the same place and for the same reason. They were similar in width and length, and all were at least a full inch thick. The salt and sun had bleached them a silver-gray, but it was clear that they were still sturdy and strong and could be used for things far more substantial than as a runway for boats on the shore.

Handing out two hammers and a handful of iron nails, he explained that these boards were not the pine, juniper, poplar, or cypress most often seen floating in the surf. These were "solid oak" and thus were hardwood; so hard that he had a little challenge for us. He would pay us an extra dime for every nail we could drive to its head into any of those boards.

Having grown up around carpenters and learned to hammer at nails before we could remember, we were eager to take him up on his offer and were confident that within another few minutes we would have more than doubled our bounty for the morning. So, grabbing his hammers and several of the nails, we bent over the pile and started flailing away. Ten minutes later, we were still flailing with dozens of bent nails strewn by our side, but not even one showing its head pressed against the lumber. Standing beside us, Uncle Earl was laughing, and the harder we swung the hammers, the harder he laughed.

Finally, he interrupted, and taking one last nail he had held between his fingers, he searched and found a grain mark in the solid oak and gently tapped the nail until it had set in deep enough to offer a final pounding blow that finished the task.

We were as astounded as we were disappointed, but not for long. Before we could even beg for another chance, he pulled two dimes out of his pocket and sent us on our way. The lesson we learned that day about hardened wood and iron nails lasted much longer than the money we hurried to show off to our friends. And the man who was our teacher remains an inspiration to anyone on the Island who has ever wondered, "What if?"

Miss Ollie & Dr. Moore

You didn't take kids to the doctor merely because they weren't feeling well. Everyone, young and old, had days when they didn't feel well, and sometimes you might be confined to your home or even bedridden. But in most cases, such illnesses were considered another normal part of life that could be endured and outlasted with no need for the help of a doctor. Every mother had her own repertoire of home remedies that applied to nearly every malady, and these were the first line of defense against any illness or injury.

If a condition persisted or worsened dramatically, the next option was to call on the neighborhood "specialist" whom everyone recognized as the best thing short of a real doctor for diagnosing and treating common ailments. At "Red Hill" that somebody was Marianne Willis, while at the "Eastard" it was Annie Rose.

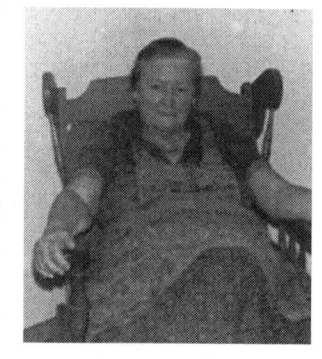

"Big Ollie" Willis

The Education of an Island Boy

In our neighborhood, that was most certainly "Miss Ollie." Ollie Willis (1902-1979), sometimes called "Big Ollie" to distinguish her from her daughter of the same name, was the wife of my father's cousin Danky (Dannie) Willis. She was as kind and gentle as the day is long, and she was so compassionate to me as a child that I have sometimes described her as the closest I ever came to having had a "living" grandmother of my own. And when it came to ailments, she had predetermined remedies for anything that could be imagined. More importantly, most of them seemed to work.

Miss Ollie used to be especially gifted at dealing with skin problems such as "ground itch," hornet stings, and the ever-present boils associated with spending at least half of your life in and around salt water. She even concocted her own "black salve" that was known all over the Island as the most potent balm anywhere to be found for dealing with such problems. In the normal hyperbole of Island talk, I have heard my parents claim that Ollie's salve could "draw an iron nail out of a piece of heart pine."

Walking barefoot on the Island's shore resulted in lots of cuts and scrapes. The bottom of my brother Telford's feet sometimes looked like the plat for a city map laid out with no concern for straight lines and easy access. The most assuredly painful "foot ailments" were those associated with stepping on the exposed nails, usually rusty ones, which were the excruciating by-product of discarded boat timbers and planking. Seemingly always, the wound would swell and harden, causing unbearable discomfort.

Eventually, someone would send for Ollie, or at least for a spoonful of her salve, and within hours, or so it seemed, the infection would ease. Her magic potion would cause the offending particles and fragments to rise to the wound's surface so that loving hands could wash it clean and complete the healing process.

Yet there were times when even Miss Ollie's salve couldn't help, and a real doctor was needed. But because any expense was often "too much," my parents made sure that all other avenues had been explored before taking us children to Beaufort to see Dr. Moore, Dr. Fulcher, or Dr. Salter — the three primary care physicians who served our area. Before it became a part of the Cape Lookout National Seashore in the mid-1970s, and for several years afterward, private individuals could maintain rustic cabins as summer and weekend getaways at Shackleford Banks. Among those was Dr. Laurie Moore. One way to avoid official visits was to wait until word came that Dr. Moore was spending the weekend at his camp at the Banks. It was assumed and accepted that calling on him there was a "personal" call, and hence, there was no obligation to offer any payment. As I grew older and came to know him better, I realized that Dr. Moore probably would not have accepted any money even if offered on such occasions.

Dr. Laurie Moore (1901-1979) lived in Beaufort but had grown up in nearby Marshallberg. His family, the "Tyre Moore crowd," named after his father, had lived at Shackleford Banks before the exodus following the great hurricane of 1899. Most of the family settled at Harkers Island, but Tyre and his children took up residence at Marshallberg. Dr. Moore had a summer camp on the Banks, near the mouth of Whale Creek Bay, close to where the old family home place had been generations earlier. His Harkers Island cousins would attend to his needs while there, ferrying back and forth across the Sound several times each day as he might need them. It generally was from them that everyone knew when he was at the Banks and open for "visitors."

Dr. Moore was considered a bona fide hero among most of the people of the Island. There were many reasons for that respect and affection, but there were two special ones. First, he was the earliest of the Banks crowd to go off to college and come back as a doctor. I was always told that it was while pulling in a net on a cold fall morning that he made up his mind that fishing was not for him. Within weeks he had moved to Wake Forest, NC, then still the home of Wake Forest College (later relocated to Winston-Salem, NC), where he eventually earned his medical degree. So, to Down Easters he was one of their own who had made it in the world doing

Dr. Laurie Moore
CSWM&HC Collection

The Education of an Island Boy

something other than living out of the water.

It was said that Dr. Moore got the money to pay for medical school at Wake Forest from a gold medal his father had earned while serving as a surfman on a rescue team at Cape Lookout before the turn of the 20th century. According to the story, his father had buried and hidden the medal soon after he received it, knowing its value, and fearing that he might someday lose it or have it stolen.

When at long last, his son decided he was not cut out for fishing, and wanted to be a doctor instead, the old man dug up his treasure and presented it to his son, saying, "Now, you sell this, and it will pay for getting you started up there." So, off to Wake Forest went Laurie Moore, and all Down East was blessed with a wonderful family doctor and friend for the next half a century.

A second reason, and most importantly, for the veneration in which he was held by so many was that he never "forgot where he came from," and was willing to care for the poor people of Down East with little or no consideration for their ability to pay him. Dr. Moore always seemed to be just another one of the ordinary folks, but one with extraordinary compassion and an ability to help.

I still can vividly recall those times when my father would take me in his boat, across Back Sound, to Dr. Moore's camp. His attention was needed most often to deal with the earaches that were so frequently a part of my youthful experience. Mama would wrap my head with warm towels and blankets and Daddy would secure me in the front of his open boat, just under the forward deck, to shield me from the wind and spray as the boat broke through the cresting swells. He would head due southwest across Back Sound into the mouth of "Bottarum Bay." There he would weave through the marshes to the shore where Dr. Moore's camp sat some one hundred yards or so up from the shore.

Daddy would carry me to the water's edge in his arms before lowering me so that together we would walk up to where Dr. Moore would be normally resting out on his porch. "Hey, Charlie Bill, which one of your youngerns is that?" he would ask, referring to the fact that Daddy had ten. My father would tell him, but I don't think Dr. Moore really listened. He had no hopes of ever knowing all of us by our first names, the mere fact that we were Charlie and Margarette's children was all that mattered to him. He would ask about Mama and the family and then about Louie, Daddy's brother, and several other of the old people in the neighborhood. But as he was talking to Daddy, he would be pulling me towards him and beginning to diagnose the problem that had caused Daddy to bring me to him.

Should I live to be a hundred, I will never forget the gentleness in his soft hands as he explored around my sore ear. Because of the swelling that usually accompanied such infections, my ear and neck would be so tender that I could scarcely allow even my mother to touch them. But Dr. Moore's hands seemed endowed with some special soothing aura that allowed him to explore and examine without causing even the slightest pain.

Charlie William Hancock Family: Sitting L-R: Lillian Michels, Ella Dee Willis, Charlie William, Margarette, and June Davis. Back L-R: Brothers Ralph, Bill, Joel, Tommy, Telford, and Mike. Missing is Denny who died in 1953.

After just a few moments, he would assure my father that there was no need for undue concern. He would then tell him what medicine and treatments he wanted to start. Sometimes, he would write out a prescription to be purchased from the drug store, but more often, he pulled something out of his little black bag and gave it to us with only his oral instructions.

The Education of an Island Boy

"Now, you go ahead and get him home and out of this wind," he would say, signaling to my father that the checkup was over and allowing us to leave gracefully with no mention of any payment or obligations. Then we would make our way in reverse order of how we had come, but with daddy, and later mama, now relieved that they had done their part to make sure nothing more than an "earache" had been the culprit.

Many others of my generation, and the ones before me, have similar memories and stories of Dr. Moore. In the days before "Social Services" and the County Health Department, he and others like him cared for the families of eastern Carteret County with a depth of feeling that made him more than just a doctor; he was part of the family.

Manus Fulcher was Headed Home

Troy Manus Fulcher (1914-1987) was one of many young men from Harkers Island who either joined or was drafted into military service during World War II. Born in 1914, he served in the Pacific and spent most of his time on the Japanese island of Saipan. After the war, he returned home, married Estelle Guthrie (1925-1995), and moved with her into a small house he built on the northeast corner of the land owned by Willie and Carrie Guthrie, Estelle's parents.

Manus was a self-trained mechanic and carpenter who, in his spare time, became the closest thing our neighborhood had to an engineer — or even an inventor. After being one of the first people on the Island to have and drive a motorcycle, he fashioned his own version of that contraption by installing

Manus Fulcher beside his home-made gas-powered bicycle
CSWM&HC Collection

Special People and Their Stories — Life Lessons Lived Large

a lawn mower motor onto a bicycle. The sound of Manus riding his lawn mower-motorbike was familiar to anyone who lived or hung out on what we called the "Old Road."

Besides doing odd jobs as a carpenter on homes and boats, he was also a gunsmith and the neighborhood handyman for sharpening saws and knives, and especially for repairing and servicing small motors. Old lawn mower engines were his specialty. It was said that he could fix any motor so long as it was still in one piece. My father once took an old "grass cutter" to Manus because he couldn't get it to "fire" and start, no matter how many times he yanked on the rope. The next time he saw Manus, he asked his friend if he had been able to get the motor running. Manus responded that not only did he get it going, but he had also been obliged to remove the wire from the spark plug "...'cause every time the door slammed and jarred his back porch, the engine would start!"

Manus was also a talented artist who used smooth boards and old paper sacks instead of a canvas to draw portraits – often full-length – of friends, movie stars, and other well-known figures. It was not unusual to walk by a boat or temporary wall he had been building and see a recognizable face that Manus had sketched with his "no 2" pencil while enjoying a break from his labor.

Late in his life, in the mid-1960s, he went to work for Julian Guthrie (1914-1998) at the Hi-Tide Boat Works in Williston, less than ten miles north of the Island on US Hwy 70. Julian's crew at that time was made up entirely of his Harkers Island friends. These included my father, Charlie Hancock, Roosevelt Davis (1903-1983), and "Danny Boy" Lewis. Then there were the Guthrie boys, including Julian's nephew, Will Guthrie (1934-2018), Willie Colon "Bonnie" Guthrie (1913-1993), and Bonnie's son, Terry, whom we all knew as "Tuck." There was also Graham Boyd "Graby" Guthrie (1944-2003) and Curvis Guthrie Sr. (1929-2010), whom everyone called just plain "E." All were accomplished

Julian Guthrie

The Education of an Island Boy

boat-builders, but Manus was among those considered to be a "finished" carpenter who could do the fancy trim work that came after the boat had been framed and planked. When his work was done, the boat was ready for the water.

Like so many of his time and place, Manus went out of his way to avoid conflict or contention. He was humble in both personality and means. After facing the anxiety and insecurity of the war, he had neither the time nor the patience for even the slightest of confrontations. I can say that with certainty because I witnessed firsthand a stark example of his passivity.

In the summer of 1968, Julian hired me and my brother, Telford, and E's son, Curvis, to help at the boathouse. One day, I was assigned to help Manus and Graby put the finishing coat of paint on the sides of a sixty-five-foot "headboat." We used an expensive brand of paint reserved for the final finish on boats just before they were launched and ready.

Standing on the typical staging of the time, a 2"x12" wooden board laid between sawhorses, the three of us were hurrying to finish the job. In our haste, one of us — most likely me — moved too abruptly, and the staging fell, spilling paint and us onto the saw-dust flooring below. We knew we had done something awful. The whole gallon of paint that we had wasted cost more than any of us, and maybe the three of us together, would have made for that day's work.

Graby and I instinctively hurried to clean up our mess, and hopefully hide the evidence of what we had done before it was discovered. As we hastily brushed more and more sawdust and shavings over the remains of the spilled paint, Graby noticed that only the two of us were helping in the cleanup. In a matter of minutes, we had the scene looking as if nothing had ever happened, but before we could resume our work, we determined to find out where Manus had gone while we were "mopping up."

Just a few moments later, Graby hollered for me to come and look out the west'ard window towards the highway that was only thirty feet or so from the door to our shop. Manus was standing by the road with his right hand held out and his thumb extended, trying hard to "bum a ride." He was weary of what might be said when

Julian learned what had happened, and he was not going to wait around to see or hear it! Manus Fulcher was hitchhiking. Manus Fulcher was headed home to Harkers Island.

Luther Willis- Mullet Fishing, an Old Man, & The War to End all Wars

There is one final account of the special people who surrounded me while I was growing up. It relates to my mulleting days with Calvin and Neal Willis, as told earlier. But more than most of the others, as I have grown older, this recollection has grown both starker and more wistful in my memory. It is about the fourth member of our crew — one who was several times older and more experienced than me. He was old, too old to work for himself. About the only thing he still could offer was to join with me in jumping overboard from the boat with the forward staff attached to the net in tow and pulling it along until we were able to join the two ends together. His name was Luther Willis (1894-1968), and he was well into his seventies by the time we spent a few weeks together in Calvin and Neal's mulleting crew. What I learned from Luther, or more appropriately, what I did "not" take the time to learn, has been seared into my consciousness as I have thought back on those mornings that we huddled and strained together to pull a cotton net along the sandy bottom of Core and Back Sounds.

No matter how hot summer days might be, it is always at least a little chilling to get waist-deep in water before the sun has had time to warm the morning air. When Luther and I climbed out of the skiff, holding a wooden staff he would grab at the top while I latched on to the bottom, we always shivered together as we stooped below the waterline.

Then, while Calvin and Neal remained in the boat and ran out the net, we might talk about how cold the water was, wonder why the boat was making such a wide turn, or marvel at the beauty of the sun rising over the Banks. Then we would strain together as he reminded me to keep the lead line on the bottom and asked if I had noticed anything jumping the net. Soon, after just a few minutes of jerking and pulling, he would lose the little energy his old body had left to spend, and he would begin to stumble as we headed for the

The Education of an Island Boy

other end of the circle. Then, several times every morning, he would exclaim to me, almost apologetically, "I just ain't been the same since France!" Not only that, as he offered his regrets, he would gasp for air at least once in each sentence. In fact, he hardly ever spoke more than a few words without seeming to struggle for his breath.

Luther Willis
Used by permission of his grandson, Michael Willis

As I think back, I must have realized that in referring to "France," he was talking about being a "dough boy" who fought in Europe during World War I. I assume I might have known that the cause for his breathing issues would have been exposure to the poison gasses that were used by both sides in the trenches of "no-man's-land." But what puzzles me now, what bothers me to no end, is why in all those hours I spent with him, alone, and with little else to occupy our time, I never asked him to tell me something or anything about what his war experience had been like.

I have spent my entire adult life enthralled by the past and by stories. I majored in history at both the undergraduate and graduate levels in college. I have poured through countless books, documents, and letters trying to understand, and even write about, how things used to be, and how they affect us even now. But for some reason, I never took advantage of what has proved to have been a once-in-a-lifetime opportunity to talk privately and intimately to someone who was on the very cusp of the one event that history has concluded to have been the midwife to the international turmoil of the entire last century.

Not that this tired and unsophisticated old man would himself have offered any profound insights into the causes or consequences of the "War to End all Wars" and "To Make the World Safe for

Democracy." That is not what I feel deprived of. Instead, I lament that I could have had him tell me what it was like to have been drafted into a European War when he had never left Carteret County. He could have outlined the experience of training for a few weeks and then being herded on board a transport ship for the long ocean crossing. Many years later, I stumbled across some US Army Transport records with his name. They showed he was aboard the Army ship "Great Northern" when it departed from Hoboken, NJ, on 22 May 1918 as a PFC belonging to Truck Company No. 5 of the First Corps Artillery Park. What was that like?

He might have explained his feelings as he arrived on the continent and saw the beautiful "City of Lights" that Paris remained despite the fighting less than a hundred miles away. He could have told of finally learning that his unit was being sent to the front, and of witnessing the devastations that years of scorched earth fighting had done to eastern France, and of why it really was a "No Man's Land." How could he have avoided being terrified at the sight of wounded, dead, and dying soldiers as he made his way forward to the trenches.

He might have explained how he became a victim of the poisonous gas that permeated the air on both sides of the battlefield. Why was he not wearing the protective gear that is so often seen in pictures of the front? Or, were the fumes so thick that even the grotesque-looking masks issued by the army could not wholly shield him? How was he treated after he was wounded? How long was the wait to be allowed to come home? What was it like to get back to Harkers Island and his family?

Those are just some of the thousand questions I might have asked, but, at least by me, never were. I assume he would never have mentioned "France" if he had been unwilling to talk about it. Just by raising the subject, he allowed me to pursue my interests in any direction I wanted. Yet that is the point. At that stage of my life, I must not have had any interest beyond catching fish, making money, and enjoying my life as a young teenager on Harkers Island. That is one of the very few parts of my life growing up on the Island that I would do differently if I had the chance to go back and do it over.

The day I married my wife, Susan — less than six months after we first met, July 6, 1974

10

Leaving and Coming Back

The fountains of my great deep are broken up, and I have rained my reminiscences for four and twenty hours.
                                                            Mark Twain

The past is a safe place. Nothing changes there! ... The choice is not between progress and no progress. The choice is whether we join the journey or not.
                              *"*Lark Rise and Candleford*"* Season 2 Episode 2

"... All we need to do now is ... get on back to [where] ... we hadn't ought to never left nohow.
                                       William Faulkner, "The Reivers"

Over the Bridge

In late August of 1966, on a warm and muggy summer's morning, I crossed the Harkers Island bridge for the first time as part of a daily routine. A few years earlier, the voters of Carteret County had approved a bond referendum that called for building two new high schools. They were to be labeled "consolidated" as they would bring together all the community high schools that had served the county for most of the previous half-century. The larger one, to be built in Morehead City, was to be called West Carteret High School and would serve students on the west side of the Newport River, a small tributary of the much larger Neuse River that was considered

The Education of an Island Boy

the county's line of demarcation. The smaller one was to be located not far from Beaufort and was for students on the east side of the Newport River.

Not everyone, especially in the east, had been happy with the decision to abandon the smaller schools. Some feared the loss of community identity the schools had provided and the intimacy of the smaller classes and groupings. Another more vocal group was bothered by the fact that the school campus was as far as thirty miles from the homes of some students living at Cedar Island and Atlantic. That necessarily would involve bus trips of more than an hour each way every day. For us, the Harkers Island bridge was more than ten miles from the new campus and more than twice as far as the Smyrna building. But the lure of a larger modern facility, and more and better opportunities in and out of the classroom, eventually won the support of enough parents and voters to carry the question.

Students living east of that dividing line in Beaufort, Core Creek, South River, and the several communities east of the North River bridge, including the Island, would attend the new East Carteret High School. This campus was built about five miles north of Beaufort on the west side of the North River bridge, the nominal dividing line between Carteret County's mainland and what was already called Down East. The plot was so low-lying that much of it appeared as a swamp. Long and wide ditches marked the borders to ensure the area remained drained during heavy rainfalls.

The school campus was surrounded on three sides by farmland, and on the east side by US Highway 70 and a long stretch of marshland that extended all the way to the North River Bridge about one mile away. There was no air-conditioning in the building, so windows were always open. In the early fall, you could hear the roar of tractors and harvesters in the adjacent fields, and easterly winds brought in the rich smell of the marshes, making some of us more than a little homesick at the beginning.

The first classes started in the fall of 1965, so I was part of the second group to spend our entire high school years at the new school. That seemed only fitting, as I had been part of the second group to start and finish at the new Harkers Island Elementary

Leaving and Coming Back

School after it opened for students midway through the school year that began in 1957.

With detours included, it was a fifteen-mile ride across three bridges to the new campus from the bus stop at Edith's store. Our bus, labeled number 27, was obliged to take a circuitous route that included several side roads along the way to pick up riders in other communities, and it seemed much longer than the actual distance covered. It was outfitted with a "speed-governor" for the accelerator that prevented it from going more than thirty-five mph, so the nominal quarter-hour ride sometimes took twice that to complete.

Leaving the Island as I headed out to start high school was like entering a new world. Until then, Harkers Island and the waters around it had been my universe "24/7/365." Occasionally, I left to play ball games, visit family on the mainland, or go shopping with my parents on some Saturdays. But getting off that bus that summer morning was stepping into "phase two" of my life. During the ensuing four years, I came to love that school, the teachers, and especially my classmates much the same as I had those on the Island. By the time I left there in May of 1970, my heart and mind were filled with memories that, just like the ones that preceded it, have influenced my life in the half-century that has followed.

Once at East Carteret and fully settled in, I became a part of a new group of more than 200 first-year students who were getting to know each other along with another 600 upperclassmen for the first time. Not only were we new faces, but many of us spoke with such distinct dialects that after a few weeks, we could tell where someone was from just by hearing them speak. That variation was not just between Beaufort and Down East. At that point, every community from Cedar Island in the north to Harkers Island in the south retained unique inflections as identifiable as hair color and height. Eventually, even though some distinctions of drawl, surnames, and traditions remained, they evolved into "distinctions without a difference" as far as most of us were concerned.

I had been a good student, at least in grades, while attending elementary school at Harkers Island. In general, that continued when I reached high school. I was assigned with other students of

The Education of an Island Boy

similar academic records to the college prep curriculum, one of the three standard groupings for students at that time. The other two were general education and vocational prep. As might be imagined, those classifications did more than determine your classwork assignments. They also helped to predetermine with whom you would spend your time during the school day.

In 1954, the US Supreme Court had ruled in the case of "Brown vs Board of Education of Topeka" that the public schools throughout the country had to be desegregated "with all deliberate speed." That process took a decade to start in North Carolina and elsewhere in the South. But by my sophomore year, Carteret County finally began implementing that decision. Beaufort and the rural areas surrounding it had a significant population of African Americans and had maintained two separate and segregated school systems, including high schools, since the onset of "Jim Crow" late in the 19th century. That separation finally ended in the fall of 1967.

So, from that point on, and for the first time in my life, I was in the presence of African Americans, both students and teachers, on a regular basis. I was not conscious of it so much at the time. Still, looking back, I realize that the criteria used to assign students to classes based on what was deemed to be our educational potential had a supplemental consequence. Using traditional but sometimes arbitrary standards allowed that even after the supposed end of the physical separation of the races in different facilities, my days at ECHS were as segregated on several levels as they had been the decade earlier at Harkers Island Elementary.

Still further, the grouping along academic ability lines also kept me apart from many of my Harkers Island friends and family who had come with me across the bridge. That group totaled less than one hundred for the four grades. That was because so many high school-aged students were inclined to drop out when they reached the permissible age of sixteen. Less than a third of us were in the college-prep classes, so I no longer had the day-to-day relationships with the entire group that had been my routine for the previous eight years. Such was among the costs of school consolidation and the added opportunities it offered. Despite that caveat, what developed because of those options and chances was wonderful for me in some special ways. But losing that daily contact with so many of those who had been my school family left a lasting hole in my consciousness and memory.

Within a week of the opening of the school year, elections were held for class officers. The first-year class had over two hundred students from four different feeder schools. Those few of us who, like me, were extroverted enough to make new friends quickly were at a distinct advantage when it came to anything resembling a popularity contest — which those elections necessarily were. I was nominated for the office of class president and won the election without requiring a run-off. I also was elected a representative to the student council. Those would be the last of my elective offices for quite a while. By the time the following year rolled around, I had become more of an athlete, often referred to as a "jock," than a student leader.

It's not that I completely abandoned my academic pursuits once I got to high school. My grades were sufficient to keep me among a higher grouping of my classmates. It's just that those concerns gave way as a priority to football, basketball, and baseball when it came to my time, energy, and focus. Fortunately, I had a few teachers who could see beyond that interest and bring me back in line regarding my studies. Especially in English and Social Studies, I continued to make the effort needed to do well in the classroom. My sophomore World History teacher, Miss Ann Salter, and my junior English teacher, Miss Margaret Todd, gave me enough encouragement and incentive while in their classes that those two subjects — studying history and then writing about what I learned —would be the focus of my later college education.

I don't recall when I made the decision that I would want to go to college or seek any type of schooling after high school. I just always assumed that I would. Similarly, I have no memory of ever considering opting for the life of a waterman and making a living as a fisherman. It quite simply never even crossed my mind. That alternative remained viable at the time and was chosen by at least some of my generation. But by the end of the decade of the 1960's, many more of us were looking for an economic, and even a social mobility that earlier had remained beyond the reach of most Island men and women.

During summer vacations while in high school, I held various odd jobs, including working as an assistant custodian at the elementary school in nearby Smyrna. The position was funded by the "Neighborhood Youth Corps," one of Lyndon Johnson's "Great Society" programs. Another summer, I worked as a carpenter with a family friend who was building a large addition to my Uncle Earl and Aunt Lillian's home.

After my sophomore and senior years, I worked beside my father and other boat-builders at the Hi-Tide Boat Works in Williston. And every summer, at various times, I worked in the water with my father and with my brother Michael. Those experiences with my father and brother were memorable and even enjoyable. But they further convinced me that fishing, shrimping, and clamming to support myself and eventually a family were not something I would enjoy doing for the rest of my life.

Off to College

Despite my time involved with high school athletics, I devoted enough time to the classroom that getting admitted to a college was not a problem. How to pay for all that venture would entail certainly was. By my senior year, I assumed an athletic scholarship was my best alternative to overcoming that obstacle. Midway through that school year in early 1970, after having had a successful final season of football, I was invited to come for a visit by the football coach at Elon College.

The campus of what is now Elon University is located some 250 miles inland from the coast near Burlington, NC. After a single work out there, I was offered a spot on the school's upcoming freshman squad with a full scholarship. Assuming that to be my best and probably my only option, I accepted their offer. All the necessary arrangements were made for me to report there in early August to begin practice and prepare for the fall semester of classes.

Later that spring, I was also offered the chance to play in an annual all-star football game sponsored by the North Carolina Jaycees to raise money for a boy's home in Lake Waccamaw, NC. I immediately jumped at the opportunity. Besides being part of what was considered a special honor, the game was to be played at East

Carolina University in Greenville, NC. ECU was the closest university and only two hours away from the Island, my home, and my family — none of which I had ever left on my own for so long as a week.

So, just a month before heading to Elon, I checked in at ECU for a whole week of practice in preparation for a Saturday night game pitting two teams of high school players from across the entire state. All practices were held on the ECU campus, and the game was played at the University's recently expanded Ficklen Stadium.

Little did I suspect at the time that a week of football practice in the middle of summer during the heart and heat of the tobacco market season would prove so consequential for my life. At that time, Greenville and surrounding Pitt County grew more tobacco than any other county in the whole country. The mid-summer tobacco market was like an extended "Black Friday" for the entire community, and so the whole town was bustling the week I was there.

Just that spring ECU had changed direction in their football program and brought in a new coach and staff to replace long-time head coach Clarence "Stas" Stasavich. The new coach, Mike McGee, wanting to make an immediate impact in recruiting new talent, had his assistants patrolling the sidelines for each of our practice sessions. I had a good week of practice and then caught several passes in the actual game, including one for a touchdown. By midweek I was made aware that one of those assistants had taken notice and inquired about me to the coach of my team and a few others. When he learned that I already was committed to another school, the matter was dropped, but not completely.

A few days after returning home from Greenville I was off to Elon for orientation with fall football practice scheduled to start the following week. Orientation lasted only three days, but that was all it took for me to realize that I was never going to be satisfied or happy that far away from home and where my cleats were scuffed with red clay rather than beach sand and crabgrass. Two days after returning home I notified the coach at Elon that I would not be coming back. Thinking it was too late to make any other arrangements for the fall, I assumed I would continue working at

The Education of an Island Boy

the boat house with my father in the short term. I intended to use that time to try and arrange financing for attending ECU for the winter quarter that would begin in December.

At that time, included in the cost of taking the SAT (Scholastic Aptitude Test) was the option to have your scores sent to as many as three different institutions at no additional fee. I sat for the exam in the spring of my junior year and ECU was one of the schools on my chosen list. When the admissions office there received my scores, they sent a letter asking me to apply for admission with a waiver of any application fees. Having nothing to lose, and not sure at that time what my plans might be, I immediately complied. Within a few weeks I received a letter of acceptance. Without much consideration — at least for the time being — I filed it away.

This is where serendipity came into play. An older student-athlete from our area, Charles Mason, was completing his graduate studies in the Health and Physical Education Department at ECU the summer I was in Greenville for the all-star game. Shortly after, while back home for a weekend, he heard from a mutual friend that I had decided not to go to Elon as planned. When he returned to Greenville the next week, he mentioned my situation to a member of the football coaching staff with whom he shared a class.

It was the same one who had noticed me during the all-star week. When the coach had inquired as to where I had played in high school, and knowing that Charles was from the same area, he had discussed with him my situation at the time. In fact, I always assumed that Charles had informed him of my earlier plans to play at Elon.

Within a few more days I was at my job in Williston, sanding fiberglass on the bow of a newly built sport-fishing boat, when I was alerted by a coworker that I was wanted on the phone, and by a voice they didn't recognize. The caller turned out to be Charles Mason. He told me why he was calling and immediately handed his phone to Coach Sonny Randle, head coach of the ECU freshman football team. (It was not until one year later in 1971 that rules were changed to allow freshmen to play varsity football at the college level.) Then and there, on the telephone amid the sounds of hammers, saws, and sanders, he invited me to come and play football at ECU. He didn't offer a full scholarship in the traditional sense. Instead, it was what he called a "financial aid package" that combined grants, loans, and smaller scholarships from several sources in an amount that would pay my tuition, room, and board for the first year. Depending on how that worked out, similar arrangements could be made for subsequent years.

With no hesitation at all, I jumped to accept the offer. Less than a week later, on a Saturday morning and the first day of August 1970, I was headed out and away from home not just for the school day, but for the foreseeable future. Instead of going west to Burlington and Elon College, I was traveling north and in the direction of Greenville and East Carolina University. It was at the start of that journey that I had ventured one more time down the path to the Landing where I would bid goodbye to my father, and where he applauded me for my effort to try and get "some kind of education."

A Serious Student

As it turned out, my career as a football player at ECU did not last long at all. My talent as a wide receiver was real, at least when it came to running routes and catching passes. But I was neither strong enough nor fast enough to compete for meaningful playing time against most of my teammates. I had come to that realization even before my coaches would acknowledge it, and within just a few weeks I was no longer playing football.

Once again, circumstances worked to my immediate advantage, as a generous and sympathetic financial aid officer, Mr. Robert Boudreaux, listened sympathetically as I explained my situation. His wife, Joan, attended our church in Greenville. The group was so small that everybody immediately became acquainted with everyone else, and when I mentioned to her that I might be leaving the football program, she immediately put me in contact with her husband.

After a few days he had arranged a package that secured additional loans and allowed me to work on and off campus to make up for most of the financial help I had been promised as a student-athlete. My heavy "high tide" accent also proved to my advantage as well. Several of the clerks in the financial aid office were so intrigued by the way I spoke that, according to Mr. Boudreaux, they would find projects and jobs for me just so they could hear me talk when I came in to get my assignments.

From that moment on, my education was no longer dependent on playing any kind of sport. Rather, it would be based on my academic projections and the financial assets, or lack thereof, of my parents. I was pretty sure that the latter would not change any time soon. My task was to make sure that the former remained constant.

In the years since, I often have reflected on how the grants and loans I received that allowed me to continue at ECU, worked out wonderfully for me, and also for the governmental programs that provided them. I graduated with honors exactly on schedule in the spring of 1974 with a BA in History. A year later I was awarded a master's degree in the same field and entered the workforce.

Within less than ten years I had paid back all my student loans. And from graduation to my retirement forty-one years later at the end of 2016, I was always employed and paying local, state, and federal taxes in amounts that were far greater than I might have paid had I not had the opportunity to earn my degrees. So, at least in my own mind, those grants and loans were an investment in me that worked out as well for the investors as for myself.

While at Harkers Island Elementary and at East Carteret, I had been blessed with exceptional teachers in my history courses. Both were from nearby Marshallberg, a secluded and picturesque community that is directly across Straits Channel from the Island. Miss Rita Harris all but adopted me during my seventh and eighth grade years and challenged me every day with special projects related to social studies. In addition, she gave me encouragement that motivated me in the years that followed as I was always mindful never to disappoint her with my progress, or a lack thereof, from then on.

In high school, the aforementioned Miss Salter assumed a role similar to the one played earlier by Miss Harris. Although she was my classroom teacher for only one year — World History as a sophomore — she continued to keep close tabs on me from then on. She regularly invited me to come by her office so she could share with me mementos and stories related to the subject we both loved. She led me to believe that my attending college and maybe even becoming a history instructor like her should be more than a wish or a dream. It was a reachable goal.

Even with the influences of those special teachers still fresh in my mind and memory, I entered ECU with no predetermined major or concentration. But during my second year there I took a course in Greek History from one of the newest professors in the History department. His name was Dr. Anthony Papalas, and he was fresh out of the University of Chicago. He loved baseball and the pop culture that had emerged in the late 1960s as much as he loved his profession. Those things were evident early on and as I grew to share those passions, he immediately became my favorite professor. His classes were, for me, both intriguing and enlightening.

By the time the year was over, I was a confirmed history major and never looked back or wavered in that commitment. By then I had latched on to Dr. Papalas as a mentor and friend. I eventually took several more of his classes and he directed my senior honor's project. He did the same for my master's thesis a year later and he has remained both a friend and a mentor ever since. Indicative of that friendship is that he voluntarily lent his hand at editing the manuscripts of this book a half century after our professor-student relationship ended.

Another professor of history whose friendship and classroom style influenced my choice of a major was Dr. William (Bill) Still. His concentration was in maritime history, and he also taught classes on the American Civil War and its aftermath. My first experience as his student was in his survey course of American history during my sophomore year. He had earned his graduate degrees at the University of Alabama and also was an accomplished tennis player. I was intrigued to learn that when he was younger, he had participated in the US Open tennis tournament when it was played at Forest Hills, NY. He eventually became a founder of ECU's Program in Maritime History and Underwater Archaeology. His love of the coast caused him to visit me at Harkers Island several times both during and after my time as a student.

The Education of an Island Boy

I optioned for Political Science as a minor at ECU. It seemed a helpful complement to History as a field of study. But two professors, Dr. Tinsley Yarbrough and Dr. John East, persuaded me that my choice could be as rewarding as it had been obvious. Dr. Yarbrough had been a clerk to Supreme Court Justice Hugo Black after graduating from the University of Alabama. He became a nationally recognized authority both on constitutional matters related to the United States Supreme Court and on the career of Justice Black. He later went into administration and served as a vice-chancellor at ECU. I still make it a point to seek him out at times when I visit the campus, and he is always gracious in inquiring about my career and family — a reminder of why he was such a successful teacher.

Dr. East was a veteran of the US Marine Corps who later graduated from the University of Florida and from the University of Illinois. He specialized in western political philosophy and was the school's designated "conservative voice" during the era of Vietnam and Watergate. He gave up his professorship for politics not long after I graduated and was elected to the United States Senate in 1980. Despite our differences of opinion on some political issues, we remained close friends.

In fact, two of my most often quoted maxims are taken verbatim from political and social discussions in his classes. The first and most important was that for matters of politics, "There are many issues about which reasonable minds may differ, and those differences should not affect a friendship." The second, and one directed at me on more than one occasion was that "In a free and open society, everyone should be allowed to defend their position — flimsy though that position may be." To his credit and my relief, he always smiled broadly even as he focused his attention in my direction.

He had suffered from polio and used a wheelchair most of his adult life. That wheelchair was the only evidence of his paralysis, but his close friends were aware that he suffered from chronic pain related to his disability. Sadly, that pain was a factor in causing him to take his own life shortly before he completed his first term in the Senate. In the years that have followed, and especially of late, I often have contemplated how much we now could use his conciliatory voice and example.

I lived in dormitories during my entire undergraduate time at college. In fact, the better part of the friendships I made while there were in that setting. The demographic of classrooms with a student body as large as ECU's was so inconstant that it was unusual to share classes repeatedly with more than just a few other individuals, even those with the same major. Conversely, at least at that time, the population of dorms was much more static and therefore long-term associations were more frequent and more intimate.

There were some friends who were my dorm-mates for successive years, and even a few for all four. It was with my dorm friends that I played intramural sports and went to movies and concerts. It also was with them that I teamed up to work on assignments and group projects. A select few of them were with or beside me when and where I spent most of my time, and where I made the single most important association of my college career — and my life — at the school's main library.

"Love in the Library" with a Shout-Out to Jimmy Buffett

Surrounded by stories surreal and sublime, I fell in love in the library once upon a time-
                          Jimmy Buffett "Love in the Library"

Even more consistent than my dormitory buddies was the group I gathered with each afternoon and evening at ECU's Joyner Library. That building, at least for me, was the heart and soul of the campus. I spent multiple hours there nearly every day of my college career. Some reference works could be used only on-premises and so the largest single room in the whole building was the "Reference Room," and that was where our group assembled while using those resources.

Eventually, I came to recognize and build friendships with others who showed a similar inclination to study surrounded by a million books. At that time Joyner Library still used the by-then already archaic Dewey Decimal System to arrange their collections. It also

The Education of an Island Boy

was a "closed stack" library, meaning that patrons perused the card catalog rather than the shelves in search of titles.

Once a book was identified, a request card was submitted to the staff to locate what was requested and bring it to the main counter to be checked out. The "stack-runners," as those who retrieved the books were called, were students working to help pay for tuition. When patrons were finished with an item, the same workers who had gathered them were then charged to return and refile them in their proper locations.

Understandably, not all the student workers were equally talented in their jobs or committed to the tasks at hand. Consequently, they were not all uniformly efficient or swift, or even as pleasant, when it came to finding and delivering the requested items. After a while and following dozens of visits to the counter to hand over requests, I came to recognize the faces and abilities of many of those runners. It didn't take long to discern who among them were the most helpful or, on the other hand, was most likely to come back carrying only a shrug of the shoulders while asserting, "I couldn't find it. It must be checked out!"

In the middle of my senior year (1973-1974) my eyes and attention began to focus on one special stack-worker who not only was among the most efficient on the staff, but also the most likable and attractive. Her name was Susan (Leggett), and shortly after returning from Christmas vacation, I garnered the courage to go out on a limb and ask her for a date. The occasion was a concert being held at the school's Minges Coliseum. The Goose Creek Symphony and the Earl Scruggs Review,

Susan and Joel shortly after meeting each other in 1974.

352

Leaving and Coming Back

two "bluegrass" bands who were quite popular at the time, were on the bill that evening. After some nervous hesitation, she finally agreed. The concert was on Thursday evening and after the show we spent the next few hours, until well after midnight, talking and getting to know each other better. Events moved rapidly after that. By Sunday evening we were engaged, and in early July, less than two months after my graduation and the end of her junior year, we were married!

We remained in Greenville for another two years. The first year we stayed in a one-bedroom, second floor apartment on Third Street just two blocks from the main campus and allowed us to make our daily commutes on bicycles or on foot. I had a fellowship as a graduate student in History while studying for my master's and received my advanced degree at the end of the summer term in 1975. Susan was able to get a job as a full-time library clerk and while working she completed her senior year with a major in Psychology.

The following year, I applied for fellowships to work towards a doctoral degree in history and was accepted at several schools, including Brigham Young University and the Universities of North Carolina and Kentucky. UK offered the best financial incentives — a scholarship as well as a teaching fellowship — and so early that summer we drove to Lexington, KY, to visit the school and explore accommodations.

Just before heading out on our journey in a Volkswagen Beetle, we borrowed from good friends, Danny and Judy Gore, we had learned that Susan was expecting what was to be our first child, our daughter Emily, and was due sometime before the new year. By the time we reached the foothills of the Smoky Mountains on our trip there,

Following my graduation from East Carolina University in the spring of 1974.

Susan began to experience the nausea symptoms of early pregnancy, making the trip more stressful than we had anticipated. Once we arrived, we spent a couple of days visiting the campus and making the acquaintance of some church friends who had invited us to be their guests for our visit. The campus was impressive, and the Bluegrass country was beautiful. We even picked out an apartment that would be our home when we returned to stay in late August.

But on the way back, the "morning sickness" that had first shown up on our way there, came back even more severely as our tiny VW Bug wove through the hairpin curves that are everywhere in the mountains of southeastern Kentucky. To help her not to focus on the winding road we had a prolonged discussion about whether we really wanted to move that far away from home and families. The worse she felt in the moment, the less appealing such a move became for the future. By the time we had reached the North Carolina side of the Blue Ridge, we had decided and determined that we were going to find some way to stay closer to home.

Within less than a week I had secured a teaching and coaching job at J. H. Rose High School in Greenville, one that would allow us to stay right where we were for at least another year. Soon after accepting that position, we moved into a new mobile home in what then was called Riverview Estates and that was located on the eastern edge of town. During that time, the much-anticipated bicentennial year of 1976, our new baby arrived, and I taught World History and was an assistant football coach, head JV basketball coach, and head girl's track coach. We didn't have a whole lot of leisure time during what proved to be our final year in Greenville.

Susan kept attending classes and working at the library until only a week before giving birth, while I had either practice or games every afternoon and evening following each day in the classroom. Our daily routine was usually saying goodbye to each other in the morning and my getting home just before bedtime late in the evening. In the fall, while awaiting Emily's arrival, Susan sometimes already was asleep by the time I got home. In the winter and spring, as Susan attended to our newborn during the day, we bedded down with the baby lying between us as soon as we were finished with supper.

In what little time for thinking we had, we together determined that we would be happiest not just in eastern North Carolina, but at Harkers Island in the place and around the people who had been and were so much a part of my, and soon our, lives and character. Susan was as willing as I was to make the move. So, at the end of the school year, less than a week after teaching my last class of the spring semester, we loaded up our 1970 American Motors Ambassador automobile that we had purchased with a loan for $500 and headed back to what has been our home ever since.

It would take several more weeks for us to settle into our own place, the mobile home we had brought with us from Greenville, on a half-acre parcel that sat beside one of the roads I had helped to cut and clear for my Uncle Earl a decade earlier. In the years since we have welcomed five more children, and eventually their spouses and twenty-one grandchildren. The mobile home was replaced by a small wooden frame dwelling in 1978, and we have renovated and expanded it several times since then. What started out as a single-story structure with three small bedrooms now is a two-story home that can sleep a dozen or more family and friends whenever that space is needed.

Providing for a growing family initially proved to be much more complicated and demanding for me than it had been for my parents and ancestors on the Island, as working the water was no longer a viable alternative except for the hardiest and most determined of fishermen — of which I was neither. So, to support them, I initially hopped around several different jobs and careers. Shortly after moving home, I was appointed county tax collector for Carteret County — a political patronage position that was a favor to my father for having been such a loyal supporter of the local party for so many years. Two years later I tried my hand in education again as a teacher and coach for East Carteret High School — my Alma Mater.

When it became obvious that I could not adequately provide for what by then was a family that included four children, I ventured into the world of business and signed on as a freight forwarder for a shipping firm at the port of Morehead City. After two years there, I was lured away with an offer to manage a mobile home sales center in Morehead City and later in Havelock. I spent several years there that were successful for me, but not for the company as it eventually failed during the economic recession of the late 1980s. Before it finally did, I left for a position that promised to be more secure; overseeing credit and technology at an international veneer plant in Lennoxville, a suburb of Beaufort that was just across a narrow channel to the west of Harkers Island.

Finally, when I was forty years old in 1992, I found what I had been looking for when I latched on to a job in insurance sales with North Carolina Farm Bureau in Beaufort, a position I retained until my retirement a quarter of a century later in January of 2017. Farm Bureau was good to me in every way imaginable the entire time I was there, and still is of a sort. One of my sons and another of my sons-in-law have followed me to work for the same company and in the same office building.

The More Things Change

It is commonly accepted that a generation is the period, considered to be about 20-30 years, during which children are born and grow up, become adults, and begin to have children of their own. With that assumption in mind, I am now at least two generations removed from the world and lifestyle I have sought to portray. That distance has, no doubt, clouded my memory of some details. But at the same time, it has sharpened my focus on what mattered most to me and to many of my contemporaries.

Living and raising a family at Harkers Island as the world around it has changed so dramatically in the last five decades has allowed me countless opportunities to reflect on how fortunate I truly was. In my formative years I was able to experience and enjoy a world and way of life that in most ways was only marginally different from the one my parents and grandparents had known for several generations. Since returning, I have not only witnessed but also been involved in what have been seismic albeit inevitable changes, and that have come much more rapidly with the passing of time and increased interaction with the world on the other side of the Harkers Island bridge.

Our family in 1989 with our six children:
Bottom: Joel Jr., Joel, Susan, Mike
Top: Alyson, Emily, Joella, and Leah.

Many of those changes were as beneficial as they have been inescapable. Standards of living have improved and brought better educational and economic opportunities, medical care, communications, and transportation. Islanders, and especially their children, who once were skeptical and suspicious of anyone who spoke their native tongue with a different accent, have learned to be more tolerant and less intimidated by the newcomers that now are part of our everyday lives. Being from "off" is no longer a reason for mistrust. Other changes were not necessarily better or worse, but often judged to be the latter, simply because they were "different." But that is a reaction common not just to natives of the Island. So, I trust that it will be understood that these final observations are not a polemic against what the Island now is or yet may become. It is, rather, a celebration of what it once was.

There is now a museum on the Island, the Core Sound Waterfowl Museum and Heritage Center, which works to preserve as much as possible of the Island's rich past. As the name suggests, its primary focus is on memorabilia and mementos of duck hunting, and especially hand carved decoys — old and new. They also sponsor educational programs, conferences, seminars, and exhibits to

The Education of an Island Boy

document and celebrate all of what has become known as the original "Down East." Their task is in many ways a race against time as the demography of the area changes so rapidly with the arrival of retirees and vacationers and the departure of younger individuals and families seeking better economic opportunities on the mainland.

What has been lost is some, but not all, of the sense of community and closeness that once was so pervasive. No longer is it common to know the stories, or even the names, of all your neighbors. Unfamiliar faces are part of most ventures to a local store or business. That change is both a cause and a consequence of our having lost so many ties with our heritage. What was once a natural by-product of always being around extended family members, especially older ones, has yet to find a modern substitute. Stories and traditions that were part of the daily routine for several generations are not so available for the ones that have followed. Even when they are, they often are considered quaint and old-fashioned.

Core Sound Waterfowl Museum and Heritage Center at the "End of the Road" on Harkers Island
CSWM&HC Collection

The Lighthouse at the Cape and its surroundings are now the centerpiece of the Cape Lookout National Seashore that extends from Portsmouth Island to the north and the Beaufort Bar to the west. Thousands of tourists and sport fishermen flock there every year. It is accessible only by boat, so nearly all the visitors use Harkers Island as their waypoint for getting there. The shoreline in front of the lighthouse is often packed with swimmers and sunbathers and in the summer months as many as a hundred boats might be anchored just beyond the tideline. The structure itself has been adopted as the symbol for the "Crystal Coast," a marketing name used by organizations that encourage visitors not just to Cape Lookout but to all of Carteret County.

All of both Shackleford and Core Banks also are part of the National Seashore. Efforts have been made to return them to their natural state — the way they were even before the first refugees from the Tidewater area of Virginia reached here three centuries ago. But nature itself, especially storms and hurricanes, have taken a toll such that many of the tall sand dunes, especially at the easternmost end of Shackleford, are all but gone. Place names that once marked the different Banks communities like Bells Island, Sam Windsor's Lump, Wade's Shore, and even Diamond City itself, now evoke images of places rather than memories of people. The persons once attached to those names are mostly forgotten except by a dwindling few who are striving to preserve their collective history.

Cape Lookout Lighthouse

Those barrier islands themselves are getting progressively narrower and in some places are as much sandbars as islands. On breezy days, depending on the wind's direction, while standing at Shell Point you can see the waves breaking on the ocean side of either Banks. Except for the horses, all the other feral livestock including cattle, sheep, and goats were removed from Shackleford once the park service assumed control. There are no longer any roundups, or what we used to call "horsepennings." A managed herd of roughly a hundred ponies has been allowed to remain as their lineage is traced farther back than when the first permanent settlers came to Diamond City. Their numbers are closely monitored both by park rangers and volunteer groups that advocate for the protection and safety of the herd.

The Education of an Island Boy

On Harkers Island there were once as many as a dozen fish houses where watermen delivered their catches and gathered each Saturday morning to get their pay. None of them remain as refrigerated trucks from Beaufort and Cedar Island have taken their place. Only a handful of families here continue to make their living exclusively in the water. The fishing boats still in use are mostly large "trawlers" that are docked together in a harbor of refuge at the foot of the Island bridge. The scores of smaller hand-fashioned wooden boats that were moored or anchored close to the shoreline now are gone or moored in protected harbors. Most have been replaced by fiberglass production models that are pulled on trailers and launched and lifted at a state-maintained ramp just beyond the bridge.

The easternmost end of the Island, Shell Point, is now the property of the National Park Service. Locals still return as a ritual, but when they do, they have to pass beside a parking lot full of cars and golf carts belonging to visitors to the Cape Lookout National Seashore. Academy Field, where we once gathered for family picnics and to watch fishing boats race just for fun, now is home to a rapidly expanding development of privately-owned houses serviced by its own sewage system and a long sound-side wharf that reaches far out into Back Sound.

Hardly any Willises are left at Red Hill, and few people even remember the spot where Boo shoveled coal and Mary Ann raked up oak leaves. The glistening bank of almost crimson sea sand that gave the place its name is now hidden behind concrete and wooden sea walls. A portion of the Sand Hole, where extended families gathered for celebrations and small children climbed and then ran down the dunes and sand hills, has been turned into a housing development. What remains is mostly cordoned off and is a playground only for the all-terrain vehicles that can evade the ropes and fences that mark its boundaries.

Modern homes, raised on stilts to protect from rising seawater, now line the northside Bay from one end of the Island to the other. What was once called "Johnson's Cow Palace," a place where young baseball players learned to judge a fly ball, field a ground ball and hit a curve ball — and older ones like "Mississippi" taught valuable life lessons, and not just with their bats — has returned to its primeval state. It now is flanked by burgeoning housing developments, and its glory days remembered only by a shrinking number of elderly men.

Neighborhoods no longer are distinguished as enclaves of extended families. In fact, there are no more Hancocks at Hancock Landing. All the little general stores, except for Billy's, now are no more. The rest were replaced by the easy proximity to chain stores in Beaufort and Morehead City, and eventually by a Dollar General near the midpoint of the Island. The theater has long since vanished. More people here now remember it as an "arcade room" than as a "show house." The REA was merged into a larger cooperative that serves the whole county. We have a municipal water supply and access to a privately owned sewer system for those who can afford it. There are several campgrounds with modern amenities and on warm weather holidays the Island can seem as crowded as some of the other "beach communities" up and down the coastline.

More than half of the houses on Harkers Island now are occupied by owners whose primary residence is or was somewhere else. Skyrocketing costs for land and homes has had the effect of "pricing out" subsequent generations of younger Islanders when it came their time to settle down with a family of their own. With prices on the Island approaching more than twice what it might be for similar property across the bridge or in Beaufort or Morehead City, most of them were obliged to choose one of the latter alternatives. None of my children, including the four who have remained nearby, have homes on the Island — although they still call the Island their home. When asked where they live or are from, both they and my grandchildren always answer, "Harkers Island."

A byproduct of that shift in housing patterns has been that the Island's demographic has trended progressively older as younger families have been replaced by retirees and seasonal visitors. There are fewer and fewer children to be educated at the Island school such that enrollment in the elementary school has shrunk so much that changes had to be made in zoning to allow it to continue. Presently, most of the students at Harkers Island Elementary School do not live on the Island.

Only one of my grade schoolteachers survives. Miss Harris, now Mrs. Freshwater, remains an example and an inspiration, for me and many others. I can still see and hear her every time I notice a grammatical mistake or a factual error or doubt my ability to accomplish any goal.

Perhaps most telling of all, the Landing, the south shore that was the fastest route between any two places on the Island, as well as the focal point and gathering place for both adults and children for as long as anyone could remember, is literally no more. Beginning in the 1980s when waterfront property values began to increase exponentially, many locals were induced to sell their waterfront homes. As land prices all over the Island also increased, not a few of the sellers ended up in mobile home parks on the mainland. By the turn of the century, hardly any of the southside property belonged to the descendants of those who first had built their homes close enough to the shoreline that from their south-facing windows they still could gaze across the Sound to see where they or their parents once had lived.

To protect their investments, the new owners began installing seawalls to halt the erosion that is an inevitable part of the natural lifespan of any barrier island. A side-effect of those structures meant to protect one spot of shoreline was that it accelerated the erosion of the adjacent beach. As a result, the neighboring properties had to add their sections of similar structures so that like "reverse dominos," each new seawall resulted in new ones being erected beside it.

Eventually the entire "Landing" was gone. Where it once was now remains visible only when the tide is at its lowest. And even then, it is all but impassable for beachcombers as piers, wharves, breakwaters, and fences block any extended movement along the shore. Barriers mark the east-west boundaries and are sometimes fortified by signs with large letters shouting "No Trespassing" to anyone who gets close enough even to see them. What used to be the "shortest distance between any two points on the Island" is now a distance too far for anything other than memories. Natives who want to "wet their feet in the sound just one more time" now must search for someone willing to let them "trespass" through their property even to see where the Landing used to be.

Leaving and Coming Back

Boats lined up at the Landing along the southern shore of Harkers Island
CSWM&HC Museum Collection

The Education of an Island Boy

Our children: Aly, Emily, Mike, Leah, Joel, and Joella
Photo by Katie Amspacher

Epilogue

"And so we beat on, boats against the current, borne back ceaselessly into the past."
                    F. Scott Fitzgerald, "The Great Gatsby"

My oldest brother, Ralph, who lived away from the Island for more than forty years before finally returning to stay, sometimes related how each time he visited home, old-timers he met would tell him, "This will probably be the last I ever see of you. The next time you come back I'll be gone." He would try to dismiss those warnings with a smile and ask, "Really, where are you going?" Then, in a forlorn voice he would conclude, "But eventually, I would come back, and they would be gone!" So, it has been with oh so many of the people I have known.

I was reminded of that when I ran across an observation made by Sam Clemens after his final visit to his hometown of Hannibal, Missouri that echoes that same sentiment. "That world which I knew in its blossoming youth is old and bowed and melancholy now. Its soft cheeks are leathery and wrinkled; the fire is gone out of its eyes and the spring from its step. It will be dust and ashes when I come again. I have been clasping hands with the moribund—and usually they say, 'It is for the last time.'"

So, it must eventually be for each of us as we cling to memories of old faces and older places. Along with the shoreline and the showhouse, also gone are all but a few of the people whose stories I have told. My aunts and uncles, and many of my older cousins have long since passed, along with most of their contemporaries. I have said my final earthly goodbyes to my parents, five of my brothers; Ralph, Tommy, Bill, Mike, and Telford, along with two of my sisters; Ella Dee and "Sister." As of this writing, just my sister

June and I are left to remember. Their passing has caused their images and examples to be seared even more deeply into my memory.

Only a few of the characters described in these pages are still around to appreciate my telling of their tales. One of the main motivations for having prepared this narrative is to preserve not just the stories, but also the memory of the unique personalities who got to live or witness them in real time. I especially hope that these pages will help to preserve their names.

I have heard of the ancient belief that each of us will die not once but twice: once when we take our final breath and then again, the last time someone says our name. They imagined that your spirit would live on as long as people kept remembering you. I hope that by telling their stories and sharing their names again, I might have given them and us just a little more time together to laugh and to love.

When I walked to the Landing that sweltering morning in August of 1970 to bid farewell to my father and move beyond, if only for a season, the world he and others had given me, I was not offering a goodbye to the lessons I had learned. Quite the opposite, the brief period I spent away caused me to recognize and appreciate even more the distinctiveness of the things I had already come to know. Now, a full half-century later, that perception has blended with the innumerable experiences I have enjoyed since I returned home. Every passing year, every lost mentor and friend, and every changed venue and scene, when taken together, serve to make even more valuable and enduring those lessons I had been taught. For me, it was more than a time and a place. It was a setting and a classroom never to be forgotten for *"The Education of an Island Boy."*

"... I conclude this record, declaring that I have written according to the best of my knowledge, by saying that the time passed away with us, and also our lives passed away, like as it were unto us a dream ..."
Jacob 7:26

All of us in 2020. Since this picture, we have added 3 grandchildren. Additionally, a granddaughter has married, a grandson is engaged, and we have said goodbye to a beloved son-in-law. The Circle of Life continues.
Photo by Katie Amspacher

Made in the USA
Columbia, SC
22 February 2025